Praise for

The Body Has a Mind of Its Own

"This is scientific reporting at its best—the sort that not only imparts knowledge, but also evokes curiosity and wonder."
—LARRY DOSSEY, M.D., author of
The Extraordinary Healing Power of Ordinary Things

"You will breeze through this accessible, practical overview of an important scientific story and will certainly agree that the body is not an innocent bystander in the mind business."
—ANTONIO DAMASIO, author of *Descartes' Error*

"A fascinating exploration of senses we didn't even know we had, this compelling account of new research findings underscores how much of our human nature is mediated not by thinking but by profoundly somatic ways of knowing. This new science strongly suggests that we can trust and train various aspects of awareness to our immediate and enduring benefit."   —JON KABAT-ZINN, author of *Coming to Our Senses*

"A marvelous book. In the last ten years there has been a paradigm shift in understanding the brain and how its various specialized regions respond to environmental challenges. In addition to providing a brilliant overview of recent revolutionary discoveries on body image and brain plasticity, the book is sprinkled with numerous insights."
—V. S. RAMACHANDRAN, M.D., director,
Center for Brain and Cognition, University of California, San Diego

"Through a stream of fascinating and entertaining examples, Sandra and Matthew Blakeslee illustrate how our perception of ourselves, and indeed the world, is not fixed but is surprisingly fluid and easily modified. They have created the best book ever written about how our sense of 'self' emerges from the motley collection of neurons we call the brain."
—JEFF HAWKINS, co-author of *On Intelligence*

"The Blakeslees have taken the latest and most exciting finds from brain research and have made them accessible. This is what science writing should always be."

—MICHAEL S. GAZZANIGA, Ph.D., author of *The Ethical Brain*

"Offers us a fascinating new perspective on ourselves . . . The subject, the interactive relationship between the mind and body, has far-reaching implications."   —*Body + Soul*

"[Includes] engaging anecdotes from the fields of psychology, sports, and medicine about how brains and bodies communicate (and occasionally miscommunicate)."   —*Seed*

"[This book presents] some of the most exciting discoveries in neuro-science. . . . Using a readable and inspiring format, the authors showcase new and classic research on neural representations, without compromising accuracy."   —*Nature*

"The Blakeslees venture deep into the mysterious folds of the brain to reveal how its representations of our physical selves aren't always accurate. . . . With captivating anecdotes and mind-bending tricks, this book shows how we often blur the boundaries between corporeal self, the mind, and the outside world."   —*Psychology Today*

"Etched in your brain are maps that correspond to your body and the space and objects around you. How these maps work and what happens when they go awry are the subjects of the Blakeslees' highly readable book."   —*New Scientist*

"This book is a must-read [not just for the general population but] for the neuroscientist also—there is currently nothing out there that manages to integrate the existing literature so well."   —*Neuron*

THE BODY HAS A MIND OF ITS OWN

THE BODY HAS A

*How Body Maps in Your Brain
Help You Do (Almost) Everything Better*

RANDOM HOUSE TRADE PAPERBACKS
NEW YORK

MIND OF ITS OWN

SANDRA BLAKESLEE
and MATTHEW BLAKESLEE

For Carl, Julia, and Lucas

2008 Random House Trade Paperback Edition

Published in the United States by Random House Trade Paperbacks, an imprint of The Random House Publishing Group, a division of Random House, Inc., New York.

RANDOM HOUSE TRADE PAPERBACKS and colophon are trademarks of Random House, Inc.

Originally published in hardcover in the United States by Random House, an imprint of The Random House Publishing Group, a division of Random House, Inc., in 2007.

Illustration credits appear on pages 227–28.

Grateful acknowledgment is made to HarperCollins Publishers for permission to reprint an excerpt from page 29 and an adaptation of pages 27–33 from *Phantoms in the Brain* by V. S. Ramachandran, M.D., Ph.D., and Sandra Blakeslee (New York: William Morrow, 1998), copyright © 1998 by V. S. Ramachandran and Sandra Blakeslee. Used by permission of HarperCollins Publishers.

LIBRARY OF CONGRESS CATALOGING-IN-PUBLICATION DATA

Blakeslee, Sandra.
The body has a mind of its own: how body maps in your brain help you do (almost) everything better / Sandra Blakeslee and Matthew Blakeslee.
p.   cm.
ISBN 978-0-8129-7527-7
1. Mind and body. I. Blakeslee, Matthew. II. Title.
BF161.B52 2007
150—dc22   2006101557

www.atrandom.com

Book design by Simon M. Sullivan

147028622

When a reporter asked the famous biologist J.B.S. Haldane what his biological studies had taught him about God, Haldane replied, "The creator, if he exists, must have an inordinate fondness for beetles," since there are more species of beetle than any other group of living creatures. By the same token, a neurologist might conclude that God is a cartographer. He must have an inordinate fondness for maps, for everywhere you look in the brain maps abound.

—V. S. Ramachandran

CONTENTS

THE BODY HAS A MIND OF ITS OWN

THE EMBODIED BRAIN

S tand up and reach out your arms, fingers extended. Wave them up, down, and sideways. Make great big circles from over your head down past your thighs. Swing each leg out as far as you can, and with the tips of your toes trace arcs on the ground around you. Swivel and tilt your head as if you were craning out your neck to butt something with your forehead or touch it with your lips and tongue. This invisible volume of space around your body out to arm's length—what neuroscientists call peripersonal space—is part of you.

This is not a metaphor, but a recently discovered physiological fact. Through a special mapping procedure, your brain annexes this space to your limbs and body, clothing you in it like an extended, ghostly skin. The maps that encode your physical body are connected directly, immediately, personally to a map of every point in that space and also map out your potential to perform actions in that space. Your self does not end where your flesh ends, but suffuses and blends with the world, including other beings. Thus when you ride a horse with confidence and skill, your body maps and the horse's body maps are blended in shared space. When you make love, your body maps and your lover's body maps commingle in mutual passion.

Your brain also faithfully maps the space beyond your body when you enter it using tools. Take hold of a long stick and tap it on the ground. As far as your brain is concerned, your hand now extends to the tip of that stick. Its length has been incorporated into your personal space. If you were blind, you could feel your way down the street using that stick.

Moreover, this annexed peripersonal space is not static, like an aura. It is elastic. Like an amoeba, it expands and contracts to suit your goals and makes you master of your world. It morphs every time you put on or take off clothes, wear skis or scuba gear, or wield any tool. When Babe Ruth held a baseball bat, as far as his brain was concerned his peripersonal space extended out to the end of the bat, as if it were a natural part of his arms. When you drive a car your peripersonal space expands to include it, from fender to fender, from door to door, and from tire to roof. As you drive you can feel the road's texture as intimately as you would through sandals. As you enter a parking garage with a low ceiling you can "feel" the nearness of your car's roof to the height barrier as if it were your own scalp. This is why you instinctively duck when you pass under the barrier. When someone hits your car you get upset—not just because of the bills and the hassle ahead, but because that person has violated your peripersonal space, no less than a careless elbow in your rib.

When you eat with a knife and fork, your peripersonal space grows to envelop them. Brain cells that normally represent space no farther out than your fingertips expand their fields of awareness outward, along the length of each utensil, making them part of you. This is why you can directly experience the texture and shape of the food you are manipulating, even though in reality you are touching nothing but several inches of lifeless metal. The same thing happens for surgeons controlling microrobotic tools using a joystick. It happens for NASA technicians controlling robotic arms in orbit. If you learned to operate a crane, your peripersonal space map would extend out to the tip of the crane's hook.

This book presents the emerging scientific answer to the age-old mystery of how mind and body intertwine to create your embodied, feeling self. In doing so, it provides clues and answers to a host of fascinating questions that, until now, seemed unrelated.

Questions like: Why do you still feel fat after losing weight? Why do you automatically duck your head when you pass through a doorway while wearing, say, a cowboy hat? Why do your kids get sucked into video games with total abandon?

Or these: How do you sense discomfort, such as heat, cold, pain, itching? How do you sense an emotion such as sadness? Do you get a lump in your throat? Do you feel dread in the pit of your stomach? Were you born with emotions or did you have to learn them? Where do they reside in your body and how do they arise?

What happens in your own brain when you observe other people moving around or expressing emotion? Why do you feel a frisson of fear when you see a tarantula walk on the pillow next to James Bond's head? Why do you wince and double over when you see someone else get walloped between the legs in a blooper reel?

Answers can be found in a new understanding of how your brain maps your body, the space around your body, and the social world. The discovery of peripersonal space mapping is but one of these fast-evolving areas of insight. Every point on your body, each internal organ and every point in space out to the end of your fingertips, is mapped inside your brain. Your ability to sense, move, and act in the physical world arises from a rich network of flexible body maps distributed throughout your brain— maps that grow, shrink, and morph to suit your needs.

The science of body maps has far-reaching applications. It can help people lose weight and make peace with their bodies, improve their ability to play a sport or influence people, and recover from a stroke. It points the way to new treatments for anorexia, phantom limbs, musician's cramp, and a condition among golfers called the yips. It helps explain out-of-body experiences, auras, placebos, and healing touch. It reveals why video games and virtual reality literally capture both your mind and body. It provides a new way to understand human emotions, from love to hate, lust to disgust, pride to humiliation.

So here it is, the untold story of your body maps and how you can apply this understanding to yourself in your life's many facets—you the athlete, you the dieter, the equestrian, the parent, the actor . . . the list goes on.

None of this is to imply that the science of body maps adds up to a Grand Unifying Theory of neuroscience. But it is a widely underappreciated piece of the puzzle. Body maps provide a valuable lens for examining ourselves as a species and as individuals. They provide a fresh and illuminating thread for telling the story of humanity's past, present, and future—with you at center stage.

CHAPTER 1

THE BODY MANDALA

or, Maps, Maps, Everywhere

I f you were asked, "Does your hand belong to you?" you would naturally say, "Of course."

But ask neuroscientists the same question and they will turn the question back on you: How do you know it's your own hand? In fact, how do you know that you have a body? What makes you think you own it? How do you know where your body begins and ends? How do you keep track of its position in space?

Try this little exercise: Imagine there is a straight line running down the middle of your body, dividing it into a left half and a right half. Using your right hand, pat different parts of your body on the right side—cheek, shoulder, hip, thigh, knee, foot. With your finger, trace a line over your right eyebrow and over the right portions of your upper and lower lips.

You are able to tell these body parts from one another because each is faithfully mapped in a two-dimensional swath of neural tissue in your left brain that specializes in touch. The same thing goes for the left side of your body: All its parts are mapped in a similar region of your right brain. Your brain maintains a complete map of your body's surface, with patches devoted to each finger, hand, cheek, lip, eyebrow, shoulder, hip, knee, and all the rest.

A map can be defined as any scheme that spells out one-to-one correspondences between two different things. In a road map, any given point on the map corresponds to some location in the larger world, and each adjacent point on the map represents an adjacent real-world location. The same holds broadly true for the body maps in your brain. Aspects of the outside world and the body's anatomy are systematically mapped onto brain tissue. Thus the topology, or spatial relationships, of your body's surface is preserved in your touch map to a high degree: The foot map is next to the shin map, which is next to the thigh map, which is next to the hip map. Whenever someone claps you on the shoulder, nerve cells in the shoulder region in this map are activated. When you kick a soccer ball, the corresponding part of your foot map is activated. When you scratch your elbow, both your elbow region and fingertip regions are activated. This map is your primary physical window on the world around you, the entry point for all the raw touch information streaming moment by moment into your brain.

This touch information is collected by special receptors throughout your body, funneled into your spinal cord, and sent up to your brain along two major pathways. The more ancient of these pathways carries pain,

---

THE FLESH-BOUND SENSES

The flesh-bound, or somatic, senses stand apart from the other senses at a deep level. In medicine, sight, hearing, smell, and taste are known as the special senses, while the somatic senses form a category all their own. Within that category there are several distinct senses, each brought to you by a separate population of receptor cells that suffuse your body's skin and inner tissues. Here is a quick run-through:

Touch. Touch receptors send your brain information about pressure. There are several kinds of touch receptor—for example, gentle pressure, deep pressure, sustained pressure, hair follicle bending, and vibration. In your daily life, touch is by far the most prominent of the somatic senses in your conscious mind.

Thermoception. When you feel the hot sun beating down on the back of your neck, or when you swish an ice cube around inside your mouth, you are making use of your skin's thermoreceptors. These receptor cells come in two types: one for warm, one for cold. When something is dangerously hot or cold, your sensation of scalding or freezing is created by pain receptors (see below) kicking in. Your deep tissues and organs are suffused with an entirely different type of thermoreceptor that lets your brain keep track of core body temperature.

Nociception. Pain is one of life's starkest and most dreaded experiences. The raw material for pain perceptions comes from your body's nociceptors (*noci-*

temperature, itch, tickle, sexual sensation, crude touch—sufficient, say, to know that you bumped your knee and not your shin, but not acute enough to tell a penny from a dime—and sensual touch, which includes the gentle maternal caresses that were vital for your body map development as a baby.

The evolutionarily newer pathway carries fine touch information—the kind you need in order to thread a needle or leaf through a book—and position-and-location information from receptors embedded in your joints, bones, and muscles.

Once these many channels of sensory information reach your brain, they are combined to create complex, composite sensations such as wetness, hairiness, fleshiness, and rubberiness. The same goes for the many varieties of pain. Through a combination of pain- and touch-related signals, you have access to the rich diversity of unpleasant experience that

is Latin for injury or trauma). As with touch receptors, there are several types: for example, piercing pain, heat pain, chemical pain, joint pain, deep tissue pain, tickle, and itch.

Proprioception. This is your inherent sense of your body's position and motion in space. This sense is what allows you to touch your index fingers together with your eyes closed, for example. There are two main kinds of proprioceptor cells. One kind is embedded in your muscles and tendons and measures stretch. Your brain uses this information to infer limb location. The other kind is embedded in the cartilage between your skeletal joints and keeps track of load and rate of slippage in each joint. Your brain uses this to infer limb speed and direction.

Balance. Unlike the other somatic senses, your sense of up-versus-down doesn't come from a population of receptor cells distributed all around your body, but from a pair of special balance organs in your inner ears. For this reason, it may seem strange that balance—aka your vestibular sense—is classified as one of the somatic senses. But as you'll see, it is an indispensable ingredient in your ability to operate your body in the world. The vestibular sense also belongs in the family of somatic senses by virtue of its sheer ancientness: The inner ear balance organ is a marvel of microengineering that is shared by all vertebrates (animals with backbones), a lineage that goes back more than half a billion years. Through that whole time it has remained virtually unchanged in its design.

includes the smarting pain of a sunburn, the shooting pain of carpal tunnel syndrome, the piercing pain of a stab wound, the dull throbbing pain of an abused knee, the itchy pain of healing, and so on.

You also have a primary motor map in your brain for making movements. Instead of receiving inputs from your skin, this map sends output signals to your muscles. Just like the touch map, this movement map is also found in both sides of the brain. It is vital to your ability to guide your body parts to make fine-tuned movements and assume complex positions in space—like doing the hokey-pokey, playing hockey, or assuming a

---

BRAIN 101

The cerebral cortex, where most of your body maps are located, is folded and crumpled around the much older structures of a more primitive brain. The cortex is divided into four lobes (main sections separated by deep folds):

The brain's gross anatomy in profile.

Occipital Lobe. Mainly dedicated to vision. In sighted people, the occipital lobe sends visual information to the parietal lobe, which contributes to vision-based body maps.

Parietal Lobe. Mainly deals in physical sensation, the space on and around the body, and spatial relations in three dimensions. Rife with important body maps.

Frontal Lobe. The orchestrator of voluntary and skilled movements, the conductor of planning and foresight, and the seat of several of the mind's most cherished functions such as moral reasoning, self-control, and some aspects of language. Rife with important body maps.

Temporal Lobe. Processes auditory input from the ears, has important linguistic and emotional functions, and participates in high-level vision.

poker face in a high stakes card game. When you wiggle all your toes, the toe and foot regions of your motor map are active. When you stick out your tongue, the map's tongue and jaw regions are active. Thanks to this map, all the low-level, mostly unconscious tasks of coordinated movement unfold smoothly without a glitch.

Elsewhere in your brain you also have a very different but no less critical body map of all your body's innards. This is your primary visceral map, a patchwork of small neural swatches that represent your heart, lungs, liver, colon, rectum, stomach, and all your various other giblets. This map is uniquely super-developed in the human species, and it gives you a level of access to the ebb and flow of your internal sensations unequaled anywhere else in the animal kingdom. You feel lust, disgust, sadness, joy, shame, and humiliation as a result of this body mapping. These visceral inputs to the psyche are the wellspring of the rich and vivid emotional awareness that few other creatures even come close to enjoying. The activity in this map is the voice of your conscience, the thrill of music, the foundation of the emotionally nuanced and morally sensitive self.

The Embodied Self

The idea that your brain maps chart not only your body but the space around your body, that these maps expand and contract to include everyday objects, and even that these maps can be shaped by the culture you grow up in, is very new to science. Research now shows that your brain is teeming with body maps—maps of your body's surface, its musculature, its intentions, its potential for action, even a map that automatically tracks and emulates the actions and intentions of other people around you.

These body-centered maps are profoundly plastic—capable of significant reorganization in response to damage, experience, or practice. Formed early in life, they mature with experience and then continue to change, albeit less rapidly, for the rest of your life. Yet despite how central these body maps are to your being, you are only glancingly aware of your own embodiment most of the time, let alone the fact that its parameters are constantly changing and adapting, minute by minute and year after year. You may not truly appreciate the immense amount of work that goes on behind the scenes of your conscious mind that makes the experience of embodiment seem so natural. The constant activity of your body maps is so seamless, so automatic, so fluid and ingrained, that you don't even recognize it is happening, much less that it poses an absorbing scientific puzzle that is spawning fascinating insights into human nature, health, learning, our evolutionary past, and our cybernetically enhanced future.

Your body is not just a vehicle for your brain to cruise around in. The relationship is perfectly reciprocal: Your body and your brain exist for each other. A body that can be moved or stilled, touched or evaded, scalded or warmed, frozen or cooled, strained or rested, starved, devoured, or nourished, is the raison d'être of the senses. And the sensations from your skin and body—touch, temperature, pain, and a few others you will learn about—are your mind's true foundation. All your other senses are merely added-on conveniences in comparison. After all, human beings can get by just fine in life without vision or hearing. Even people like Helen Keller who lack both these senses can thrive both mentally and physically. The brains of people born deaf don't develop auditory maps, and the brains of congenitally blind people never form visual maps, but even deaf-blind people have body maps. In contrast, vision or hearing without a body to relate sights and sounds to would be nothing but psychically empty patterns of information. Meaning is rooted in agency (the ability to act and choose), and agency depends on embodiment. In fact, this all is a hard-won lesson that the artificial intelligence community has finally begun to grasp after decades of frustration: Nothing truly intelligent is going to develop in a bodiless mainframe. In real life there is no such thing as a disembodied consciousness.

The sum total of your numerous, flexible, morphable body maps gives rise to the solid-feeling subjective sense of "me-ness" and to your ability to comprehend and navigate the world around you. You can think of the maps as a mandala whose overall pattern creates your embodied, feeling self. All your other mental faculties—vision, hearing, language, memory—hang supported in the matrix of this body mandala like organs on a skeleton. Developmentally speaking, it would be impossible to become a thinking, self-aware person without them.

If some of this sounds a little overheated, consider this. If you were to carry around a young mammal such as a kitten during its critical early months of brain development, allowing it to see everything in its environ-

WHAT IS A MANDALA?

In Hinduism and Buddhism, a mandala is a geometric pattern of images that symbolically maps out the universe from a human perspective. Mandalas are often used as a focus for the mind during meditation or for theological instruction. There is typically a central figure surrounded by other scenes and figures in a concentric arrangement.

A mandala is both an appealing metaphor and a convenient shorthand for referring to your brain's far-flung yet tightly integrated network of body maps. Following this analogy, the peripheral figures of the body mandala are your many cortical body maps, the large and the small, all intricately interconnected. The central figure is their composite product: the seamless sense of a whole, indivisible, embodied self.

ment but never permitting it to move around on its own, the unlucky creature would turn out effectively blind for life. While it would still be able to perceive levels of light, color, and shadow—the most basic, hardwired abilities of the visual system—its depth perception and object recognition would be abysmal. Its eyes and optic nerves would be perfectly normal and intact, yet its higher visual system would be next to useless.

How can this be? If an animal grows up seeing, shouldn't its brain's network of visual maps develop along normal lines? Shouldn't full exposure to visual information about form, shading, motion, color, parallax, size, and distance be enough to compensate for a lack of self-mobility? The surprising answer is no. Another ingredient is needed: The ability to use one's body freely to explore the world, even if it's only a small corner of it. As a young mammal in its formative stages moves around, feedback from its own bodily movements provides meaning to what it sees. Each step forward, each pause in its tracks, each quickening of its pace sends critical sensory information streaming up through its network of body maps, which in turn feeds its developing visual system the information it needs to make sense of all the otherwise meaningless blobs, colors, and shadows streaming in through the eyes. If an animal is exposed to high-quality visual information but only as a passive observer, its brain will never learn what any of that visual information is supposed to mean.

From this you can begin to appreciate how vision is indeed a hanger-on, a humble symbiote, within the body mandala. The same goes for all the "special" senses: The body mandala is their central integrator, the mind's ultimate frame of reference, the underlying metric system of perception. Sensation doesn't make sense except in reference to your embodied self.

Now that you've gotten a sense of the big picture, it's time to rein in the scope and look at the basics—the primary sensory and motor maps that prop up the rest of the body mandala like a foundation. So let's get started. When you were moving your hands over your body to get a feel for your body maps based on touch, did you brush against any really interesting spots? If you're a woman who likes to shake her booty at men, where is your rump in your brain? If you're a guy, where is your penis in your brain? Does it have a permanent location in your gray matter? If so, who discovered that fact—and how?

CHAPTER 2

THE LITTLE MAN IN THE BRAIN

or, Why Your Genitals Are Even Smaller Than You Think

Tall, with ramrod posture, piercing blue eyes, and buzz-cut blond hair, Wilder Penfield was the sort of doctor who inspired fanatical trust in his patients. For good reason.

In the 1930s, Penfield, a surgeon at the Montreal Neurological Institute, pioneered an operation in which he sawed through his awake patients' skulls, pulling away half of each brain casing like the flap on a Fabergé egg. Then, using an electrode, he probed their brains for hours at a time looking for abnormal tissue, such as a tumor, that might be causing their epilepsy. This entire procedure was a prelude to the actual surgery, which involved cutting out the abnormality.

A black-and-white film of an operation that took place in the late 1940s records one of these sessions. Penfield strides into the cavernous, shadowy operating room at his hospital. Spotlights fall directly on the assistant surgeons and nurses, who wear heavy white cotton gowns. Their faces and heads are mummy-wrapped in white gauze with only nerdy black glasses perched over bandaged noses.

A patient—let's call her Mary—is wheeled in, her head already shaved and marked with black ink. She lies on her left side and her head is secured in a metal frame, exposing the right side of her head to the surgical team. Nurses drape her with sterilized sheets. For the next twelve hours she'll remain in this little tent world, talking and joking with Penfield, who works above her, on the other side of the sheets.

Penfield reasons that if he can find the focal point of Mary's seizures, he can cut the offending tissue out of her brain. But first he must make certain he won't remove healthy tissue that would result in paralysis, or lack of speech, or damage to her memory or personality, or some other horrible loss. He has to be patient and he has to be careful. In his day, relatively little is known about the functional organization of the brain.

Since the brain has no pain receptors, all Mary needs is a local anesthetic. This is a good thing, because it is vital that she stay lucid throughout the procedure so she can report to Penfield exactly what happens in her mind while he explores her naked brain with his electrode. A surgeon's assistant administers the anesthetic, then starts cutting the skin. She peels and clips it back with what look like a dozen giant roach clips.

Next, using a special saw, Penfield removes a circular panel of bone, about the width of an orange, from Mary's head. He puts it aside. Three more protective layers of tissue between skull and brain are cut and fastened back with more clips, exposing the brain's gray, cauliflowerish surface. Every so often a nurse spritzes a saline solution onto the glistening tissue to keep it moist.

Penfield gets to work. Holding an electrode that looks like an electric toothbrush with a wire dangling from one end, he begins probing Mary's brain. She has no way of knowing when he is touching her brain, because the electrode is silent. He zaps a spot less than an inch behind the great fissure that divides the front part of Mary's brain from the back and says, "What do you feel now?"

Mary says she feels a tingling on her left hand. She does not believe that someone is touching her there; she just notices the sensation.

Penfield puts a small numbered ticket—like a tiny Post-it note—on the spot. He also dictates the result to a secretary who sits outside the operating room, watching through the glass. If Mary reports no sensation in a particular spot, that too is recorded.

Penfield tries another spot a short distance from the first. This time Mary feels the tingling on her left wrist. Another. She feels it on her left forearm. Another. She feels it on her left elbow. And so he goes, like the man in the cell phone ad—"Can you hear me now?"—only he says, "Feel anything now?" Penfield zaps dozens of points in this area of Mary's brain, and each creates illusory sensations in one or a few parts of her body: cheek, back, side of her tongue, toes, throat, and so on. Some regions seem to overlap one another—notably the hand and face regions—

but overall these neural representations of all Mary's different body parts are remarkably discrete.

Over the next twenty years, Penfield described similar reactions from scores of patients as he probed the same strip of brain tissue. He found spots for toes in ten patients. He found feet more often, but they tended to be mixed with a lower leg or heel. He found sensations "in the leg," or spanning thigh to knee, or knee to ankle, and so on. Only four people felt stimulation on their hips. Heads, arms, shoulders, elbows, forearms, and wrists were felt in many combinations.

A twenty-seven-year-old patient had areas of this body map that gave rise to a tingling in her left labium, left breast, and nipple. The labial sensation was also accompanied by a sensation in her left foot. Some male patients also reported sensations induced on one side or the other of their penis and often in association with foot sensations. Even stranger, Penfield found surprising discontinuities in the body maps. The representation of the penis and vagina are not located at the junction of the representations of the torso and thighs, but beyond the tip of the toes. This fact has been suggested as an explanation for the prevalence of foot fetishes. (One recent study claims that Penfield got it wrong, however, and argues that the map representations of the genitals are located between those of the legs and the trunk, just as they are in real bodies. The researchers suggest that Victorian mores may have led people to say they felt stimulation in the leg or trunk because they were embarrassed to mention genitals. But other evidence still supports Penfield's original map. The jury is still out.) "Curiously enough," wrote Penfield, "we have never produced erotic sensations of any sort by stimulation."

Meanwhile, the representation of the face is next to the hand, not the neck. Hands reacted vigorously to Penfield's electrode. He induced scores of sensations in the little finger, ring finger, middle finger, index finger, and thumb. The nose and face were much less sensitive, but the lips responded tremendously. So did the teeth, gums, jaw, the roof of the mouth, and, above all, the tongue.

From all this patiently collected data Penfield catalogued a complete brain map of the body's surface. Penfield playfully nicknamed this map the "homunculus," an obsolete term from medieval philosophy that means "little man" in Latin. This was the first-ever map of a human being's primary touch map, or somatosensory cortex, which lies along a narrow strip

A HOMUNCULUS BY ANY OTHER NAME . . .

Sometimes one philosopher will savage another by charging him with the "homunculus fallacy." In philosophy, that's a serious offense. Since Penfield's use of the term is quite different, it's worth a few words to clarify the distinction.

The premodern idea of the homunculus was akin to the helmsman of a one-man submarine. Just as the helmsman senses the world outside through a periscope, sonar screen, and various gauges to inform him of fuel levels, external temperature and pressure, and so on, the homunculus is presented with sensory information from the eyes, ears, skin, and gut, which are piped into his bridge through neural fibers. And just as the helmsman has an array of buttons and levers that let him alter his vessel's bearing, speed, depth, and so on, the homunculus has the power to send impulses out through the neural fibers of the brain's motor system to make the body move in whatever ways it deems appropriate.

Obviously, a literal reading of this idea leads straight to a paradox of infinite regress. It utterly fails to explain perception, understanding, and action: How does the homunculus perceive, understand, and act? The only way to "explain" the homunculus's abilities is to posit another, smaller homunculus inside "him." But then the same problem pops up, and you're left with an endless series of Russian doll homunculi.

No one who is serious about philosophical rigor subscribes to a straightforward homunculus model of intelligence anymore. But there are subtler forms of it. A philosopher (or a neuroscientist) commits the homunculus fallacy whenever he "explains" something important about how the mind works by sidestepping the real difficulties of the problem and shifting them to another, unspecified level of explanation—where it remains just as mysterious as ever.

Similarly, the cartoonish overlays that are commonly used to depict the warped "anatomy" of a homunculus may tempt you to imagine "him" as a tiny impish pilot, sitting behind a control panel eating pizza and calling the shots. But it's nothing like that. All the action takes place in cells and their interactions. Nevertheless, the cartoon figures are helpful because they remind you of the fact that even though there are some areas of overlap and some non-body-realistic discontinuities, these are the brain's maps of your body.

Penfield named his body maps "homunculi" as a term of art, not as a metaphysical statement. Penfield revived the archaic term because it was a cute and concise way to refer to the maps. In neuroscience the term is still used in this way—as shorthand for referring to a maplike representation of the body in the brain.

In the modern neuroscientific view there is not one homunculus, but many. No single one of them is particularly smart or skillful.

Our amazing physical intelligence springs not from any one of these dumb little homunculi, but from the web of interaction between them. There is no one "highest" homunculus among them, no one single node that could be destroyed to bring down the whole remainder of the network. No homunculus is at the "center" because there is no center. No body map could claim to be the "essence" of the embodied self because there are no such things as essences, at least not as far as science has been able to determine. The brain is highly interactive. Each part—each map—imprints its own unique stamp into the character of the mind's psychic churnings of mental processing.

less than an inch wide that runs from ear to ear across the crown of the head. You can see it on the left side of the illustration below.

Penfield also explored his patients' motor cortexes and found a similar body map. Electrical zaps to this sector of the brain engendered not sensations, but movements. When he touched one spot, a foot jerked. Another spot made a knee flex. Another arched an eyebrow. Patients sometimes moved their hips or their whole trunk. Fingers moved a lot, often together. And here again, the lips showed hair-trigger sensitivity. Penfield mused that the lips are the most important extremity in the

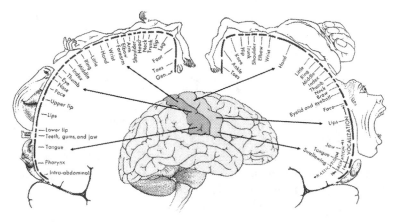

Penfield's homunculi. At left, the primary somatosensory area, a body map based on touch and related sensations. At right, the primary motor area, your basic body map for voluntary movement. Shown here is the brain's right hemisphere; the left hemisphere contains a near identical pair of the same maps.

brain's map of body movements. He noted that the newborn baby's sensorium (the world as experienced through its senses) is all mouth and lips, rooting for the mother's nipple. Under the electrode, jaws moved. Tongues twitched. Necks turned. Penfield could make people swallow or gag. He found a spot that elicited highly practiced chewing motions. Often the head turned as if looking toward nonexistent sights or sounds. But he could not find a spot to produce an urge to pee or cry.

Penfield found it notable that most of the movements he induced by stimulating this map were motorically primitive, unrefined, unpurposeful—the very kinds of movements newborns make. They are gross, he wrote, "like the sound of a piano when the keyboard is struck with the palm of the hand."

Eventually Penfield compiled a complete output map of the human musculature, which is shown on the right side of the illustration. When cells in this map fire, signals are sent down the spinal cord to particular muscles or groups of muscles. A foot moves, a hand clenches, the lips smack. There is substantially more overlap between neighboring regions in this primary motor map than in the primary touch map. It is somewhat "blurrier," less crisply defined, a fact that reflects the greater complexity of coordinating contraction and relaxation in dozens of interrelated muscles. Nevertheless the degree of order is striking and fundamental to the grace and precision of your movements.

After nearly two decades of exploration and surgery, Penfield was at last ready to compile his findings in a book, *The Cerebral Cortex of Man*, published in 1950 with his colleague Dr. Theodore Rasmussen. He also hired an illustrator, Mrs. H. P. Cantlie, to draw the cartoons pictured in the illustration on page 19. These grotesque, rather bizarre-looking manikins were a hit with the public and quickly become iconic—the $E = mc^2$ of neuroscience. They have been reprinted and redrawn countless times in textbooks and popular science writings through this day. They titillate the imagination. Many sculptors and other artists have been inspired by them as well, as shown in the photographs on page 21.

Penfield's now-classic book includes data on more than 520 human brains, each marked by sticky notes as he explored many other cortical regions. For example, he found areas where movements are planned, and others where strong feelings—sinking, floating, nausea, choking, a racing

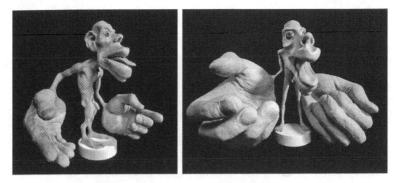

It is also possible to render Mrs. Cantlie's motor and sensory homunculi as three-dimensional sculptures. Both of these models are on display at the Natural History Museum in London. Left: the somatosensory homunculus. Right: the motor homunculus.

heart—are aroused. Poking around just above the ears in forty of his patients, he found areas that conjured memories—voices from the past, scenes from childhood, a certain song, reveries. Penfield believed he had found the physical basis for what he called the "engram"—an enduring change in the brain that accounts for the persistence of memory. Ironically, while he thought his findings on memory were his crowning contribution to science, a few decades after his death they were overturned by a more sophisticated theory of memory. But Penfield's homunculi live on.

One of the most striking features of the Penfield maps is how comically misproportioned they seem: giant lips, tongues, and hands; tiny heads, arms, and trunks. It is a grotesque parody of the human form. Why should this be?

The answer is straightforward. Take the primary touch map. The sensory receptors in your body are distributed unevenly. They are densely concentrated in the body parts where you need high acuity and dexterity, and sparse in parts where superior sensory resolution isn't paramount. This is why your fingers can easily distinguish the individual nubs of velvet on an armchair, while your buttocks give you only general information about the chair's firmness, temperature, texture, and the presence or absence of thumbtacks.

But the situation up in your cortex is quite different. Here your brain cells are packed together at a uniform density, like a honeycomb. It is this simple fact that accounts for the homunculi's ridiculous proportions. Your finger maps take up one hundred times as much cortical real estate as your torso map because there is a hundred-to-one ratio of touch receptors in your fingers compared to your torso. The actual surface area of your skin where the sensations originate is irrelevant in apportioning your homuncular map; all that matters is the incoming sensory bandwidth. Hence your huge lips and hands but scrawny arms and legs and disappointing rear end.

The distortions of your primary motor homunculus exist for much the same reason. The muscle groups in your mouth and hands, which are used in fast-changing, highly coordinated ways, receive far richer projections from your motor cortex than do less dexterous muscle groups like those in your back, knees, and hips.

Many people seeing the sensory homunculus for the first time comment on (even object to) how small the genitals are. They expect that these organs would merit an allotment of territory commensurate with their sensitivity and the disproportionate mindshare they command. The confusion comes from the multiple meanings of the word "sensitive." Sensitive can refer to high acuity. Your fingers, lips, and tongue are sensitive in this sense: generously packed with somatic receptors of every type, able to make extremely fine discriminations. Your genitals are extremely sensitive in a different sense. A penis and a clitoris can tell the difference between one finger and two, but they can't read Braille. Instead, the genitals are sensitive in the sense that just a little bit of stimulation marshals a huge share of your attention. The exquisite pleasure you get from having them stimulated by the right person in the right way is not a function of their acuity, but of the unique way they are wired up with your brain's pleasure and reward circuitry.

After Penfield

Penfield explored all over the brain and found a handful of other, smaller body maps as well. Even before he zapped the brain of his first patient, he knew that he would find touch and motor maps, since his contemporaries had already found them in cats, dogs, monkeys, and other mammals. By the same token, Penfield also knew of a few other maps he should look for, and found them.

For instance, he was able to locate a region known as the secondary somatosensory cortex, which performs a slightly higher level of shape, texture, and motion analysis than the primary touch map. Yet he found this secondary map much harder to explore and understand. For one thing, it is quite a bit smaller than the primary map, and its neurons have larger receptive fields that are wired to make more complex sensory discriminations. (Every neuron in a given body map receives information from a specific group of "downstream" neurons, known as that cell's receptive field. Receptive fields in your primary touch map are made up of receptors in the skin itself. For cells in most other body maps, receptive field inputs come from other, lower-level body maps elsewhere in the cortex.) Penfield's difficulties were compounded by the fact that the secondary touch map is difficult to access, half-buried where the parietal lobe plunges beneath the temporal lobe like a tucked-in bedsheet.

Penfield had better luck in the frontal lobes. Just in front of the primary motor cortex he found a small, higher-order body map where action plans are made. It is imaginatively known as the premotor cortex. Penfield found that stimulation to this map produced far more complex movements than he could get out of the primary map. While stimulating the hand region of the primary map causes random jerking of the fingers and wrist, stimulating the premotor hand area brings forth more complex and fluid action fragments, such as moving the hand smoothly up to the mouth. To extend Penfield's piano metaphor, if zaps to the primary motor map are like the discordant din of notes from a palm striking a keyboard, then zaps to the premotor homunculus reel off simple melodies like musical scales or "Chopsticks."

Higher-order motor maps like those in your premotor cortex also afforded one of the earliest glimpses into the neural mechanisms behind intentionality and free will. Penfield's patients reported that the movements induced through the primary motor cortex felt involuntary—like something that had been done *to* them. But the actions produced by stimulation to the premotor cortex were accompanied by an inkling of intention—like something being done *by* them. Or sometimes Penfield would stimulate a spot and no movement would be produced, but the patient would report a sudden desire to perform some simple gesture or action.

OTHER BODY MAPS: THE CEREBELLUM

Most of this book is about the body maps of the cortex—the newest, and in humans the largest, part of the brain and the seat of intelligent perception and thought. But there are also body maps outside the cortex, which play just as vital a role as cortical body maps in creating your embodied sense of self and your physical intelligence.

A prime example can be found in the cerebellum, an extremely ancient structure that sits at the bottom rear of the brain attached to the brain stem. Originally it served as the brain's chief motor coordinator. But as the cortex expanded, it took over much of that role, and the cerebellum moved into a new role as a kind of motor outsourcing hub, fine-tuning, smoothing, and rapid-sequencing the action commands of the cortex. The cerebellum looks small, but it contains nearly half the neurons in the brain. It also contains a pair of body maps.

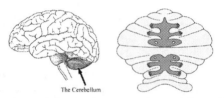

The Cerebellum

On the right: The cerebellum has been opened up and flattened like unfolded origami. Two distorted body maps were recently found along its central axis.

These motor map signals are the basis of modern brain-machine interface systems, by which a paralyzed person can have electrodes implanted in his or her motor cortex and learn to move a cursor or a robot arm through pure thought. More on this later.

Before moving on—and for fun—let's take a look at the body maps of some other, nonhuman critters whose body maps are very different from yours and your fellow primates'. Generally speaking, the primate lifestyle requires sensitive, dexterous hands and mouths that are suitable for patient, deliberate acts of peeling, prying, and probing food items, accurately grasping branches and judging their suitability for climbing in the treetops, and methodically combing through each other's hair and crushing lice between the tips of the fingernails.

But other creatures make their way in the world very differently. Their body maps tell the story:

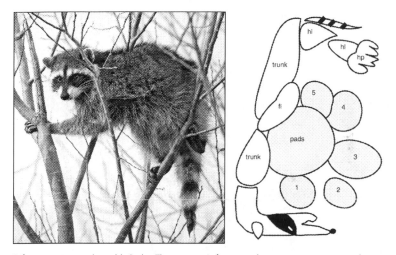

Left: a raccoon in the wild. Right: The raccoon's forepaw dominates its primary touch map. Digits numbered 1–5, "fl" = foreleg, "hl" = hind leg, "hp" = hind paw.

The raccoon, like the monkey, lives or dies by the sensitivity of its hands. Within each dainty little forepaw are packed as many touch receptors as there are in the entire human hand. Its representation in the primary sensory cortex is easy to spot: An entire bulge of brain tissue is devoted to each digit. All told, about 60 percent of a raccoon's neocortical surface is taken up by the fingers and palm.

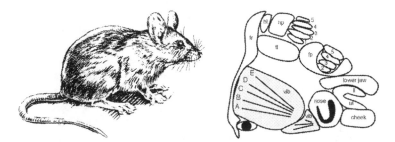

Left: a mouse. Right: the mouse's primary touch map. Digits numbered 1–5, whiskers lettered A–E, "tr" = trunk, "fl" = foreleg, "fp" = forepaw, "hl" = hind leg, "hp" = hind paw, "ll" = lower lip, "ul" = upper lip, "vib" = vibrissae, or whiskers.

The mouse's main sensory organs are its whiskers. Fully half of its sensory cortex is devoted to them. Mice sweep their whiskers back and forth constantly as they nose their way through the world, and from the ways the whiskers bend and vibrate, they can get an instant sense of an opening's width or an object's size and even useful information about its shape and consistency—all that from a few stiff little hairs. The mouse's sensory cortex has special sectors studded throughout known as "barrels" (because under a microscope they look like, well, barrels, evidently). Each barrel finely processes information from just one of those exquisitely sensitive whiskers. Each section of a barrel contains a map in which cells are systematically organized to indicate the direction of whisker deflection.

Top: a star-nosed mole poking its head and forepaws above ground. Bottom: artist's rendering of the same creature with its body parts drawn in proportion to their share of its primary somatosensory cortex.

The star-nosed mole is an odd beast indeed. Like all moles, it digs tunnels, has underdeveloped eyesight, and seldom ventures above ground. Its most striking feature is its nose, which is ringed with twenty-two small, writhing, tentacle-like protrusions. These "rays" are so sensitive that the mole can detect an earthworm shifting around through several inches of soil. A star-shaped somatosensory map dominates the mole's cortex. The nose is so richly represented that its star shape is apparent to simple naked-eye inspection of its cortex.

The pig brain sports a supersized snout region. An entire circular bulge of brain tissue in each hemisphere is devoted to it, and at the center of that bulge is a dimple where the nostril lets in to the animal's powerful airways. Such snout-centrism is entirely befitting an animal that roots for a living.

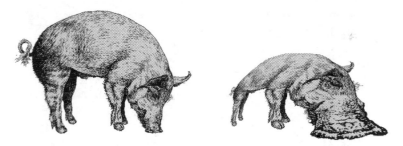

The humble pig meets the world head-on with its snout, jaw, and powerful neck.

It is fascinating to imagine what it is like to be one of these other mammals. How would it feel to have your body awareness focused and distributed so differently from the primate norm? What is it like to be that pig, with your keen sense of touch so concentrated in your snout, your head backed by powerful neck muscles, moving nose-first and jaw-ready through earth and underbrush, questing after whiffs picked up through your phenomenal sense of smell? How different that is from the prim hand-to-mouth, fondle-at-a-distance MO we use.

CHAPTER 3

DUELING BODY MAPS

or, Why You Still Feel Fat After Losing Weight

Have you ever seen a fat person who was comfortable in his or her own skin? Think of Jackie Gleason high-stepping across a stage like a tutu-clad hippo on pointe. If you're too young to visualize the inestimable Gleason, consider the contemporary American comedian Jack Black, who, despite a propensity to chubbiness, moves gracefully, athletically, self-lovingly around a movie set.

And now consider talk show megastar Oprah Winfrey before and after her lionhearted battle with yo-yo dieting. She reveals the whole story in a video, *Make the Connection*—how for twenty years she lived her life unconsciously, how she felt out of control, ashamed, lonely, filled with self-loathing. Afraid to confront her traumatic past, she ate compulsively to dull the pain. Once, sitting near ringside watching Mike Tyson in a world heavyweight championship fight, she was shocked to realize that they both weighed the same—216 pounds. So she starved herself, dropping 67 pounds. And then ballooned back up to 226 pounds.

Famously, in 1992, Oprah decided she had to take control of her life. With the help of a professional trainer, Bob Greene, she began a daily regimen of intense aerobic exercise plus a low-fat diet. The rest is history. As chronicled on her television shows, books, and videos, Oprah conquered her weight problem, with occasional minor backslides, through vigorous physical conditioning, hard work, and determination.

No doubt the exercise played a major role in Oprah's weight loss. But there is another explanation for her success that has never been brought to light. Apart from all that time spent in the gym, the 6 A.M. workouts, the sweat and suffering, the weaning from deep-fry and chocolate, her transformation can also be described as a story of dueling body maps, of how she used one body map to remodel a second body map.

To understand how this works, you need to understand the nature of both maps. One, called the body schema, is a felt sense based on physical properties of your body. The second, the body image, stems from learned attitudes about your body.

The Body Schema

You already know about your body maps, à la Penfield, based on touch. You have sensors all over your body surface that are responsive to gentle caresses or pressure or pain or heat or cold. But there are two other ingredients to your body's felt sense, or body schema, that operate almost entirely outside consciousness. And while scientists have known about these sensory channels for decades, they are only now being traced to specific regions of the brain. One reads signals from inside your body. The other reads signals from your inner ear to give you a sense of balance.

Take a moment to form a mental picture of your body's muscles, bones, joints, and tendons. These tissues are endowed with specialized receptors that detect tiny movements—the twitch of a muscle fiber, mechanical stress on a bone, angular rotation of a joint, or stretch of a tendon. Whenever they sense change, these sensors send the information up to your brain to update your sense of where you are in space and how your body is configured. The signals are first mapped in your primary touch map, then branch and filter upward through other, higher-order maps in your body mandala. These maps guide your body movements and expectations about those movements.

The weight of your body and its postures are calculated by these sensors, providing what is called proprioception, meaning "perception of one's own." If you fail a sobriety test—you can't walk a straight line or touch your finger to your nose—it's because your sense of where you and how your limbs are located in space is impaired. During growth spurts, some children and teenagers temporarily lose this body sense and feel as if their feet or legs are missing. When you learn a new skill or sport, you re-hone this body sense through practice.

Your body schema is also informed by a library of what many people

OFF OUR ROCKERS

Of all your body senses, the one you tend to underappreciate most is your sense of balance. You only pay attention to it if you happen to lose it, which for most people is a rare happenstance. Miss that last step, spin yourself around, jump from a dock onto a bouncy boat, and you'll feel a sudden loss of balance. But then, if all goes well, you'll regain it in an instant. Of all your senses, balance is the most intangible. You can point to eyes, ears, skin, and other organs to explain the five primary senses, but balance is somehow different. It's difficult to bring whatever "balance" is into consciousness by thinking about it. You can never switch it off. It's just there.

Balance is with you constantly because balance is all about dealing with gravity. From the moment you exit the warm floating world of your mother's womb, you are bathed in the force of gravity. Gravity exerts an attractive force on your body every living, breathing moment of your life.

In the beginning, you are helpless against it. But as you gain control over your limbs, you find that you can roll over and—voilà!—sit up. You start balancing your body. Nobody builds a two-legged chair, because it's not stable, but you, as a human, learn to walk on two legs by calibrating Earth's gravity with your head, body, and limbs. Soon you are off and running.

Balance is achieved by integrating numerous brain maps, but one you may not know much about is called the vestibular system. Just as you have eyes for seeing and ears for hearing, you have three little canals, tiny stones, and "hairs" inside your inner ear that specialize in detecting gravity and acceleration.

The canals, or semicircular canals, are fluid-filled tubes that lie on three axes—up and down, left and right, forward and back. As you move your head, the fluid sloshes around in the canals, and tiny sensors, called hair cells, pick up the direction and speed of movement. Your brain uses this information to develop a clear model of the world in three dimensions and to figure out where your head is moving in relation to gravity.

Of course you don't achieve balance with your head alone. Vestibular signals are integrated with other sensory systems for you to have a functioning whole body schema. For example, vestibular signals go to your eyes. This is why you can shake your head while reading this page and still track the words. Your eyes work with vestibular information to correct for your head movements.

Vestibular signals are intimately tied to touch. Try this little experiment: Stand next to a wall on one leg, let your arms dangle, and close your eyes. See what happens. Now assume the same posture, touch the wall with the tip of one finger, and close your eyes. See what happens this time.

Nothing stabilizes balance better than light touches and contact with the environment.

Vestibular information also goes to vomiting centers in your brain stem and up to higher brain areas involved in body perception, self-motion, the space around your body, and that biggie, self-awareness.

As you know from experience, balance is dynamic. Gravity is constant, but you are recalibrating all the time.

When astronauts return from space and do deep knee bends, they get the feeling that the ground is rushing up under their feet. Their brains have adapted to zero gravity and need time to adjust.

When you are on a boat all day, bobbing up and down on the waves, you may feel wobbly back on land because your vestibular system is still tracking the motion. Some people get motion sickness due to a highly sensitive vestibular system.

But people who gradually lose their vestibular organs as a result of injury or disease will never, no matter how hard you try to make them, be motion sick. They can navigate, but must rely on vision and pressure on their feet to calibrate balance, although they have trouble walking on sand or in the dark.

But the most common reason people lose their sense of balance is aging. All brain systems decay with age, along with failing eyes and diminished hearing. But there are ways to reverse wobbly postures: Treat the bottoms of your feet.

The soles of your feet have touch receptors that send signals up to your brain every time you stand and put pressure on the ground. These signals are combined in higher brain maps with vestibular, visual, and other touch information to keep you nimble on your toes.

But these foot signals can blur as receptors become less sharp with age. Diabetes and poor blood flow can deaden the foot. You begin to sway. But as James Collins, a biomedical engineer at Boston University, discovered, if you add a faint vibration to the bottom of the foot—he invented insoles that do just that—your brain will automatically pick up degraded signals from your feet. With his insoles, eighty-year-olds can stand as straight as thirty-year-olds.

You don't necessarily need electronic gadgets to keep your vestibular system in tune, however. Walking on cobblestones is a low-tech, proven route to the same end. Studies in Europe have shown that balance deteriorates more slowly in elderly people who walk regularly on cobblestone than in those who use only modern sidewalks. The Chinese have known about this for centuries. Go to almost any park in any city in China, and you will find thousands of cobblestones laid out in lovely patterns on the ground. People take off their shoes and walk on the stones to achieve better health. The science of body maps explains why it works.

call "muscle memories," although the term is rather inaccurate. These memories actually reside in the brain's motor maps, not down in the muscles proper, as the term would seem to suggest. These muscle memories give you an intuitive understanding about how your body is able to move and what it is capable of. This implicit knowledge includes things like how far you can bend over, what parts of your back you can reach with your hands, and which objects on the dinner table are within arm's reach without leaning. The vast majority of these understandings and judgments are unconscious. Your body mandala is constantly computing them and using them to update your schema. (Just to be clear on the distinction, your body mandala is the physical network of body maps in your brain; your body schema is the felt experience of your body constructed by these maps.)

You also have special receptors within each ear that are sensitively attuned to where your head is with respect to gravity, three-dimensional space, and motion. When you walk down the street with your head bobbing up and down, you can still read signs on buildings thanks to this so-called vestibular system. When you feel dizzy or nauseated on a rough boat ride through choppy seas, it's because signals from these receptors have reached your conscious awareness. In your brain, two small areas combine this gravity-sensing system with input from your eyes and body so that you know where you are at all times.

Your body schema is a physiological construct. Your brain creates it from the interaction of touch, vision, proprioception, balance, and hearing. It even extends it out into the space around your body. You use it to help locate objects in space or on your body—to swat a mosquito on your arm, to grasp a doorknob, or duck out of a dodgeball's way.

Again in your imagination, put out your hand, palm up, fingers pointed straight ahead. Now rotate your hand until your fingers point to the right. Rotate it again, fingers pointing to the left. You can do these movements without vision because you have an online mental representation of your body. When you reach out to grasp a coffee cup, you don't have to think about where your hand is or where it is headed. Your body sense automatically plans and directs the movements. When in the middle of the night you grope your way to the bathroom, your body sense guides you there.

Your schema is updated constantly by the flow of sensation from your skin, joints, muscles, and viscera. Your continuous sense of inhabiting a body embedded within a larger world stems in large part from this mental construct.

Moreover, you are rarely aware of sensations from your body. They occur automatically. While you can close your eyes and cover your ears, you can't turn off your body sense. If you are born blind, other senses can compensate for vision. But if you were born without receptors that map your body, you would not know you had a body.

Loss of proprioception in adulthood is rare, but it has happened. For example, in 1972 a nineteen-year-old Englishman named Ian Waterman contracted a rare disease. While the nerves that carry information from his brain down to his body, instructing it how to move, were intact, the nerves that carry information from his body back up into his brain were destroyed. Imagine how this feels. Waterman can see but not feel where his body is located, whether he is moving or not moving. At first he was a mess, like a living rag doll. Gradually, he taught himself to move again by watching and guiding his actions visually. But the second he closes his eyes, he collapses in a heap.

The idea of the body schema was first proposed in 1911 by two British neurologists, Sir Henry Head and Gordon Holmes. Head and Holmes figured out that, like touch information, signals from your body's musculoskeletal system are carried into your brain to determine your posture and the position of your limbs. According to Head, we build up internal postural models of ourselves in conjunction with models of the surface of our bodies. He dubbed this the body schemata (now just called body schema), defined as "organized models of ourselves."

Head and Holmes also realized that, wondrously, your body schema expands with the clothes you wear.

"Anything which participates in the conscious movement of our bodies is added to the model of ourselves and becomes part of the schemata," Head wrote. Thus, "a woman's power of localization may extend to the feather in her hat." In Sir Henry's day, the Edwardian era, women wore hats with wide brims and large swoopy feathers. The feather, he observed, was incorporated into the woman's body schema.

The next time you see a person wearing a cowboy hat, watch how he ducks down when he passes through a doorway. Better yet, if you have a

ILLUSIONS OF THE BODY

Your body schema feels reliable and stable most of the time, so you may be surprised at how mutable it can be under the right conditions. Using certain tricks, you can induce somatic illusions to make parts of your body feel like they are growing, shrinking, bending, embodied in foreign objects, or otherwise warped or displaced in impossible ways. Armed with these illusions, you can be the life of the party—but bear in mind, some people are immune to them. They will miss out on the fun.

A whole family of these tricks involves the use of small vibrators, or buzzers, that can be taped or held against your body. (Researchers often use standard 100 Hz physiotherapy vibrators, but many kinds of small personal massagers should work.) The buzzers work by confusing the stretch-sensing fibers, called muscle spindles, in your muscles. Spindles sense the length, and changes in length, of your muscles. Their constant reporting to your brain plays a vital role in your body schema.

Like all the senses, proprioception is fallible. The vibrations "fool" your muscle spindles into informing your body maps that the tendon is slackening. At the simplest level of interpretation, this corresponds to the feeling that the joint is bending, even though it isn't. You have a discrepancy between what you see and the proprioceptively sensed position of your limb.

But simple bending isn't the only illusory sensation buzzers can fabricate. The brain is a very clever and willing rationalizer. When combined with other sensory signals that don't jibe with the tendon-stretch information, rather than conclude that that information is faulty, your body mandala will try to come up with an integrated interpretation, even if that interpretation is physically impossible.

Here's one of the simplest examples. Tape a buzzer to your triceps tendon, lean against a wall with just that arm, and close your eyes. You soon feel that your arm is growing longer, and your head feels as if it's moving away from the wall! Now tape the buzzer to your biceps tendon (in the crook of your elbow), and you get the opposite sensation: Your arm feels as if it's shrinking. If you wait long enough, you may even feel your forehead tingle with anticipation as it passes ghostlike through the wall. Of course, in reality, your arm and body are motionless, as you can confirm by opening your eyes at any point.

Or consider the Pinocchio illusion. Tape a buzzer to the biceps tendon, touch your index finger to your nose, and close your eyes. It feels as if your nose is growing two feet long! Here's why: Your body mandala needs to reconcile two contradictory pieces of data. Your finger is in constant contact with the tip of your nose, and your elbow is extending away from your face. The best-fit rationalization is that your nose is magically lengthening.

Next consider the shrinking waist illusion. Tape a buzzer to each triceps tendon, put your hands around your waist, and look up at the ceiling. After a few moments, you will feel your waist begin to shrink! It draws closer and closer toward a point in the pit of your stomach. You expect your fingers to meet each other in front and your thumbs to touch behind your back, but because your waist isn't actually shrinking, they never do. (Sorry, miracle diet seekers.)

You get the idea. The list of buzzer-based illusions goes on. If you vibrate both your Achilles tendons, you will feel that you're pitching forward on rubbery ankles. Vibrate the muscles at the base of your neck, and you'll feel as if your head is swiveling into an anatomically impossible position, looking back, like a ghoul in a horror film.

And if you don't mind being in a pitch-black room, you can, with the help of a friend, try this little experiment on yourself. The room must be utterly dark. (Another great place to try this is inside a cave where there are no photons whatsoever.) Stand in a comfortable position and wave your hand in front of your face. You will have the powerful impression that you can see your hand. Now lower your hand and ask your friend to wave his hand in front of your face. You will not be able to see it. The reason? When you move your own hand, the multisensory part of your brain that combines movement and vision is activated. An accurate visual prediction of your hand's movements percolates through your body mandala into your visual centers, creating the sightlike experience in spite of the darkness. But when your friend moves his hand, your visual areas are not co-stimulated. You may imagine in your mind's eye what your friend's hand must be doing out there in the dark, but the experience is not at all the same.

Other illusions don't require you to close your eyes, such as the doorframe illusion children around the world enjoy at slumber parties. Stand in a doorway and press the backs of your wrists outward against the frame as hard as you dare for thirty seconds or so. Then relax your arms, step forward, and it feels as if your arms are being levitated.

But this is child's play, a super-low-tech way of fatiguing your proprioceptors. Some of the most interesting somatic illusions involve the combination of vision and somatic sensation, which happens in the posterior parietal lobe. Let's consider two of them:

First, imagine a periscope tube that hangs from the ceiling and snugs down over your head like a helmet. But unlike the periscope in a submarine, you keep your hands in your lap and can pivot your view simply by turning your neck. Furthermore, this periscope is rigged up in an unusual way: For every one degree your neck turns, your view rotates by two degrees. Thus, at the extreme, if you turn your head all the way to the left or the right, you actually end up seeing the view behind you. What do you experience wearing this thing? It's called the rubber-neck illusion: It feels as if your neck has become twisty like an owl's. Building one at home is probably beyond most readers, though it's entirely possible to do.

Finally, one more great illusion that you can more realistically perform at home is called the rubber-hand illusion. What you need is a fake hand (from a mannequin or a Halloween store, for example), a freestanding cardboard partition, a table, two chairs, and a friend. Sit down and lay the rubber arm facing away from yourself, palm down, on the table in front of you. Lay your real hand palm down next to it, making sure the orientation of both hands is the same. Now place the partition between the two hands, hiding your real hand but leaving the false one in plain sight. Next, have your friend sit down at the other side of the table and gently manipulate both hands in the same way with identical timing while you watch the fake hand. For example, on both hands your friend taps the third knuckle twice, then drums her fingers on the pinky finger joint, then makes a long stroke down the length of the index finger, and so on. Soon, if you're like the majority of people, you will feel those sensations coming from the false hand!

The kicker is that the fake hand prop is not really needed. You can sometimes get the same illusion—if not always as vivid—using other objects that only vaguely or abstractly resemble a hand, such as a small kitchen broom or a twig from a tree. You may even do it with no fake hand at all, just the tabletop.

How does it work? Visual and tactile stimulation converge in combined vision and touch maps in your posterior parietal lobe, and because they are well correlated in time, those maps will accept the interpretation that the tactile sensations are actually coming from the inanimate thing you are watching.

Interestingly, people show different degrees of ability to experience this illusion. Some people feel it vividly and almost instantly, while others take a long time to start experiencing it and may "lose the feel" for it. Neuroscientists are just starting to search for the basis of these individual differences, which may end up having practical implications for prosthetics, virtual reality, neurotherapy and rehabilitation, and anorexia treatment; anorexics are immune to the rubber-hand illusion.

Stetson or can borrow one, try it yourself. Walk through a door and notice your posture. Did you stoop down ever so slightly? Unless you are very tall, the hat probably cleared the doorframe with inches to spare. Yet you still felt the need to bend your knees or duck your head. A hat is an inanimate object. Yet you act as if it were a part of your head. As far as your body schema is concerned, it is part of your body. If you wear the hat regularly, you will gain precise though largely unconscious knowledge of its height and width, and will pass through doors with an automatic, tiny tilt of your head that's just right to miss the doorframe by a hair.

When you work with instructors of dance, yoga, tai chi, Pilates, Alexander Technique, Feldenkrais, or dozens of other kinds of movement training, you are basically working on body schema awareness. These methods teach you to purposefully attend to the many core elements of your schema as a means of self-exploration.

Personal trainers say that they can often identify thin people who were previously overweight, noting that such individuals still have the body language of a fat person, with shoulders forward, head tilted down, legs slightly splayed. Their walk is heavy, their movements cumbersome. On the other hand, a fat person can have the body language of a ballerina, with a straight back, erect shoulders, lightness of step, and fluidity of motion.

Finally, your shadow binds extrapersonal space to your body, which is why many people are superstitious about stepping on shadows. As far as your brain is concerned, your shadow is a part of your body, as real as skin. If you walk down a path with your eyes down and a shadow looms into your peripheral vision, your brain sounds the alarm. Your space is being invaded. Time to pay attention.

A Paean to the Parietal Lobe

To better understand how your body schema emerges, it is helpful to know a little bit more about your parietal lobe. If you place your hand toward the back of your head and over your ear, your parietal lobe is beneath your hand. This area's upper rear sector, called the posterior parietal cortex, is chock full of maps of your body and the space around your body. Like the mighty Mississippi, it lies at the confluence of several great tributaries. Highly processed information converges in the posterior parietal from all your major senses—touch, proprioception, vision, hearing, and balance—plus a constant stream of information about movements and action plans flowing in from your frontal motor maps. Probably more than any other region of your brain, this area constitutes the center of your embodied self embedded in a wider world. Here is where your body schema, sense of balance, and feeling of physical wholeness "come together." Parietal neurons are not concerned with identifying things in terms of their names, identities, or meanings. Rather, they are concerned with the composition of space and your body's relationship to its surroundings.

Many of the maps in the posterior parietal cortex represent your body in different coordinate systems, or frames of reference. Some maps "think" in head-and-neck-centered coordinates; some are trunk-centered; some are arm-and-shoulder-centered; some are eye-centered; some are hand-centered; some are whole-body-centered. Your parietal lobe juggles these many coordinate systems, all the while keeping them tightly integrated with the activity of your motor maps, to produce the impression that your body is whole and unified in purpose. It creates your (usually) seamless understanding of where you are in the world and how you relate to it. That last point is worth emphasizing: The mental map you keep of the world around you is represented not in dry, referenceless, x-y-z coordinates, but in terms of your bodily relation to it.

It is amazing enough to know that this system works during a mundane action like getting up off your sofa and heading for the kitchen to start dinner. At the height of human skill and talent it is even more astounding. Imagine soccer star Mia Hamm in the thick of a skirmish. She is hurtling toward the other team's goal just a few meters ahead. She is running and dribbling the ball between her feet. She is so well trained and talented, the ball is at one with her inside her peripersonal space, as integrated into her body mandala as her own feet. She knows the ball's position and speed each fraction of a second. All around her are other players running in different directions at different speeds. A few of them are closing in fast. She feels it the instant they penetrate her peripersonal space. Her eyes sweep the field. Her head and body pivot, and the balance organs in each inner ear send precise information about the angle, velocity, and acceleration of her head into her vestibular cortex, where it is immediately integrated in her body schema. Her arms arc and twist to keep her balanced. Her legs dance. Her feet sense the texture of the grass beneath her. She hears other people's footfalls and heavy breathing as well as her own. In a split second she sees an opportunity. For another split second the motor intention forms in her parietal and motor body maps, and with a deft kick the ball rockets off toward its target.

Body Image

So here's an interesting question. Let's say you go on a diet and lose twenty-five pounds. You are thinner. Your thighs are less bulky. You don't feel your legs pinching the seams of your too-snug jeans or that roll of fat over a tight waistband. Your belt is a notch smaller. Given the fact that your body schema arises from the motion of your body as it makes contact with clothes and other objects, shouldn't it reflect the fact of your hard-won thinness in the way you feel and perceive yourself? Shouldn't you now be getting constant signals telling you that you are svelte? Shouldn't you feel less fat?

But as most yo-yo dieters can attest, at some deep level you have not changed. Mysteriously, you still feel fat. As you gaze in the mirror at your newly trimmed-down body, something is giving you a different message.

That something is your body image. In the world of weight loss advice, body image is often mentioned but rarely explained in ways that can help you keep off excess pounds. In contrast to your body schema, which is mostly unconscious, your body image is the more conscious perception of your body: how you see yourself and how you present yourself to the world. It is not about being tall or short, fat or skinny, good-looking or homely. It is about your attitudes toward those traits in yourself, your emotional response to how you experience your body, including how you dress, pose, move, and believe others see you.

Like your body schema, body image has its basis in many of your brain's body maps. But there are some important differences that explain why diets often fail. Your body schema is more confined to specialized circuits, while the ingredients for your body image—which include the beliefs you have about your body—are spread more widely throughout your brain, wherever memories are stored. Beliefs are ultimately as tangible as the cells in your brain, because that is where beliefs are created, stored, and, with new information, updated or reconsolidated. Beliefs are embedded in the physical interconnections between neurons, which are organized by experience into stable networks. Beliefs are held in brain circuits that fire in response to your expectations and predictions about how the world operates.

To grasp how this works, you need to know a bit more about how the

FAT

People are overweight for many reasons. They have fat parents, eat terrible diets, and don't exercise. Their bodies—actually their gut bacteria—are super-adept at absorbing calories. They watch a lot of television with ads that depict heaping portions of high-calorie food and come to see those amounts as normal. They are too poor or overworked to join a gym or buy fresh fruits and vegetables. They overeat because they were abused, physically or emotionally, and food alleviates their pain. They feel an emptiness inside and reach for food to fill it.

Actually, food is addictive in the sense that heroin is addictive. Like drugs of abuse, the sight or smell of food increases levels of a brain pleasure chemical called dopamine. But like drug addicts, many obese people have a relative dearth of dopamine receptors, which makes them more sensitive to the reward properties of food. The brain's pleasure circuitry can be co-opted by many stimuli, such as cocaine, gambling, sex, or food.

One study of obese people found that a sensory region of the brain devoted to mapping the mouth, lips, and tongue is overactive. Thus they may get extra pleasure from eating.

A study of craving, or an irresistible urge to consume, found a specific pattern of activity in the brain's frontal lobes. The cravings could be suppressed by zapping these regions with a special magnet.

brain is organized. Almost all of your higher mental functions are carried out in the cortex—a thin sheet of tissue that is wrapped around older brain structures. About the size of a formal dinner napkin, it is massively folded so it can fit inside your skull. The entire cortical sheet has six layers of cells, each as thick as a single business card.

Although the cortex physically resembles a thin sheet, it is functionally organized into regions that specialize in different tasks, such as vision, hearing, touch, movement, and making plans. Furthermore, these regions are organized in hierarchies. Imagine a deck of cards laid out, faceup, side by side. Functionally the ace is higher than the jack, which is functionally higher than the eight, which is functionally higher than the two. The functional hierarchies in your brain are far more complex than playing cards, but the analogy should give you an idea of how hierarchies can exist in a nearly two-dimensional plane.

In the cortex, so-called lower areas absorb raw sensory information and pass it over to higher areas where it is processed and then passed over to still higher areas. But there is no ultimate top area where everything "comes together" (remember the "homunculus fallacy" from chapter 2). On the contrary. Once information reaches higher regions, it is fed back down the hierarchy. Anatomists have found that in most areas of the cortex, for every fiber carrying information up the hierarchy, there are as many as ten fibers carrying processed information back down the hierarchy.

Researchers are still exploring the meaning of this massive feedback architecture, but one function is now clear: Your mind operates via prediction. Perception is not a process of passive absorption, but of active construction. When you see, hear, or feel something, the incoming information is always fragmentary and ambiguous. As it percolates up the cortical hierarchy, each area asks: "Is this what I expect? Is this what I predict? Does this conform to what I already know is the case?" So your brain is constantly comparing incoming information to what it already knows or expects or believes. As higher areas make sense of the input— "Yes, this is something I have seen before"—the information is fed back to lower areas to confirm that what you believe is happening really is happening.

But in many cases it goes beyond mere confirmation, and the back-fed prediction or belief actually alters the upward-flowing information to make it conform. The fact that the information travels "backward" down the cortical hierarchy all the way from higher, mentally sophisticated regions into lower levels of basic sensory processing means your predictions and beliefs can work against you. They do this by interfering with your ability to see things afresh, or even notice major contradictions between your expectations and what is actually present to your senses. For example, pity the ubiquitous husband who totally fails to notice that his wife has come home with a new hairstyle.

In other words, your understanding of reality is a far cry from reality itself. Your understanding of reality is constructed in large part according to your expectations and beliefs, which are based on all your past experiences, which are held in the cortex as predictive memory. This is worth repeating: Many of your perceptions—what you see, hear, feel, and think is real—are profoundly shaped and influenced by your beliefs and expectations. And this includes beliefs about your body.

The term "body image" was introduced in 1935 by Paul Schilder, an Austrian American neurologist who felt that the body schema concept did not capture the full nature of bodily experience. The body image, Schilder said, refers to the mental pictures we have of our bodies or the way our bodies appear to us. If you added a pair of cowboy boots and a turquoise belt buckle to that Stetson, you would have a distinctive body image. As a psychological construct, it is the set of beliefs you hold about yourself. (Maybe this is why Halloween is such a popular event in our culture. You get to dress up in outrageous costumes and change your body image, if only for one night a year.)

Your body schema and your body image both evolve as you grow up. The changes in the schema are pretty universal. Your arms get longer. Your reach is greater. Your legs lengthen. Your center of mass rises. Your stride increases. Your proportions fall into place. Hormones kick in. Girls grow breasts. Boys bulk up.

But while the schema is largely a function of body parts in motion, your body image draws on a larger web involving your lifetime's library of personal experiences and memories. Your body image is an amalgam of beliefs—attitudes, assumptions, expectations, with an occasional delusion thrown in—that are likewise embedded both in your body maps and in the parts of your cortex that store your autobiographical memories and social attitudes. Your family, peers, and culture provide the content; you provide the interpretation.

For most people, important beliefs about the body begin to bubble into consciousness in early adolescence. By the end of the teenage years, these beliefs have congealed into a coherent body image, right along with religious beliefs, political attitudes, and stereotypes. All are highly resistant to change later in life.

Now, it would be great if typical adolescents had body image experiences that resulted in boys and girls saying to themselves, "I am lovable. I have a very nice body that encompasses the real me. I am happy with the way I look." But teens hold all sorts of unhealthy beliefs about their bodies: "I am too fat." "I am not muscular." "My ears are freakishly huge." "I am flat-chested."

And for people like Oprah, who experienced sexual abuse in child-

BODY IMAGE AND CULTURE

Not all cultures promote thinness for women. In Belize, there are *two* ideal body types for women. You can be shaped like a bottle of Coke with hourglass curves, or you can resemble a bottle of Fanta with less at the top and more at the bottom. For women in Belize, shape is more important than size, and it's shape, not size, that they dress to accentuate. Little girls are given these words of advice: "Never leave yourself."

Similarly, not all cultures promote muscularity for men. A Harvard psychiatrist, Dr. Harrison Pope, recently developed a computerized measure of body image perception called a somatomorphic matrix. A subject sees an image of a male body that he can adjust on a computer screen through ten levels of muscularity and ten levels of fat, for a total of one hundred images. He is asked to choose the images that best match his own body, the body of an average man his age in his own country, and the body he thinks that women would prefer.

American, French, and Austrian men picked an ideal body image that was twenty-eight pounds more muscular than themselves. In fact, the women preferred a male body size that was much closer to that of the average man, with little added muscle. Taiwanese men, on the other hand, rarely wanted to be more muscular. Asked what women like, they said, "Someone who looks like me."

hood, the body image can be drenched in shame. Such wounds are deeply buried and soothed by comfort foods far into the night.

If you lose weight and still feel fat, it may be because of a gaping mismatch between your body image and your body schema, which is a reflection of the body proper. Your body schema has drifted remarkably out of touch with your body image, and you experience an internal psychic disconnect. Your body image is dueling with your body schema. Your beliefs about your body are out of sync with what your body maps or even your eyes are reporting to you. And being at war with yourself, even when it is all happening beneath the level of your conscious awareness, is a miserable experience.

Like your political and religious beliefs, your attitudes about your body are obstinate, headstrong, all but immutable. When you learn that a trusted politician has been lying to you for years, you don't switch parties. When you find out that intercessory prayer does not make people heal

CULTURAL EFFECTS

Cultural beliefs can also produce pathological changes in body maps. For example, *koro* is seen in parts of Asia and Africa. It begins when a man who is emotionally upset goes to urinate and observes that his penis is becoming smaller. He grabs his genitals before they can retract into his body and he runs for help. Those afflicted with *koro* believe that their penis is shrinking, and that when it disappears, they will die. Epidemics have occurred in Singapore, Indonesia, and China. In Senegal, foreigners have been accused of being penis shrinkers. A handshake is all it takes.

In Japan, people suffer from a syndrome of intense fear that one's body, body parts, or bodily functions are displeasing, embarrassing, or offensive to other people in appearance, odor, facial expressions, or movements. It is a motivation for suicide.

Koreans can suffer from *hwabyung*, in which victims complain of a periodically rising abdominal mass and sense of dying from asphyxiation. Nigerians complain of extreme heat in their heads when they feel anxious, whereas Cambodians suffer painful neck tension, ringing in the ears, and body weakness, called "wind overload," when they are stressed. Such symptoms are related to cultural beliefs about which body systems are most vulnerable in a person.

faster, you don't stop praying or give up religion. And when your body schema gives you different, thinner signals about your body size, you don't give up your beliefs about your body.

Recall that your body schema is composed of dynamic sensory signals flowing through your body mandala, plus a database of muscle memories distributed among your body maps. As your skin rubs against your clothes in a smaller size, you have a new set of information about your proportions. You have to work less hard to lug your body around your house, which also testifies to the changes you've achieved. But your belief-ridden body image has not changed. Beliefs can be enormously potent, potent enough to drown out your new-felt body sense. If only the "thin person screaming to get out" of the fat body could triumph. But the reverse is more often the reality: A fat body image trapped inside a slimmed-down body wins the conflict. Being thinner hasn't solved your problems. All the psychological reasons you have for overeating have not gone away. You overeat because you hate yourself and you hate yourself because you overeat. Such is the recipe for yo-yo dieting.

Fortunately, there are ways to break the cycle. The thin person screaming to get out of the fat person is actually your body schema, masked and muted beneath a rubble pile of false belief. The trick is to find ways to listen to that person.

The Wisdom of Wobble Boards

Now, you could spend years in talk therapy, Woody Allen style, combing through your past, getting to the bottom of your painful feelings, poking holes in your self-hatred. But talking about your problems is not a good way to get in touch with a body schema that has been trumped by die-hard beliefs. You need to try something more direct, more dynamic, more tactile, more proprioceptive, more vestibular. More to do with body maps than with strolls down memory lane.

Jeff Della Penna, a personal trainer in Santa Fe, New Mexico, has two primary goals for his clients. One is for them to get in touch with their body schema—to learn to feel their muscles without straining, sense the movement of their joints, and balance while standing on a wobbly board. Second, have fun. Enjoyment is essential to a good workout, he says, and so Della Penna often takes his clients on hikes and adventure trips where they get constructive aerobic exercise.

Many of Della Penna's clients are overweight. They come for help, he says, because they've hit three hundred pounds, have dangerously high blood pressure, or can no longer walk up their front steps. They are very frightened. Most of them tell Della Penna that they can trace their weight problem to some traumatic event in their lives—a death, an accident, an abusive childhood, or the like. For many years they have felt dissociated, as if body and brain inhabit mutually exclusive worlds.

Della Penna's first task is to try to bring his clients' bodies and minds back together—to fire up their body schemas. But he is more often than not astonished by the extent to which his clients are not in touch with their physical bodies. He'll gently tap a major muscle in the back, arm, or abdomen and ask the client to contract it. They cannot. He puts them in front of a mirror and they won't look. He asks them to twist at the waist so their shoulders are at a right angle to the mirror. They cannot perform the motion. He asks them to throw their shoulders back by flexing the muscles that pull the scapula together. They have no idea of how to begin. When they try to stand on one leg, they cannot do it. They are completely unable to perform many of the basic skills that so many of us take for granted, he says.

Della Penna focuses on overcoming this body-blindness by getting his clients to experience their bodies from the inside out. He has created a series of proprioception and balance exercises designed to trigger minute neuromuscular responses. After establishing an initial contraction, he builds on the exercise program until his clients are connecting their entire body to the required movement. One method is to have them lift very light weights, very slowly, with many repetitions while pretending they are lifting hundreds of pounds.

"I want them to feel each muscle fiber and each neuromuscular response," he says. "I tell them that their muscles don't have a dimmer switch, that we want to trigger all of the neuro-senders and that they need to learn to fire all their muscle fibers while lifting light weights to tone the muscle. Lifting big weights will just make big muscles. I get them to concentrate on their abdominal muscles hundreds of times a day to retrain their bodies to use core muscles in every movement they make. The slower they go, the better they do."

And then Della Penna brings out the wobble board. His is a homemade affair consisting of an 18-inch-square board mounted on a two-by-two piece of wood, like the blade on an ice skate. You stand on it and try to keep it from wobbling. Your task is simply to maintain your balance the best you can. In terms of body maps, the wobble board provides a powerful entry into body schema repair via stimulation of the vestibular cortex. By putting balance at the center of attention, your body schema cannot be ignored.

When Della Penna's clients first step onto his wobble board, they have a difficult time keeping it centered. But, he says, "people adapt to it very quickly. After a while, I toss them a ball and have them toss it back. Then I toss two balls simultaneously, which they catch and throw back. As they begin to relax and maintain balance, some get really, really scared. They are getting in touch with their body schema." Some people become so frightened, they leave the training, he says. Others use the newfound sense to begin to transform their relationship with their body image. It can go either way.

If you have lost weight or toned up, consider ways to broker a truce between your dueling body maps. By getting in touch with your slimmed-down schema, you may be able to keep the pounds off for good.

Waking the Tiger

In 1969, the somatic psychotherapist and stress researcher Peter A. Levine met a woman named Nancy whose experience captures other ways the body can become trapped in past trauma. Nancy, a graduate student, was not battling a weight problem. Her problem was severe, crippling, and, to her mind, completely inexplicable panic attacks.

As Levine recalls in his book *Waking the Tiger*, he began their session with the standard approach of relaxation training. Nancy sat in a chair, quietly listening, but she did not respond. As Levine pressed on, trying to help her relax, Nancy suddenly imploded, gripped by a full-blown anxiety attack—paralyzed, pallid, unable to breathe, heart pounding.

Levine remembers being drawn into her nightmarish attack. It was palpable, contagious. Then, without warning, he had the fleeting vision of a tiger, crouched, ready to leap toward them. It just appeared in his imagination. Swept along by the experience, he commanded, "Nancy! You are being attacked by a large tiger! See the tiger as it comes toward you! Run toward that tree! Run, Nancy, run! Climb up! Escape!"

To Levine's astonishment, Nancy's legs started trembling in running movements. She stayed in her chair, but her legs shook as if in full escape. She let out a primitive scream that brought in a passing police officer. Then Nancy began to tremble, shake, and sob in full-bodied convulsive waves. The shaking went on for an hour and ended with soft trembling.

This event was an epiphany for Levine. Nancy told him that she had, for the first time in her life, recalled a terrifying memory from her childhood. At age three, she had been held down and strapped to an operating table for a tonsillectomy.

Under the anesthesia, which might have been incomplete, Nancy felt she was suffocating. Terrifying hallucinations gripped her mind. The event, etched deeply in her being, was not subject to conscious recall.

Like other traumatized people, Nancy felt threatened, overwhelmed, and psychologically stuck. Her body had resigned itself to a state where she could not escape. Hence the panic attacks.

At the time, Levine was studying animal predator-prey behaviors, which may explain the tiger image. He observed that when prey animals are captured—say, an impala is brought down by a cheetah—they drop to the ground and freeze. In the moments before death, prey animals are entirely immobilized and their brains are flooded with natural painkillers. But if they are lucky enough to escape—say, the cheetah does not kill instantly and the impala gets away—the animals will run to safety and then literally shake off the residual effects of the immobility response. Their bodies convulse with paroxysmal spasms.

Looking at Nancy, Levine realized that her shaking was an instinctive and long-overdue response to her being immobilized and terrified as a little girl. He also understood that her panic attacks were not caused by the triggering event itself. Rather, they stemmed from the frozen residue of "energy" that had not been resolved and discharged from her body. After a few more visits and further gentle shaking, Nancy's panic attacks vanished.

With this insight, Levine, a pioneer in the field of what has come to be called "somatic psychology," went on to develop a method called Somatic Experiencing. The method helps people access their bound-up energy and release it in a gradual, titrated way by tracking felt sensations in the body. Unlike conventional talk therapy, which can sometimes retraumatize a person, somatic psychology gradually delves into the body state moment by moment. In a way it amounts to turning psychotherapy inside out and upside down. The treatment does not directly address beliefs about the body, or body image. Instead, it focuses on fluctuating internal sensations as embedded in the body schema. If the patient's posture or body language changes while talking about her past, the therapist makes her aware of it. Or he may ask her to note what visceral sensations she is having while she talks about herself. As her awareness of the connections between her thoughts, memories, emotions, and body states grows, so does her self-possession. In short, somatic psychotherapy uses body sensation as the key to healing trauma. Like the wobble board, it recalibrates your body maps so that you can feel yourself from the inside out.

The Stolen Cat Suit

When the psychologist Martin Grunwald lived in Jena, East Germany, working at Friedrich Schiller University, he kept his experiments simple. Grunwald is interested in the sense of touch—how it is processed in the brain and how it interacts with other senses. So as part of his doctoral dissertation, he blindfolded people and asked them to trace sunken figures with their index fingers. Imagine a triangle or an *X* or a more complicated squiggle carved into a piece of wood. That is what his sunken figures look like. After the subjects ran their fingers over each shape, they opened their eyes and drew it on a piece of paper.

It's an extremely easy task, Grunwald says. You simply have to transform what you feel into what you see. You do this all the time without thinking, as when plunging your hand into your car's glove compartment in search of a hairbrush or sunglasses. A quick slide of the fingertips usually identifies objects immediately.

While the subjects touched the sunken figures or drew them on paper, Grunwald measured the electrical activity in their brains. "I just wanted to observe the kinds of brain signals associated with the understanding of active touch," he says. Nothing fancy. Just basic curiosity.

With one exception, every person in the experiment drew the shapes accurately, Grunwald says. While their *X*'s might be a little crooked or their wavy lines a bit off center, they could easily draw what they had touched. The exception was a young woman from Jena University's psychology department. She was a total, abject failure at the task. Her cramped, tortured drawings bore little or no resemblance to the actual shapes. She seemed incapable of understanding the structure of even the simplest sunken figures.

Grunwald was intrigued. What was with this young lady? As a university student, she was undoubtedly literate and probably quite intelligent. Might she have some odd physical disability that prevented her from being able to feel the sunken figures? Nothing made sense. The mystery deepened when Grunwald tried to set up an interview with the student and she flatly refused to return to the lab. She would have nothing more to do with the experiment, period.

That would have been the end of it, except for an astute observation made by Grunwald's laboratory assistant. Her notes indicated that the woman's skin was a very pale gray color and covered with fine soft hairs. And she was extremely thin. Grunwald went to the library and checked the research literature. What kind of illness, he wondered, could produce abnormal touch and such strange skin? He found the answer in a paper on the physical characteristics of women with eating disorders. Her skin was the giveaway. The young woman was profoundly anorexic.

The experts agree that biological and cultural factors are involved in anorexia nervosa, a mental disorder of self-starvation that kills up to 18 percent of its victims. But beyond that, the consensus frays. A leading explanation for the disorder is similar to what people used to say about autism and homosexuality, namely, that it is a learned behavior. In the case of self-starvation, they say, young women do not build a strong identity early in life. That leaves them feeling uncertain, confused, or dissatisfied about who they are. To feel valuable, they fixate on being thin. The oversexed popular culture of billboards and *Cosmo* covers and tautmidriffed teen pop divas serves to reinforce the fixation. The explanation is entirely cultural and psychological.

But that theory fails to explain one of the most intriguing observations about these sad women who willingly starve themselves to the brink of death. If you give a pair of calipers to an anorexic woman and ask her to estimate the size of her upper arm, she'll look straight into the mirror and open the pinchers wide enough to encompass Popeye's biceps. She literally sees her upper arm as grossly fat when it is frightfully thin. Her eyes—or more accurately, her misperceiving brain—tell her what no one else sees.

And she is not making it up.

Such drastic misperception looks suspiciously like a mismatch between body maps. With this clue, neuropsychologists are now starting to investigate anorexia along these new lines.

In 1996, Grunwald moved to the University of Leipzig, where he decided to investigate abnormal touch perception in anorexia patients. Since touch is integrated with vision and other senses in the parietal lobe, he wondered if anorexics have abnormalities in this region of the brain.

When Grunwald repeated his earlier experiment with ten anorexia patients, not one of them could draw the shapes correctly after feeling them. Looking closely at their brains' electrical activity, he saw that each person's right parietal cortex was working hard but without success. Sensory information was not being integrated. Could this be why they did not perceive their bodies as appearing skinny in the mirror?

Grunwald believes that anorexia is fundamentally a body pattern disturbance. And he has some ideas as to its source. The disease is seen almost exclusively in women and girls, which points to the effects of sex hormones on the developing brain. It is known that testosterone plays a role in the enhanced spatial abilities of males, which are located in the right parietal lobe. Female brains, by contrast, show subtly different patterns of organization; the right parietal lobe is less specialized for spatial awareness. This trait may be more pronounced in anorexia patients.

Added to this anatomical variation is the fact that early brain development is dependent on human touch—possibly more so in girls than in boys. It could be a genetic trait linked to the female X chromosome. It could have to do with basic sex differences in how emotion develops in the brains of each sex. There are other proposed explanations as well, including insecure attachment. The jury is still very much out. But the final effect, in Grunwald's view, is unhealthy or incomplete map integration in the right parietal lobe of a disproportionate number of girls. Hence as they grow up, their body schemas are unreliable, while their body images become more and more distorted by social influences.

Anorexia patients hate to be touched, Grunwald says. They do not like physical therapy or massage, and they leave situations in which they are expected to have body contact with others. But what if he could flood their brains with full-body stimulation? Could a powerful input of touch sensation help overcome their distorted body image?

Grunwald, who is thin and gets easily chilled in cold water, had begun using a neoprene diving suit while on holiday with his family. "My daughter is an enthusiastic swimmer and loves to romp and play with me in the waves," he says. The suit allowed Grunwald to spend many hours with her in the sea water. But in wearing the suit, he noticed distinct bodily perceptions. On land, the suit pressed on his skin and muscles as he moved. In water, he felt less compression. After thinking about these sensations for a few years, Grunwald wondered if a diving suit could help anorexics who have an abnormal response to touch. When he mentioned the idea to a friend, he learned that full-body latex suits are popular among some people for enhancing sexual experience.

And that is how Grunwald got the idea of putting an anorexic patient into a full-body neoprene suit—a cat suit—to see if it would send new, perhaps corrective, signals to her brain.

The patient was a nineteen-year-old artist who agreed to wear the cat suit three times a day, for an hour each time, for fifteen weeks. It fit under her clothes as she went about her normal activities. She liked the idea, Grunwald says. She was relieved that the treatment did not make her talk about her childhood or deal with other psychological issues. Anorexia, in Grunwald's view, is a disorder rooted in a brain anomaly and not in mommy-daddy issues.

During the experiment, the researchers recorded the artist's body weight thirty-nine times and assessed the quality of her body representation using several measuring techniques. They also recorded the electrical activity of her brain. Before she wore the suit, when she was starving, her left hemisphere was dominant. After she wore the suit—and had gained several pounds—brain activity shifted to her right hemisphere, particularly to the parietal lobe. She said she loved wearing the suit, Grunwald says, and felt some panic when summer arrived and she had to take it off.

Unfortunately, the effect of the cat suit was not permanent. A few months after the student stopped wearing it, her brain asymmetry returned. She lost weight. Tests showed that she once again failed to represent and evaluate her body realistically. Not long afterward, the woman moved to France and took the cat suit with her, Grunwald says. The suit was expensive and he has asked her to give it back, but she has refused. And for the time being he does not have funding to carry out more tests with other patients.

What Is Wrong with Michael Jackson?

If Grunwald is right, many so-called psychiatric disorders stem from an unhealthy or inadequate representation of body feeling. Anorexia is one. Another is bulimia, which also involves an overestimation of body size. Men suffer from a related condition called reverse anorexia, also known as "bigorexia" or muscle dysmorphia. These are guys who work out obsessively in gyms to the exclusion of a social life. They gaze at themselves in the mirror dozens of times a day, and guess what they report seeing? Instead of recognizing the incredible hulk in front of them, they see someone who looks scrawny and underdeveloped. Could there be a similar brain abnormality causing their perceptual errors?

Men and women with body dysmorphic disorder, or BDD, are painfully focused on the belief that certain parts of their bodies are grotesque. They are tormented by the notion that some piece of them—nose, ears, mouth, jaw, eyebrows, chin, rear end, genitals, you name it—is ugly, abnormal, and deformed. Like having a really bad hair day, they can't stop thinking about the defect and spend hours secretively looking in the mirror and trying to camouflage it with makeup, hats, wrappings.

Body dysmorphic disorder afflicts one to two percent of American men and women. A quarter of them have had plastic surgery. It can easily spiral to extremes. Think Michael Jackson.

Like anorexics, when people with body dysmorphic disorder look in a mirror, they literally see the exaggerated defect. Their rear end is disproportionately huge. Their chin is completely missing. They have gorilla-like hair on their faces. Their hands and fingers blow up in size, then shrink, before their eyes. Again, they are not making this up. They truly see themselves this way.

Neuroscientists recently discovered an area of the brain, with connections to the parietal region, where body parts—legs, hands, arms, trunks without heads—are visually recognized. Could defects of this region of the brain (the extrastriate body area) be involved in body dysmorphic disorder? There are, in addition, other visually dominant body maps in the parietal lobe itself. The mind uses these maps to recognize its own body and tell its own body parts and movements apart from those of others.

But in anorexics, bulimics, even in many normal dieters, and perhaps in those with body dysmorphic disorder as well, somehow top-down beliefs and expectations (from the body image) cannot get in harmony with the bottom-up flow of unbiased sensory information from the body and eyes. The parietal lobe, with its gaggle of visual body maps, may be the bottleneck where the communication is breaking down. But while the clues are tantalizing, neuroscience research on the question has just begun.

CHAPTER 4

THE HOMUNCULUS IN THE GAME

or, When Thinking Is as Good as Doing

I n the early 1980s the sports world was seduced by a new set of ideas for how to juice up physical performance. With the help of audio and video tapes, athletes could learn how to relax, set goals, solve problems, assert themselves, concentrate, induce self-hypnosis, and rehearse their skills. By engaging in what was loosely called "mental training," they could throw farther, leap higher, skate faster, sink more of their shots, and otherwise perform much better in their chosen sport. It became a major trend. For example, more than half of the finalists and two-thirds of the medal winners for the 1980 Swedish Olympic team had used mental training.

And yet, according to William Straub, a now-retired sports psychologist at Ithaca College, many of the claims of mental training's efficacy were anecdotal. And mental practice is a broad rubric, a mishmash of techniques. While many coaches and athletes believe that relaxation, visualization, and imagery enhance physical performance, they have a glut of programs to choose from: symbolic rehearsal, modeling, covert practice, cognitive rehearsal, imaginal practice, dream work, hallucination, hypnosis, visuomotor training, ideomotor training, introspective rehearsal, implicit practice, sofa training. Assuming mental training did work—which was the first thing Straub needed to establish—what aspects of the training made a difference? Which programs did a better job? How comparable were the techniques to physical practice?

Straub, who was teaching a course in kinesiology and biomechanics at the time, decided to find out. He had ample laboratory space, enthusiastic students, and three commercial mental practice programs to test. In choosing a sport, Straub considered several criteria. It should be easy to learn, simple to score, and permit individuals to improve over time. So he settled on darts.

Straub recruited seventy-five undergraduates, male and female, for an eight-week experiment. On day one they assembled in a large, well-lit room with a regulation dart board and spent ten minutes warming up. Then they made fifty dart throws each to establish their baseline scores.

A dart board is divided into numbered sections that score from one to twenty points. Circular wires divide each pielike section into areas that earn single, double, or triple points. The red bull's-eye scores fifty points. After throwing fifty darts, a player can score between zero and 3,000 (that is, if each dart hits the triple zone of the twenty region, you get 50 times 20 times 3, which equals 3,000).

The students were then assigned to one of five groups. The first, a control group, was instructed never to play darts; they only needed to return after eight weeks to throw another fifty shots. The second group threw fifty darts for thirty minutes a day, five days a week, for two months, and kept track of their scores. The remaining three groups were assigned one of the three mental training programs. They alternated between mental training and physical practice. They would spend one day throwing the fifty darts for half an hour, and the next day they would wear headsets, relax, and listen to training tapes for thirty minutes.

Each training program emphasized body awareness, imagery, and relaxation. In one of them, students were told to visualize themselves sitting in a big easy chair facing a large viewing screen. They should see themselves positioned at the throw line and then feel the dart in their fingers, feel it release, see and hear the dart enter the bull's-eyes, and experience the pride and satisfaction that comes with performing well.

After eight weeks, seventy students (five had to drop out due to scheduling problems) took a post-test of fifty dart throws, and their scores were tallied. As expected, the control group showed no improvement. The group that threw darts daily improved, on average, by 67 points. The three groups that practiced along with mental training improved, on average, by 111, 141, and 165 points.

Even today, Straub says these results surprise him. He never expected to find that mental practice could play such a powerful role in skill acquisition. His study, which is widely cited in sports psychology journals, was one of the first to show that the effect was real. The next task was to tease it apart and figure out the relative contribution of each exercise to overall performance.

Practice Makes Perfect

Alvaro Pascual-Leone is a professor of neurology at Harvard Medical School and director of the Center for Noninvasive Brain Stimulation at Beth Israel Deaconess Medical Center in Boston. Born in Valencia, Spain, he trained in his native country, Germany, and the United States before joining the Harvard faculty in 1997 with the goal of exploring the brain using powerful electromagnets.

The technique he uses is called transcranial magnetic stimulation, or TMS. The doctor wields a heavy wand with a figure-eight-shaped coil on the end. When he holds the wand over a volunteer's scalp, the magnet discharges, which induces a weak electrical current an inch or so below, down in the cortex itself. It's like a magic electrode that can probe and zap the brain remotely. Wilder Penfield would have been green with envy.

What do you think happens when a TMS magnet is used to stimulate, say, the ankle region of a volunteer's primary motor map? At high power it induces a twitch in the ankle, just as Penfield described in his patients. At low power you may not see a twitch, but it still has an effect. The homunculus is still sending a signal down to the ankle muscles each time the TMS coil goes "pop," but the signal doesn't quite reach the threshold required to trigger a full-blown twitch. Still, the muscles respond by tensing ever so slightly, and this tension can be measured by electrodes taped to the skin. By probing around people's primary motor maps in this way, Pascual-Leone can map out the location and size of their homuncular ankle region, elbow region, neck region, you name it.

Among other things, Pascual-Leone is interested in using TMS to see how the primary motor map changes when the brain learns a new skill. "The brain changes with anything you do, including any thought you might have," he says. Any time you learn something new, any time your brain deems an experience worthy of remembering over the long term, new connections sprout between cells and previously existing connections are strengthened. The process is called plasticity.

As a self-described "fanatical" soccer player and "avid" tennis player, Pascual-Leone decided to investigate how the brain changes with physical practice. Specifically, what happens to your motor maps as you improve your skills at a sport or an instrument?

In 1994 he ran an experiment to find out. He started screening volunteers and accepted only right-handed people who neither played a musical instrument nor had ever learned to touch-type. The subjects came to the motor control laboratory at the National Institutes of Health, where Pascual-Leone was working, on five consecutive days. They were taught to perform a five-finger exercise on a piano keyboard connected to a computer. It went like this: thumb, index finger, middle finger, ring finger, little finger, ring finger, middle finger, index finger, thumb, index finger . . . repeat. They were instructed to perform these finger movements fluently, without pauses, without skipping any keys, and while paying special attention to the steady interval and duration of each key press. They had to perform at a fairly fast pace marked by a metronome.

Before training began, Pascual-Leone used TMS to measure the size of each subject's finger maps in his or her left cerebral hemisphere (which controls the right hand). Every day after that, they practiced for two hours and then were tested to see if they could do twenty repetitions of the five-finger exercise without errors. Everyone got better as the week progressed.

Their cortical finger maps were remeasured each day. Lo and behold, by the end of the week, the maps for each set of muscles for each finger had increased significantly in size. Physical practice literally increased the size of the brain map involved in acquiring a new skill, piano playing. Plastic remappings like this occur when you learn or improve at any physical skill, be it guitar playing, golf, tennis, baseball, or dancing.

That was phase one of the experiment. The following week, the subjects were divided into two groups. One continued daily practice for another four weeks. The second group stopped practicing. In the non-practicing group, the finger maps returned to pre-practice size after one week. In the group that kept practicing, the enlarged finger maps also got smaller, even as their performance continued to improve. That may strike you as a very odd and inconclusive result: The map shrinks with no practice, and the map shrinks with practice. What to make of that?

Pascual-Leone says the motor maps involved in any skill—those that send commands to your muscles to perform a task—are reorganized by physical practice. In early practice sessions, while you are still a novice, your finger maps grow in an exuberance of neural rewiring, seeking and strengthening any connection patterns that maximize your performance. If you then stop practicing, your finger maps stop adapting and slump back to their original size. But if you stick with practice over time, you reach a new phase of long-term structural change in your maps. Many of the novel neural connections you made early on aren't needed anymore. A consolidation occurs: The skill becomes better integrated into your maps' basic circuitry, and the whole process becomes more efficient and automatic.

There is one more level to all this, and that's true expertise, or virtuosity. People who practice complex motor skills day in, day out, for years on end, always striving for perfection, show motor maps that are again increased in size. For example, a professional pianist like Gary Graffman unquestionably has enlarged hand and finger maps. His maps are larger than average because they are crammed full of finely honed neural wiring that gives him exquisite (and hard-earned) control of timing, force, and targeting of all ten fingers. A violinist like Itzhak Perlman will also have an enlarged hand map—but only one. The hand map that controls his string-fingering hand, to be exact, is like the pianists'. But his homuncular bow hand is indistinguishable, at least to the naked eye, from any nonmusician's. His bow hand is deft, yes, but the level of coordination involved is not nearly the same, and the map does not get beefed up beyond normal.

Here is one more interesting fact about expertise: As you gradually master a complex skill, the "motor programs" it requires gradually migrate down from higher to lower areas in the frontal cortex and to subcortical structures. Imagine a guy who signs up for ballroom dance classes. Like all novices, he is terrible at first. During his first several lessons, he is processing his dance-related movement combinations up in his higher motor regions, such as the supplementary motor area. This area is important for engaging in any complex and unfamiliar motor task. The dance moves are at first very complex for him. He needs to pay attention to them constantly, and even so he often loses track.

He sticks with it, though, and after a couple of months he is getting a lot smoother. He is using his supplementary motor area much less for his dancing these days. Many of the motor command sequences he is using now have been transferred downward in the cortical hierarchy, to reside mainly in his premotor cortex. He's become a competent dancer. He's not Fred Astaire, but he needs to pay less attention to the basics now. He makes far fewer mistakes. He can improvise longer and longer sequences.

Finally, if he practices often for many months stretching into years, eventually his premotor cortex delegates a lot of its dance-related sequences to the primary motor cortex. Now he can truly be called a great dancer. Dance has mingled intimately with the motor primitives in his fundamental motor map. The dance has truly become part of his being.

Imagining Versus Doing

As a weekend athlete, Pascual-Leone says he was curious about mental practice and sports. "Anybody who likes watching sports can see that certain athletes appear to mentally rehearse what they are about to do," he says. "You can see it when they're preparing for a free throw or getting ready to bomb down a slope in a ski slalom race. Before they get going, they prime themselves."

Many famous musicians do the same thing. Vladimir Horowitz practiced mentally before concerts to avoid disturbing his motor skills; feedback from pianos other than his own Steinway was upsetting. Arthur Rubinstein, eager to enjoy life and practice as little as possible, used mental rehearsal to minimize time spent sitting at the piano. A violinist who spent seven years in prison and practiced playing in his mind every day gave a flawless performance the night he got out of jail. Injured ballerinas have been known to lie on the floor running through dance steps with their fingers to retain their skills.

So Pascual-Leone repeated his five-finger exercise with one specific form of mental practice: internally generated motor imagery.

Imagery takes different forms that are important to distinguish. You know what it is like to imagine an object. Close your eyes and picture a hippopotamus. Now imagine a belly dancer. This is visual imagery. You are the spectator. Visual imagery engages parts of your brain involved in visual perception and conjures up pictorial memories of what you have seen with your eyes.

Motor or kinesthetic imagery is the process of imagining a movement. Imagine yourself erasing a blackboard, signing your name, or washing a dish. You are the actor. You perform the movement, virtually, in your mind. You aren't using your mind's eye so much as your mind's body. Motor imagery engages a subset of your body mandala, including maps involved in motor planning and proprioception. It simulates the inner feeling of an action.

Using the same setup as before, Pascual-Leone's new subjects spent two hours a day five days a week imagining the five-finger piano key strokes. They were told to repeat each finger movement mentally, as if they were playing. They could rest their fingers on the keyboard but were not allowed to move them in any way.

The results were astonishing. After one week, motor imagery practice led to nearly the same level of body map reorganization as physical practice. As far as your motor cortex is concerned, executed and imagined movements are almost identical.

The "almost" is fascinating. When you mentally rehearse a movement, all but one of the brain regions that control your movements become active in the absence of movement. You imagine throwing the dart but your body is immobile. You imagine pressing the piano key but your muscles are still. So motor imagery is the off-line operation of your brain's motor machinery unfolding as if it were happening in real time. It takes you about as long to imagine walking across your bedroom as it would if you actually did the walk. Such a walk takes longer if you imagine yourself carrying a heavy box. If you imagine yourself running, your breathing speeds up and your heart rate increases. If you imagine moving your little finger for ten minutes a day, after four weeks it will be up to one-fifth stronger.

Coaches and athletes of every skill level mustn't ignore this. While many types of mental practice are undoubtedly helpful, motor imagery is the only technique that alters your body maps in the same way physical practice does. Visual imagery (as from a spectator's point of view), relaxation, hypnosis, affirmation, prayer, and other techniques may help you in one way or another, but will not alter your motor maps. Remember, the students in Straub's dart experiment who improved the most were those who carried out motor imagery.

The Emulator Within

Your motor system has many more components than the primary motor homunculus. The primary motor cortex contains your body's "motor primitives"—the most basic building blocks of intentional action. It is up to a gaggle of higher-order body maps to come up with useful and appropriate combinations of those primitives. These maps are also involved in planning and transforming goals into action. And importantly, they let you engage in motor imagery. When you imagine a movement, your primary motor cortex is inhibited. You do not move a muscle. Yet your higher motor regions are screaming along at full speed, carrying out familiar motions.

Another interesting thing about these higher-order maps is that they represent all your movements before you carry them out. Your actions, and your ability to imagine them, are driven by internal models in the mid- and high-level echelons of your body mandala, rather than directly by what is happening in the world outside your body. These models are locked and loaded and ready to deploy by the time you become consciously aware that they are, in fact, what you intend. This has profound implications for people who are paralyzed by a stroke, lose a limb, or sever their spinal cords. Some people also see it as a threat to traditional ideas about free will.

Rick Grush, a neuroscientist at the University of California at San Diego, calls this phenomenon faux proprioception. When you move your limbs for real, signals are sent to your muscles, your muscles move, and your brain receives feedback from your touch receptors and proprioceptors. Your body mandala integrates this to give you a felt body sense of the motion.

But during motor imagery, no signals are sent to your muscles. Instead, they pass through what Grush calls an emulator—a brain circuit that mimics the motor action. When you engage this circuit, your brain experiences a faithful copy of the movement, or faux proprioception.

Why have an emulator? One reason is that you would be a hopeless klutz without it. The environment changes rapidly. You need to predict what is happening in the world to cope with its complexity. For example, let's say you're playing with a fast, wriggly puppy and it starts to run away from you. You want to catch it, and as fast as you can, you formulate a motor plan to make it happen: Reach out, grab collar, pull. But it takes a tenth of a second for that motor command, carried as electrical impulses, to travel down your spine and out to your hands. By the time you reach out to grab the puppy, your hand is guided by information that is already at least a tenth of a second old. If the puppy is a spry one, you just claw the empty air.

But your brain has a clever solution. It overshoots its reach. Like a quarterback throwing the ball ahead of a running receiver, your visual-motor maps make up for the delay by acting on a prediction instead of what you can immediately see. Perception and action are inherently predictive. Your brain creates mental models of your body and the world, and is constantly updating those models with newly arrived information from the senses and constantly extrapolating predictions from them.

Sometimes your brain adds more lead time, beyond what it needs to send a command down your spinal cord. If you tap along with a rhythmic noise or flash of light, you will initiate the tap a split second ahead of the actual rhythm. Your brain uses this extra anticipation as a way of coping with an erratic, changing environment—as on the playing field of almost any sport.

For example, if you were going by immediate sensation alone, a tennis serve would be too fast for you to react to. But the reason you can return at least some of the serves dished out against you is you read the body movements of your opponent. You start moving in the correct direction before her racket touches the ball.

The world-famous Brazilian soccer player Pele developed a trick that reliably won penalty shots. As Pele approached the ball, the goalie would read his body language and begin hurling himself to the left or right to make the interception. But Pele made a small stop, called a *paradinha*, a fraction of a second before he kicked the ball. It was enough time for him to see which way the goalie was moving and to kick in a different direction.

Golf and the Brain

A few years ago, when he worked at the Cleveland Clinic Foundation, Dr. Jeffrey Ross, a neuroradiologist now at the Barrow Neurological

THE BRAIN-MACHINE INTERFACE

A paralyzed man sits in a wheelchair and controls a computer cursor with his thoughts. He can answer e-mail, turn on his television, and move objects with a robotic arm—simply by thinking of those actions.

A physically active fourteen-year-old boy, who is being evaluated for epilepsy surgery, plays "Space Invaders" without using a joystick or lifting a finger. He merely thinks of blasting aliens off the computer screen, and zap, they're toast.

You may have read accounts of these seemingly amazing feats and wondered, How in the world do they do that?

Easy. It's simply a matter of knowing how to read signals from your body maps and convert them into a language that a computer or a robot can comprehend.

Recall that your movements are computed at multiple levels of your motor cortex—before you take any action. The direction and path that your arm will follow in reaching out to pick up that book lying on the table is calculated in advance of the movement.

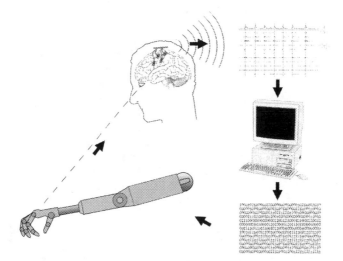

The basic setup for a brain-machine interface to control a robotic arm. Microelectrodes implanted in the brain radio their readings of neural activity to a computer, which remaps the neural data into a digital control signal that drives the prosthesis. Visual feedback from the eyes and eventually tactile feedback from the arm, which will be piped directly into the brain's primary touch map through another set of implanted electrodes, will create a closed-loop system—in other words, complete integration of the robotic arm into the patient's body schema.

Other regions of your brain (prefrontal and parietal) deal in even greater abstractions. They transform vision—*I see the book in front of me*—into planning how to reach for and grasp the book. Basically, they figure out your intentions and goals and pass commands down to your motor areas to do the desired deed.

It is possible to insert electrodes into these brain regions and record the firing patterns of neurons at work. Some patterns reflect the activity of cells involved in limb movement. Other patterns reflect intended actions. In either case, the information is mathematically translated into computer code that can operate a cursor or robot arm.

Most such experiments have been carried out in rats and monkeys. For example, healthy monkeys have learned how to bring food to their mouths via a robot arm that is operated by their thoughts. Once the monkeys realize how easy it is, they let their healthy arms go limp. It is as if the robot arm has been completely absorbed into their body schemas.

In developing effective brain machine interfaces for people, researchers face huge hurdles. They do not yet know how many neurons—tens, hundreds, thousands?—they need to record from to get the best results. Implanting electrodes directly into the brain is invasive and inherently dangerous. Electrodes are not compatible with human tissue. The body coats them in scar tissue and they fail. Infection is a constant threat.

It is safer to read electrical signals from the scalp, but these systems tend to be slow and somewhat clumsy in terms of how users adapt to them. Such electrodes listen to signals from millions of neurons all over the brain, resulting in less precise information.

The greatest success thus far has come from implanted electrodes. Matt Nagle was paralyzed below his shoulders after being stabbed in the neck during a mêlée at a beach in July 2001. In 2004, when he was twenty-five years old, he had an array of ninety-six electrodes pasted directly onto his motor cortex. Researchers asked him to follow a moving cursor with his eyes while imagining that his hand was moving it. The electrodes picked up patterns involved in his imagined movements and sent them to a computer. At first, Nagle had trouble moving the cursor to a target. But with practice he gained enough control to flip switches, retrieve e-mail, and send simple commands to a robot arm.

After nine months, the device came out. Nagle says that he is happy to have volunteered.

Another temporary user of implanted electrodes is an unnamed fourteen-year-old boy from the Midwest who was being evaluated for epilepsy surgery. To prepare for surgery, physicians implanted an array of electrodes and waited for a seizure to occur. That way they could map the exact location of the abnormal tissue involved.

While waiting, researchers asked the boy to move his limbs, talk, and then imagine moving his limbs. They matched brain signals to each act. Then they asked him to play a video game, "Space Invaders," by imagining his movements.

The boy learned to play the game instantly by moving the cursor with his thoughts. He mastered two levels of the game without breaking a sweat. Later, the electrodes came out and he got on with his life.

In the future, researchers say they want to add feedback—artificial senses of touch and movement—from robot arms or artificial limbs directly into the user's brain. Ultimately, they might be able to bypass a broken spinal cord and rewire the body to restore natural movement. Or build artificial limbs that act like real arms or legs.

Such therapies could help people with all kinds of problems—spinal cord injury, stroke, Lou Gehrig's disease, muscular dystrophy.

Or, brain-machine interfaces, assuming they are safe, could be hooked up to your normal brain. Just think, you'd be able to make a robot do your bidding. Any ideas of what you would do?

Institute in Phoenix, Arizona, wondered what would happen if he put golfers of various skill levels into a brain scanning device and asked them to imagine their golf swing. In such scanners, called functional magnetic resonance imaging machines, or fMRI, brain regions that consume the most energy "light up" the brightest, in what is thought to be a surrogate for effort.

Five men, aged twenty-four to fifty, were scanned as they used motor imagery to imagine themselves on a practice tee taking golf swings one after another for several seconds. The players held different handicaps between zero and 13 (the lower the handicap, the better the golfer).

Ross confirmed what neuroscientists had been saying: Imagining a skilled movement activates exactly the same brain regions that become active during real play—namely, action planning areas—minus the primary motor cortex. He also found that the brains of the better golfers used less energy than those of the duffers. The better you get at golf, the more efficient your brain is while playing it.

To understand why, think how complex systems in the natural world are built from simple parts. Language is composed of sentences, which are built out of words, which are built up from consonants and vowels.

Likewise, your movements are built out of motor primitives that are combined into simple actions that are combined into goal-directed action sequences, and so on. If you really excel at a sport or an instrument, you almost certainly began playing it before you entered puberty. The complex motor skills required for mastery became deeply ingrained in your body maps as a child. If you kicked a soccer ball around the streets of São Paulo from the age of three, you have better eye-foot coordination than a kid from Kansas who developed superb hand-eye coordination from throwing baseballs in Little League.

Basic movements in any sport can be described and taught. In tennis, your bones and muscles have many degrees of freedom for playing the game. A teacher breaks it down: You throw the ball, move your pelvis forward, bend your knees and elbow. Transitional states are explained: Rotate your upper body, accelerate your racket, stretch your whole body, hit the ball, flap your wrist, bend your body forward, let the racket flow through with the motion. As you learn a tennis serve, each component is stored, mapped, and activated when you attempt the movements.

Among novices, the shape or configuration of each piece of the action is clunky and poorly coordinated. You throw the ball too high, your pelvis tilts back, your wrist does not bend with sufficient force. You're struggling to put all the parts together, verbalizing each step in your mind.

Coaches say that people should not try motor imagery at this juncture because they don't have the basic motor maps required for the movements being learned. You cannot mentally practice a skill until it is actually related to your muscles. You can only imagine movements you have done previously and have a minimum level of competency with. For example, you can play at imagining you are able to bang out an intense piano concerto, but unless you can actually play the piano to begin with, you're not going to get a rehearsal benefit.

It is when movements are fluid, automatic, synchronized, and tuned that imagery becomes a useful tool. Indeed, there's a saying among golf coaches: If you want to make a good golfer into a bad golfer, ask him whether he breathes in or out before hitting the ball. The fact is it doesn't matter; but it can be something that simple that ruins a player's game. Golf is played at the limits of the nervous system's ability to consistently reproduce precise movements. A critical component of golf mastery—and more than a few other sports, for that matter—is the ability to perform without thinking. You need attention at the beginning of training, when the movements are being orchestrated by your supplementary motor cortex; but as the skill migrates down to your lower-level motor maps, attention tends to just get in the way and muck things up. It is like a tech-illiterate CEO who decides to head down and start micromanaging things in the IT department. Assuming you aren't a novice, your body schema just doesn't need your conscious thoughts or second guesses trying to interfere with your well-practiced motor programs. You don't need to pay attention to your breathing, limb position, or other postural minutiae. An expert plays for the goal of the action, not its components.

Mama's Loving Touch

Many athletic prodigies have naturally high sensorimotor integration between and within their frontal and parietal lobes. These are the graceful and sure-footed folks, the ones who own the basketball court when they're on it, or could find their way around the machine shop with their eyes closed, or have the enviable ability to pick up tricky new dance moves after seeing them done just once. On the flip side are the klutzes, those who seem to keep only a very sketchy, anemic map of the space behind them when their back is turned, whose proprioception is conspicuously poor, who kick their own heels as they walk and backhand glasses of water off dining tables.

Little is known about the organic differences between naturally high body awareness types and the congenitally clumsy, but neuroscientists are certainly keen to get a handle on this question. One thing that's safe to say is that, as with just about every other complex human trait, it's not a question of nature versus nurture, but rather how nature and nurture get woven together.

On the nature side, there is clearly genetic variation between different people's brain wiring. The same area of cortex can vary twofold in size among normal people. So how much does size matter? Scientists recently discovered genes that lay down the primary motor and touch maps before birth. By manipulating these genes in the lab, the scientists produced mice with miniaturized or supersized body maps and noted that both the under- and overendowed animals were klutzy. The key turned out to be not absolute size but relative size compared with other brain areas they were connected to. Such results are a good though modest first step toward decoding the underlying differences between the Mozarts and the Salieris of many arts and disciplines.

Biology is part of destiny, but not all of it. Early experience and rearing clearly play their part. To be truly world class you need a double hit of luck: You need the biological endowment of high-quality circuits for sensorimotor integration in your body mandala, and you need the opportunity to get lots and lots of practice starting when you are young.

Seth Pollak, a psychologist at the University of Wisconsin and an expert on child development, shows just how important movements are to normal brain development. But he begins with an unusual video clip—the one that inspired him to study children raised in Eastern European orphanages and who were later adopted by American families.

The film depicts mothers and babies in Mali. People in Mali have a strong cultural belief that babies with crooked legs are unattractive, Pollak explains. But of course, all newborns have scrunched-up legs from being in the womb. So what do Malian mothers do? When they bathe their infants, they stretch out their legs with a firm stroking motion. In the video, a mother yanks at her baby's feet as if she were pulling taffy. Then she grabs his ankles and hangs him upside down.

"Look at that," Pollak marvels. "It's amazing." A mother is swinging her tiny infant by the feet, upside down.

"They do this for months, and do you know what happens?" Pollak asks. He fast-forwards the video. "Look at that!" The camera pans around a group of mothers and children where the youngest, who are merely six- and seven-month-old babies, are walking. They toddle along as if they were twice their age.

Babies in Mali walk at younger ages than babies anywhere else in the world, Pollak says, because the part of their brain that controls movement gets hyperstimulated. Their motor and touch maps reach early maturity, thanks to all the help they get from their attentive parents—who naturally want attractive, straight-legged children. (It's definitely not a good idea to try this at home unless you get expert instructions from Malian parents!)

Pollak says the babies in Mali got him to thinking about an opposite problem. Babies born into Romanian and Russian orphanages after the Soviet empire imploded were often kept two or three to a crib. With not enough caretakers to go around, they received very little personal attention—no gentle touches, no soft kisses, no snuggly hugs. They were not allowed to crawl. Most remained in their cribs, looking out at the world but unable to freely explore or interact with it. If they did become mobile, many were tied to cribs or chairs. This was not done to abuse the children, Pollak says, but to keep them from harming themselves. Adult attention was in short supply.

Fast-forward several years, after hundreds of these children were adopted by middle-class American families, many of them settling in Wisconsin. Most had lived the first twelve to twenty-four months of their lives in such orphanages.

Pollak wondered about the consequences of not being allowed to crawl. "We used to think the motor system is hardwired, that people are destined to move in certain ways," he says, "but that's not so." You need to interact with the physical world to build normal body maps, and you need to do it during a sensitive developmental window in infancy.

To see the effects of early deprivation on body maps, Pollak ran a pilot study. Twenty-two of the Romanian and Russian orphans aged three to four came to his lab to undergo standardized tests. Their language and general IQ were fine, he says. But in eight domains of motor development, they were two to three standard deviations below the norm.

"That is a whopping statistic," he says. "These kids are not just a little delayed. In comparison, only one percent of the children in the world should score that badly. And all twenty-two of these kids scored that low."

The children were asked to put one hand on their shoulder and one at their waist, then change sides: Right hand at waist goes to right shoulder while left hand at left shoulder goes to waist. They could not do it, Pollak says. They had to bring one hand completely down before they could raise the other. The children were asked to stand on one foot, like a flamingo. They all toppled over when they tried.

But perhaps the adopted kids had not been in the United States long enough, with good public schools and homes with jungle gyms. So Pollak and his colleagues recruited eighteen ten-year-old Romanian and Russian orphans who had been adopted eight or more years ago. Surely they would have made up the deficit by now.

Kids everywhere love to walk on railroad ties or curbs. But the orphans, when asked to walk a balance beam placed on the floor, could not take more than one step. They toppled to one side instantly. Asked to swing their left arm and leg back, right arm and leg forward, they could not do it.

These studies, which now include 150 children, show that body maps for balance, body sense, and movement can fail to develop normally when babies are not allowed to move freely. If you were raised in an under-staffed Romanian orphanage, your body maps are stunted.

As for the rest of us, odds are that if you have a sport or a similar motor-intensive hobby, you understand you missed the boat to superstardom long ago and just play for fun and health. (You may take some solace from the fact that basketball superstar Michael Jordan could not play baseball very well.) Nevertheless, weekend warriors can exploit knowledge of body maps to improve their game, within some limits. There is such a thing as natural talent. You will never be able to run as fast as athletes from the Kalenjin tribe in Kenya, who possess gene variants that affect the mass and shape of their leg muscles. Their cellular metabolism is more effi-cient. They need 8 percent less energy to run a kilometer than most of their competitors. Physically, you will never be Tour de France legend Lance Armstrong. He has a higher oxygen-carrying capacity in his blood, less lactic acid, a bigger heart, and better slow twitch muscles (the kind of muscle you need to carry you through long, sustained aerobic work-outs) than most human beings. And like all great athletes, he trains harder, longer, and better than most of his competitors. He has a mental toughness that puts him in a class by himself.

Meanwhile, the rest of us mortals can apply lessons from the neuro-science lab. For example, Pascual-Leone found that the level of perfor-mance after five days of motor imagery was equivalent to three days of physical practice. But when he added one day of physical practice to five days of motor imagery, his subjects were as good as those who practiced only physically for five full days. This means motor imagery can give you a distinct advantage in your training. You can get better with less rather than more physical practice. And it's gentler on the knees.

CHAPTER 5

PLASTICITY GONE AWRY

or, When Body Maps Go Blurry

On a sunny afternoon in Rochester, New York, in June 1956, the U.S. Open golf championship had reached its climax: just two holes and two contenders left. Ben Hogan was in pretty good shape. He needed to sink a two-and-a-half-foot putt—child's play—and then either make par on the final hole to tie with Cary Middlecoff or a birdie (one stroke under par) to win. Hogan was one of the most celebrated golfers on earth at the time. Seven years prior, he had been propelled to world-class stardom as the only man ever to win the first three legs of the Grand Slam (the top four golf tournaments in the world) in a single year. Perhaps more than anybody else, Hogan's impressive string of victories, reported around the world on black-and-white newsreels, made golf into one of America's top sports.

Spectators stood in hushed anticipation as Hogan lined up his putt. He assumed the perfect posture: feet apart, shoulders set, putter gripped in both hands just so. He tried to putt . . . but he couldn't get the action started. His body wouldn't respond properly. He took a step back to refocus, then again eased back up to the ball. This time he got the putt in motion. The putter arced gently back, then smoothly swung forward—and suddenly, just before the blade tapped the ball, out of nowhere his right wrist made a wild jerk. The ball sailed past the hole and stopped more than six feet away. The championship went to Middlecoff.

At first Hogan chalked this colossal blunder up to nerves, to simple buckling under pressure, but in fact he had come down with the dreaded yips—a condition that triggers uncontrollable spasms or other involuntary movements during specific swings, especially putts. After that U.S. Open tournament, Hogan's star began to set. And he was far from alone; the yips often robs a golfer of the ability to sink even the most routine putts. It has kicked the legs out from under the careers of a more than a few golfing greats. Then there are the legions of devoted amateur enthusiasts who have been forced to give up their beloved sport in frustration.

The yips—so named by the great golfer Tommy Armour—afflicts different golfers differently. The most common problem is a jerk of the right wrist during the putt, but for some players it takes the form of an involuntary jump backward, thrusting the putter into the green, tremoring or wrenching of both wrists, or tensing up the shoulders. For most of the yips-tormented, it is the short putts—those less than five feet—that suffer the most; but for some it's long putts, for some it's chipping, and for a few it's their long drives.

Having the yips is like having an invisible imp riding around on your shoulder, always ready to reach out and jinx your stroke. You know it's coming, you know what's going to happen, and there's almost nothing you can do about it. Another well-known golfer and trick shot artist, Peter Longo, who in the late 1970s dropped out of the PGA tour into extremely early retirement because of the yips, compared it to the devil following him around between the putting greens. A case of the yips usually adds about five strokes per game. This may not sound like much to golf virgins, but it's hair-ripping aggravation for those who have spent thousands of hours perfecting their game only to watch their scores marching upward as their yips worsens. The yips often does worsen, growing more entrenched and severe, and in many cases "spreading" to curse a widening range of strokes.

Originally, people thought the yips was purely psychological, a form of "choking" (which in sports refers not to a blocked windpipe, but missing a routine shot or play due to performance anxiety). There is some truth to this: Stress and anxiety demonstrably exacerbate or even provide a trigger threshold for the yips. For example, most golfers say their yips are never a problem during practice, but then, as sure as the sun will rise in the east, the yips strikes as soon as there is a real game on.

But as you'll see, the root cause of the yips is not purely psychological, but neurological. In many cases it appears to be a peculiar form of body map disorder.

The Dreaded Yips

You know about normal plasticity and learning. Whenever you practice an action, you lay down brain maps that enable you to throw a ball, kick a can, use chopsticks, type at ninety words a minute, salute the flag, hit a tennis ball, ride a skateboard, you name it.

But this highly flexible, dynamic process can go awry. There is such a thing as overlearning, as in too much plasticity. If you repeat a movement too often and throw in some biological vulnerabilities (which we'll get to later), you can end up with frozen, fused, malformed, or disturbed body maps. Your motor programs become tangled together. When you try to tap a golf ball or play an arpeggio, your muscles contract involuntarily. When you assume a familiar posture to perform a highly skilled action, your afflicted body parts may spasm, jerk, tremor, freeze, cramp, or twist up into extreme or unusual positions. While the muscles you intend to engage refuse to obey your commands, many other unrelated muscles in their vicinity receive a "go" signal from your brain. It's as though you ask your brain to play a beautiful track of music, but instead it plays five tracks all overlapping one another at the same time. The result is a cacophony of random muscle contractions that can result in painful and pointless tugs-of-war.

Such conditions are known as dystonias, a motley group of body map disorders involving abnormal muscle tone and control. It is one of those medical categories defined by its symptoms rather than its underlying causes, which can differ case by case. When spastic movements are acquired through repetitive behavior—as seen in golfers, musicians, writers, surgeons, even auctioneers—they are called occupational dystonias. When they show up early in life, dystonias are hereditary; children assume twisted body positions that interfere with normal living. Other dystonias appear with aging and the decay of central nervous system timing. Still others can arise from several kinds of brain injuries, including blows to the head. Some affect almost the entire body, some involve a related group of body parts, like the face and neck, and some, called focal dystonias, are specifically confined to a small region such as the eyelids or the hand. The latter conditions can often be treated with botulism toxin—aka the Botox used to relax facial wrinkles—or electronic devices implanted into the brain.

Golfers who come down with the yips are never going to have devices implanted into their brains to treat what is, after all, just the ability to play a game. And because so many muscles are involved in putting—hand, wrist, shoulder, back, legs—Botox injections are not practical. To devise a treatment, researchers first need to know what is behind these strange career-destroying jerks and twists that bubble up at the worst possible moments. How do your body maps get yipped?

Think about the golf putt. First, it is devilish by its very nature. Most golfers agree that no single putting technique is superior. There are simply too many variables involved in sinking putts. Putting surfaces are rarely completely flat, which means that all putts will curve one way or another. To sink a putt the golfer not only must estimate the "break" and determine how much the ball will curve one way or the other on the way to the hole, but also hit it with the just the right force. Hit it too hard and it won't "take the break"; hit it too soft and it will break too much. Other factors that affect putts are the type of grass (there are several, all with different textures), the length to which the grass is cut (putts roll faster on shorter grass), the moisture of the grass (putts are slower on damp greens), the grain of the grass (many types of grass tend to grow in one direction or another), time of day (grass grows), and the smoothness of the greens (the tiniest bumps or indentations in the surface can deflect putts).

According to John Milton, a neuroscientist who studies human movement at Claremont College in Claremont, California, some golfers are excessively process-oriented. They try to control every micro-aspect of every shot, including knowing the status of every blade of grass on the putting green, while betting on every hole. They constantly ask themselves, "What is the angle of my upper hand? What is the angle of my lower hand? Are my feet the right distance apart? Did Pete just buy a new golf club? Oh, jeez, now I have to go buy a new golf club, too! Wait, did my finger drift just then?"

Milton has a hunch that the incredibly intense, control-freak golfer is more prone to yips. On the other hand, golfers who focus more on the goal of the shot, who simply visualize where the ball is supposed to go and let it happen (what some call cave man golf: *See ball, hit ball*), may be less prone to yips, although Milton is not sure. Age definitely plays a role. Like hearing and vision, body maps can degrade with passing years. Even though a dedicated player will practice putting thousands of times each year, the fidelity of his or her motor maps declines, often with downward spurts and rebounds. The result is intermittent yips that, for some, gradually becomes full-blown. Moreover, all dystonias worsen with anxiety, which is why a real game is so different from benign practice.

Treatments for the yips are still evolving. Milton has had some success in helping some yippers, though not the really hard cases, by "rebuilding" their games. By that he means convincing them that "it's really a game of thinking about the goal rather than process." They need to go with the feeling in their body about how the stroke should go, and when it feels right, putt—and lo and behold, the ball goes in.

Many yips-afflicted players try changing grips on the putter, adopting a new putting stance, or switching to one of several brands of unorthodox putter that are specifically designed to overcome the yips. One of these newfangled putters has a long, broomlike handle, for instance, while another is shaped like a shepherd's crook. The idea is that by changing the putter's weight, balance, thickness, shape, or length, the golfer is forced to adopt postures and limb motions that are significantly different from the stance and swing of canonical putting. Thus he won't engage that messed-up tangle of mutually conflicting motor sequences in the hand and arm regions of the motor homunculus. Unfortunately for the truly dedicated, very few of these alternative putters are permitted in tournament play.

Changing stances is another obvious choice. "Slammin' Sam" Snead, who was one of Ben Hogan's chief rivals back in their heyday, was yet another pro golfer to get the yips. Snead was determined not to let it drive him out of the game and sought ways around it. At first he compensated by switching to a highly unorthodox croquet-style stance while putting. He would stand facing the hole with the ball midway between his feet and swing the putter between his legs. This indeed got around his dystonia problem, because the movements and postures he had to use were very different from those associated with the standard putting stance. Unfortunately for Snead, the United States Golf Association subsequently outlawed the croquet-style stance in the late 1960s. Again Snead adapted and settled on a "sidesaddle" stance, whereby he stood to one side of the ball, still facing the hole. He used a pendulum motion to hit the ball, but the ball was to his right rather than between his feet. Although his putting was never again as good as it had been, Snead stuck around the pro circuit far longer than most.

Another solution is the "claw grip," which has eliminated yips for some players. Rather than grip the putter like a bat, the player changes hand position. Your left hand grips the top of the club normally while your right hand holds the club between your thumb, which is near your body, and your fingers. Gripped this way, the club is pushed with your right hand so that your right wrist is taken out of the motion.

Different people have different luck with different combinations of these strategies. But unfortunately, even switching to a new style of putter that takes your wrist out of play, or altering your stance, is often only a stopgap. As soon as the golfer starts getting good with it, the yips often comes back to haunt him. In these cases it spreads almost like a creeping disease, claiming one golf stroke after another.

So what's a chronic yipster to do? Start praying? Go to tournaments just to watch? Or, God forbid, give up golf? Research shows that between a quarter and half of golfers who play for twenty or more years have experienced the yips. Their problem is less about choking and more about trying to deal with an abnormal brain map caused by abnormal plasticity.

While there are no proven treatments yet for restoring normal plasticity in widely distributed motor maps—again, muscles in the wrists, arms, shoulders, back, and hips may all be involved—ideas for how to go about fixing such maps do exist. One involves tweaking your body maps involved in balance, proprioception, vision, posture, and movement. What if you could send a strong corrective signal into the brain of a person suffering from yips? Could it, would it, help rectify the abnormal motor maps?

One approach, not proven but intriguing, involves having the golfer wear a pair of vibrating insoles in his or her shoes. Such insoles contain tiny electrical devices that send randomly fluctuating vibrations up through the feet. The vibrations, which are detected by the vestibular cortex, produce resonant changes that (as noted in chapter 3) have been shown to improve posture and balance in the elderly. Whether such an intervention could lead to improved motor control in golfers remains to be tested.

A second approach involves wearing the Brain Port, a device developed by the late Paul Bach-y-Rita, a neuroscientist at the University of Wisconsin. Bach-y-Rita long ago realized that all sensory information entering the brain via nerve fibers is nothing but patterns, and therefore at some level is all equivalent. In vision, images of the world pass through the retina and are converted into impulse patterns that travel up the optic nerve into the brain. In hearing, sounds pass through the ear and are converted into patterns carried by the auditory nerve into the brain. In touch, nerve endings on skin translate touch sensations into patterns carried into the brain. Could the brain, which maps vision, hearing, and touch, effectively translate between these different sensory maps?

Sensory input patterns travel to primary input maps in the cortex where they are interpreted as sights, sounds, and touch sensation. Bach-y-Rita built a device that would transfer any familiar sensory pattern to the tongue (which is loaded with touch receptors) and found that your brain will interpret the patterns correctly. For example, a blind person wears a camera mounted on his head. The camera sends images of real-world scenes to a strip of plastic embedded with sensors that the blind person wears on his tongue. Visual patterns from the camera are sensed as vibrations on the tongue. The blind person's brain interprets these felt patterns as a crude form of vision—enough to make out a doorway or a sidewalk curb. Blind people who are proficient at using the tongue display unit report that they feel orderly touch sensations on their tongues when a transcranial magnet is applied over their visual cortex.

In another example, a person who loses her sense of balance due to loss of her vestibular system wears a kind of carpenter's level on her head. When she moves her head, signals from the sensor are sent to her tongue and reinterpreted as balance. And, in a military example, a Navy SEAL wears the Brain Port to help him maintain his bearings in murky water as sonar signals are "read" by his tongue.

And yips? Bach-y-Rita and others say that motor feedback signals from the muscles involved in putting could easily be rerouted to the tongue. The golfer would place a plastic strip with sensors on his tongue while his putter is wired with sensors that detect the position of the club in motion. When the putter is jerked, say, two degrees to the right, that amount of error or deflection would be sent immediately to the tongue.

You would feel the error via little tongue-tickling sensations. By lining the sensations up on the middle of your tongue, you would line up your putting muscles to hit the ball correctly.

Research into the neurological basis of yips is just getting under way, including a program at the Mayo Clinic in Scottsdale, Arizona. If yips turns out to be a true dystonia, researchers say, it will be a movement disorder that affects tens of thousands of otherwise healthy adults.

A-Rod's Woes

Golfers are far from alone in their yips woes. Occupational dystonias have been documented in players from a wide variety of sports including billiards, basketball, the javelin, tennis, and cricket. In the world of dart throwing it is known as "dartitis." A dart player with dartitis can still use his throwing hand fine for writing, pointing, opening doors, and just about anything else hands are good for, but the instant he takes up a dart and stands there aiming at the bull's-eye, it's as though the hand is possessed. Either he can't release his dart at all, or his rhythm and accuracy are completely off, and his mates had better stand back and be ready to duck.

One of the most dumbfounding things about occupational dystonias is how very specific they are. The dystonic symptoms jam up your body only when you try to perform a particular well-practiced skill while maintaining a certain posture or limb position. A baseball player can perform any action on the field except one; he loses the ability to make accurate throws from third base to first base. But not always. The player might throw accurately when he fields a difficult ground ball and has to throw the ball while he is running and off balance. But when he has ample time to throw the ball, using his exquisitely sculpted third-to-first-base motor program, he screws up.

This happened to the Yankees star Alex Rodriguez, or A-Rod, in 2006 when he led major-league third basemen in errors. Rodriguez made flawless throws during practice, but in games his throws to first would sink or sail before reaching their target. In a similar vein, the former Yankees second baseman Chuck Knoblauch had trouble throwing from second base to first base, while his other plays were unaffected. Both players' troubles were chalked up to mental problems and not yips, but then not many baseball players have ever heard of an occupational dystonia.

Surgeons and dentists who specialize in certain delicate operations sometimes come down with the yips and are no longer able to safely wield their drills and scalpels in those procedures. Butchers and assembly line workers who repeat certain motions with robotlike precision can also de-

THE PEBBLE-MOUTHED ORATOR

Their diversity aside, most dystonias seem to be rooted in one kind or another of body map dysfunction. Many patients with focal dystonia discover some kind of sensory self-stimulation trick that can dispel their symptoms. Dr. Allan Wu, an assistant professor of neurology at the University of Southern California at Los Angeles, likes to describe a patient of his who had dystonia in his face and neck. The man's face would contort, slurring his speech, and his neck would twist around to the left as though being drawn taut by a winch. But luckily he was able to release himself from this posture by reaching around with his right hand and lightly touching the left side of his face. The moment he did this, the twisted posture vanished and he was back in full control.

For this sensory trick to be successful, it was essential that the fellow touch himself, Wu said; someone else touching his face wasn't of any use. His own hand was special. How? His own hand was integrated with the rest of his body mandala; other people's hands were not. It was an inside job. The sensory and motor maps representing his left face and neck were misfiring, haywire, out of sync with the rest of the maps. When he willed his hand over to where he knew the cheek was and felt the light-touch sensation it created there, his face and neck were reintegrated into his body schema. This sort of thing is common with dystonias.

Another of Wu's patients had dystonia of the mouth. His lips would snarl up to the right side of his face and his tongue became a crude flap of meat he could barely control. This man informed Wu that he was able to overcome this by putting small items in his mouth, such as coins or crushed ice. As his mouth parts moved the small objects around, he was stimulating the sensorimotor feedback loops between the mouth-part representations of his body mandala in a way that broke them out of their locked-up state.

Ancient history buffs may note that Dr. Wu's patient brings to mind Demosthenes and his pebbles. Demosthenes was one of the greatest orators in classical Greece. The story goes that before he became a dazzling public speaker he had suffered a lifelong severe speech impediment, which he overcame by practicing his speeches with pebbles in his mouth. This tale has always had an air of the apocryphal about it; it is hard to imagine a mouthful of rocks leading to improved articulation. Hard to imagine, that is, until you learn about dystonias and body maps.

velop abnormal hand and arm maps that produce clumsiness, tremor, and fatigue.

And lest you get the impression that occupational dystonias are all about hand-eye skills, consider the case of "auctioneer's jaw," which causes those professional fast-talkers to stumble over their syllables whenever they try going into "patter" mode. Auctioneers with dystonia of the mouth can talk, eat, kiss, and do everything else with their mouths that the rest of us can, but as soon as they start to drift into the mesmerizing rapid-fire speech of their trade, they become hopelessly tongue-tied.

When occupational dystonia hits a virtuoso musician it's called musician's cramp. Musician's cramp can afflict players of many kinds of instrument—pianists, violinists, banjo pickers, woodwind players, and drummers, to name just a few. Whenever they try to play, their movements become uncoordinated, their wrists may twist into strange positions, and their hands and fingers cramp, twitch, and tense. It may be simply that the demands of ultra high-speed, high-precision skills such as playing violin solos brush up against the limits of your body maps' sensorimotor integration abilities. When the demands made on the motor system go beyond what evolution was ever pressured to prepare it for, neuroplasticity starts to actively degrade the neural representations of the body parts involved rather than hone them.

Styles of playing an instrument can also affect brain maps. Pianists who learn the Russian school engage in hammerlike movements and forceful playing with the fingers bent. Those who learn the French school engage in a softer style of play with extended fingers "caressing" the keys. The Russian style is associated with dystonia more often than the French.

Like the dart player who can do anything with her hands except throw a dart, pianists with musician's cramp don't have any trouble signing their checks or using their knife and fork, but sit them down before their keyboards with their fingers in position, and their hands just seize up. They can play the Moonlight Sonata on an organ, but not on a piano. Fingers that used to fly gracefully over the ivories hitting twenty keys per second suddenly seize up or clench, and completely thwart the ability to play. Voluntary motor control is gone. Finger maps degrade. Coordinated hand postures in which various fingers function as a unit (as in arpeggios) induce changes in finger maps, blurring segregation of the fingers.

A bit of tidy support for this interpretation comes from an experiment in which several monkeys' fingers and palms were bombarded for days on end with fast, repetitive tactile stimulation. Eventually their movements became dystonic in ways very reminiscent of musician's cramp. When the researchers examined these hand areas inside the monkeys' brains, they found the maps of the fingers and palms had grown enormously: A finger area now encompassed multiple fingers and joints. The boundaries between the monkeys' finger maps had blurred.

In other experiments, researchers stitched together two monkey fingers and observed the hand map change: Two distinct finger maps merged into a single map. Neurons in the double-finger area responded to touch on either finger.

Meanwhile, other scientists looked at the hand maps of dystonic musicians, and observed much the same pattern. In a study of five patients and seven normal controls, they noted that in those with dystonia, the same brain region responded to touch on more than one finger. Guitar players can get cramps in either hand, one for finger posture and one for fine alternating finger movements. In a rather clever experiment, five guitarists with musician's cramp practiced finger movements on a guitar neck made especially for a functional magnetic brain scanner. The "instrument" was a six-string classical guitar neck constructed with no metal parts so it could be safely used inside the ultra-powerful magnet. Although the guitar had no body, the neck had true dimensions, texture, and string tension. As the musicians did the finger movements that triggered their dystonia, the main researcher, Jesús Pujol at the Magnetic Resonance Center of Pedralbes in Barcelona, Spain, noted that their primary hand maps (on the side of the brain opposite their actual hands) showed a greater than normal activity while their motor planning areas on both sides of the brain were underactive.

So the explanation runs like this: The demands of virtuoso performance surpass the limits of sensorimotor integration. Under these conditions, neuroplasticity messes up rather than hones the hand representation. Somatotopy, defined as the orderly mapping of your skin to specific parts of your brain, breaks down, and your brain comes to represent the entire hand as one big smear. Profound sensory ambiguity exists at the lowest level of the sensory cortex. Without constant and accurate feedback from your touch maps, your motor maps can't do their job. And so a feedback loop of mutual degradation is set up: Your touch map worsens, so your motor map worsens, which worsens your touch map even more. Your hand maps can no longer coordinate all those precisely timed, pressure-controlled rapid-fire movements. As the circuits in your motor cortex become disorganized, their outputs to the body are accompanied by a barrage of unrelated and conflicting commands to other muscles as well.

Many famous musicians suffer from dystonia but you might never know it, says Victor Candia, a leading researcher in musician's cramp at the Collegium Helveticum in Zurich, Switzerland. They're artists at fakery, he says, using tricks like changes in fingering or holding the instrument in a different position. Most are not willing to talk about their dystonia publicly for fear it might hurt their reputations.

Many students and instructors at major music conservatories know about dystonia and are frightened of it, Candia says. It may seem odd that a neuroscientist can go in and tell them how to move their hands so as to avoid these abnormal body maps—but that is exactly what Candia is starting to do. For example, he tells them: You should give up playing similar instruments, like guitar and electric bass, if symptoms appear. That accelerates the problem. Playing more slowly is not the solution. You may still be able to play fast, but you need to retrain your brain by using the very same mechanisms of neural plasticity that screwed up your body maps in the first place.

Here's how: Let's say you have musician's cramp. In a technique called sensorimotor retuning, some fingers are immobilized in a special splint while other fingers practice contracting in predefined sequences and postures. You learn to do this with different configurations of splinted and nonsplinted fingers for two hours a day for at least eight days. The idea is that this will reestablish your fingers' individual identities in your motor maps by reeducating your brain to properly keep track of, and make predictions about, which sensation from which finger part is the result of which motor command. The outcomes still vary. Some musicians make a modest degree of recovery. Others return to their full former virtuosity. Brain scans reveal that their finger maps have indeed been restored to somatotopic order. Interesting to note: This finger immobilizing technique worked best for pianists and guitarists, least well for brass and woodwind players. It has been impossible thus far to retrain the lips, Candia says.

Of course occupational dystonia is relatively rare. Only between one and five percent of professional musicians will develop musician's cramp in their mid to late careers. Only a minority of golfers come down with full-blown yips. So another piece of the explanation for occupational dystonias must lie in genetic differences between individuals. It seems that some people are more vulnerable than others.

Not surprisingly, monkeys are the same way. In one experiment, monkeys who were made to perform repetitive tasks with levers and switches hundreds of times per day for weeks on end developed the same kinds of spasms, jerks, tensions, and pains that are seen in assembly line workers with occupational dystonias. But not every monkey became dystonic. Like humans, it seems, some monkeys are more prone to abnormal plasticity than others.

Why some are resistant is illustrated by another kind of occupational dystonia called writer's cramp. For those afflicted, simple handwriting becomes difficult or impossible. Merely assuming the hand posture for writing brings on spasms and cramping, as though invisible marionette strings were jerking painfully at the fingers and wrists. Now, most of us can imagine how hammering through Rachmaninoff piano solos over and over again for hours and hours each day might upset the balance of something or other in the brain and lead to problems in performance—but handwriting? Handwriting is nowhere near as precise, as demanding, or as rapid as Rachmaninoff. Billions of people on earth handwrite a significant amount each day for decades and don't end up with disordered body maps, so why should it happen to these poor souls?

This question led researchers to look for biological differences between people who get writer's cramp and those who don't. There are now fairly solid indications that some basic brain-wiring differences exist between the two groups. For example, people who develop writer's cramp are bad at mentally rotating images of hands but not of feet, which could be a clue to how their hands are misrepresented in their brains. And it seems the writer's crampers have a defect in cortical inhibition, which simply means their brain's braking system is out of balance. They have trouble creating "brakes," or inhibitory connections, in their somatosensory and motor maps. The lack of good brakes could be why their body part representations get easily fuzzed up. It could also explain why the motor commands issued in their motor maps are received too broadly, leaking "go" signals to many more muscles than just the narrow set that was intended. If cortical inhibition were stronger in these people's motor maps, activation would not spread out so widely; the muscles rightfully involved in the intended action would not be overactivated.

Alvaro Pascual-Leone, who wields the TMS magnet with consummate skill, applied low frequency magnetic pulses over the motor cortexes of six patients with writer's cramp. Such pulses, which produce long-lasting decreases in cortical excitability, resulted in clear but transient improvement in all of them.

Fortunately, therapies for abnormal plasticity are starting to blossom in laboratories worldwide. There are treatments for ringing in the ears, called tinnitus, and for a problem with reading, called dyslexia. Both conditions stem from aberrant mappings of sound in the primary auditory cortex. A third of people who fracture their wrists develop complex regional pain syndrome. While they wear a cast, their brains send signals to their wrists telling the wrists to move. But of course the wrists are immobilized. The muscles and joints cannot comply, abnormal plasticity sets in, and a pain signal is returned to the brain. But when the cast comes off, the learned pain lingers.

At Candida McCabe's lab in Scotland, patients with this kind of chronic wrist pain are being treated with a so-called mirror box (as illustrated on page 91). The mirror box is a simple contraption that fools the brain into thinking that an injured arm or wrist—or, as we'll see later, a painful phantom limb— is actually okay, and not in any kind of pain. It works like this: You put your good arm into a box that contains a mirror positioned in such a way that you see what appear to be two arms—your good arm and a mirror reflection of your good arm. Your bad arm, meanwhile, is resting on the other side of the mirror, completely out of sight but proprioceptively positioned exactly where the reflected good arm appears to be. When you move your good arm and wrist, as if conducting an orchestra or swatting at flies, you see two healthy limbs. And if you perform these waving motions in the mirror box once or twice a day for several weeks, something extraordinary happens. Your wrist, muscle, and joint maps become normal again. Your brain is tricked into resetting your body schema. The pain in your injured wrist vanishes.

The Power of Plasticity

Until recently, scientists and physicians believed that body maps were set in stone by late adolescence. They likened it to chiseling a statue from a block of marble: The block initially holds a vast number of possible statues within it. With every stroke of his hammer and chisel, the sculptor rules out certain possible statues from the block, but it is all in service of working toward one perfectly finished, polished work of art. So one block of marble gets turned into Michelangelo's David while another gets turned into the Pietà. One block is Wilder Penfield, the famous neurosurgeon; another is Ronaldinho, the Brazilian soccer star.

This view made sense in the light of everyday clinical experience. The immature brain has what are called critical periods, when it is broadly tuned to acquire complex skills like language or gymnastics. When these critical periods end, by late childhood or early adolescence, most people have great difficulty learning a second language without an accent and would probably never dare take up competitive acrobatics. When children sustain a brain injury, they often recover fully. The younger the age of injury, the fuller the recovery of function. A young child can lose half his or her brain and still turn out a nearly normal adult! But when adults suffer strokes or other blows to the brain, they often remain paralyzed, unable to talk, clumsy, or confused. Scientists reasoned that this could only be due to diminished plasticity. Otherwise grandpa would bounce back just like junior.

This conclusion made no sense to Michael Merzenich, a neuroscientist at the University of California at San Francisco School of Medicine, who more than any other researcher has revised our understanding and appreciation of adult brain plasticity.

When Merzenich set up his laboratory in San Francisco in the early 1980s, virtually everyone believed that plasticity was for kid brains. Merzenich did not believe it and made bets with several of his colleagues that adult brains could undergo profound change. Merzenich was the first to perform a now-classic experiment in which he took an adult monkey, temporarily sewed two of its fingers together, waited a few weeks, and then took a look at the hand representation in its brain. Where there had been distinct maps for its index and middle fingers, now there was one single finger map for both fingers. Two fingers had been fused into one, at

THE BLIND PAINTER

Monet wished he had been born blind, because he believed that it would have enhanced his artistic perception of the world. Picasso stated that painting was a blind man's profession, as blind people have a clearer vision of reality. So what do blind people "see" that makes great artists jealous?

Esref Armagan is a fifty-two-year-old Turkish painter who has been blind in both eyes since birth. His art hangs in museums around the world. He can render objects, people, animals, landscapes, and the shadows they cast with utmost precision.

Two years ago, Armagan went to Pascual-Leone's laboratory to have his brain scanned while he drew freehand. He was given objects to feel—a coffee cup, a toy elephant, a toothbrush—and asked to elaborate them on paper from memory.

"What we saw in the scan was amazing," Pascual-Leone says. "Esref's visual cortex lit up during the drawing tasks as if he were actually seeing [the objects]. His scan, to the untrained eye, might look like the brain of a sighted person."

But Armagan's eyes were useless. No patterns of reflected light swept up his optic nerve and into his visual cortex. No colors, edges, lines, or shades of gray penetrated his gray matter. But, as Pascual-Leone observed, the blind man's visual cortex was not dormant. It was buzzing with activity.

The explanation: plasticity. Without input from his eyes building up visual patterns of the world, Armagan's visual cortex was not called upon to see. But it did not lie dormant. It did not become a black hole.

Without input from the eyes, Armagan's visual cortex was recruited by other senses—primarily touch, but also hearing and the rest of the body mandala. Without formal training, Armagan taught himself to translate his acute sense of touch into images in his mind's eye. From there he was able to render them on canvas.

Pascual-Leone says that when blind people read Braille, their visual cortex lights up as their fingers trace the raised bumps encoding written language. If he temporarily knocks out the visual cortex of a Braille reader with a transcranial magnet, the person can no longer read fluently.

When sighted people wear blindfolds for five days and practice learning to read Braille, their visual cortex lights up. But two hours after the blindfolds come off, their visual areas no longer respond to touch.

Plasticity happens rapidly, Pascual-Leone says, too fast for the brain to grow new connections. It's more likely that unused pathways are unmasked when sensory inputs are changed, as from wearing a blindfold for five days. Over time, such plasticity changes can become permanent, allowing blind painters to exploit their newly wired brains in unexpected and delightful ways.

least as far as the monkey's brain maps were concerned. After the sutures were removed and a few more weeks went by, the sewn finger map split itself back in two separate finger maps. Merzenich won the wager.

In a related experiment, Merzenich removed a monkey's middle finger and took a look at its brain map. The finger's suddenly vacant map in the homunculus was rapidly taken over by the index and ring fingers. He won the bet a second time.

By the end of the 1990s, Merzenich's work proved that far from being structures that congeal into their final, permanent form at the end of childhood, your body maps are dynamic structures, constantly shifting and adapting on scales both large and small. Unlike innocence, neuroplasticity doesn't leave you at some point, never to return. Nor is it a process like scabbing that only kicks in when you get injured. The old picture was of body maps settling into a fixed configuration like fired clay. The new picture is one of dynamic stability. Neuroplasticity continually reshapes your brain in response to experience; the fact that it seems static merely reflects the consistency of your experiences throughout most of your adult life.

Think of it as the plume of water in a fountain. From a distance it looks pretty much the same from moment to moment because the conditions that affect it are constant: water pressure, gravity, atmospheric temperature and pressure, the shape of the nozzle. But zoom in and you see that the plume is actually renewing itself continually, and its fine-scale shape is not at all constant. Change any parameter and the plume will assume a new size and shape. So too with the representations in your body maps.

You can feel plasticity at work in everyday experience. The next time you cut your fingernails too short or break a nail, you are likely to run your fingertips over the nail bed to feel the change in your body's fingertip maps. Suddenly it's difficult to pick up certain objects because your grips and your grasps are thrown off a tiny bit. This sensation goes away once your brain has remapped your fingertips.

Phantom Limbs

V. S. Ramachandran speaks in a thunderous baritone and rolls his *r*'s with gusto. He is a captivating speaker with one after another ingenious experiment up his sleeve. Working from his laboratory at the University of California at San Diego in La Jolla, he studies, among other things, the nature of metaphors, new ways to treat autism, how senses can become intertwined so people "hear" colors or "taste" sounds, and, in pioneering work, how phantom limbs come into existence.

In his 1998 book, *Phantoms in the Brain*, Ramachandran explains how he came upon the idea of using an ordinary Q-tip to explain phantom limbs—arms or legs that linger in the minds of patients long after amputation. A colleague, Tim Pons of the National Institutes of Health, was studying monkeys with an injury similar to one observed in motorcyclists who are thrown from their bikes at high speed. Upon impact, the cyclist's arm is torn from the shoulder. Nerves from the arm to the spinal cord are crushed. The cyclist's arm hangs limp, paralyzed, useless, and may in fact be amputated to keep it from being deadweight that just gets in the way.

Years earlier, another group at NIH had experimentally severed the nerves in the arms of several monkeys to study this type of injury, and now Pons had access to the animals. He wondered what had happened to their body maps when their arms could no longer send or receive signals to or from the brain. You would not expect to detect signals from the area of the brain where the paralyzed hand map should be located, Ramachandran says. If you touch the paralyzed hand, the "hand area" should be silent, right?

Indeed, when Pons stroked the useless hand, there was no activity in the hand map region. But to his amazement, he found that touches made on the monkey's face caused cells in this "dead zone" to fire vigorously. Cells corresponding to the face area also fired when the face was touched, but that was expected. It looked as though sensory information from the monkey's face went to two places in the brain—to the face map and to the missing hand map.

Ramachandran immediately grasped the implications of Pons's experiment. In Penfield's homunculus, the hand is right next to the face. Thus the hand map zone does not die or go numb after sensory loss. Rather, fibers from an adjacent part of the body map—in this case, the face—will invade the hand area. Plasticity sets in right away, over long distances.

Because monkeys cannot talk, Ramachandran found an amputee who was willing to come into his laboratory for a new experiment. The patient, Tom, had lost his left arm just above the elbow in a car accident. Tom said that he was distressed by itching and painful sensations in his phantom fingers. Maybe Ramachandran could help.

In the experiment, Tom sat blindfolded in Ramachandran's basement laboratory. Ramachandran took a regular Q-tip and stroked various parts of Tom's body surface, asking him to say when and where he felt the sensations.

He swabbed Tom's cheek. "What do you feel?"

"You are touching my cheek."

"Anything else?"

"Hey, you know, it's funny," said Tom. "You're touching my missing thumb, my phantom thumb."

Ramachandran moved the Q-tip to Tom's upper lip. "How about here?"

"You're touching my index finger. And my upper lip."

"Really? Are you sure?"

"Yes. I can feel it both places."

"How about here?" Ramachandran stroked Tom's lower jaw with the swab.

"That's my missing pinkie."

Ramachandran soon found a complete map of Tom's phantom hand—on his face! He was seeing the human version of what Pons had seen in the monkeys. Eventually Ramachandran explored Tom's entire body surface with the Q-tip. When he touched Tom's chest, right shoulder, right leg, or lower back, Tom felt sensations in only those places and not in the phantom. But he soon found a second, "beautifully laid out map" of Tom's missing hand tucked into his left upper arm, a few inches above the line of amputation. This second map existed because the brain's hand area is also flanked by the upper arm and shoulder area.

With this simple experiment, Ramachandran was able to explain the basis for phantom limbs. Before he did so, phantoms were invoked to support dualism—the idea that you possess both a material body and an ethereal soul, the phantom being proof of the latter. But Ramachandran revealed the true nature of phantoms. Every time Tom's face or shoulder is touched, the missing arm and hand area in his brain is activated. When Tom shaves, puts on clothes, or simply moves his stump around, the phantom is created.

Eventually, Ramachandran and others went on to show that if you lose a limb, your brain begins to remap your body within hours. A phantom is born as plasticity reorganizes touch maps and motor maps in the Penfield homunculi. Sometimes phantoms go away, presumably because the brain learns to predict and accept sensations from the newly fused brain maps. Some phantoms persist for decades. Some are paralyzed. In other cases, amputees report vivid sensations of movement in their phantoms, which they have to ignore lest they try to steady themselves with a nonexistent arm or leg. And, to the misery of many amputees, some phantoms produce unrelenting pain.

In a remarkable case in France, a man called C.D. had both his hands amputated in 1996. The hand maps in his brain were quickly co-opted by his elbow maps. Four years later C.D. got two new hands in a transplant operation. Within a few months, his hand and elbow maps returned to normal, as they were before his accident.

Ramachandran notes that remapping cannot be the whole story behind phantoms. For one thing, it does not explain why Tom and other patients experience the feeling of being able to move their phantoms voluntarily or why the phantom can change its posture. Where, he wondered, do these movement sensations originate?

The explanation, Rama says, is found in Tom's intact motor maps. When Tom decides to move his arm, his motor maps—which do not know the arm is missing—send out normal commands. These instructions continue to be monitored by other parts of the brain and are felt as movements. But they are phantom movements carried out by a phantom arm.

When a person's arm is held in a cast or sling for several months before amputation, he or she may experience a paralyzed phantom. According to Ramachandran, this is due to a strong dynamic established in the brain before the surgery. Motor areas command the real but immobilized arm to move. But the eyes know better. Each time the command to move is sent and the visual system fails to register movement, a kind of learned paralysis sets in. The arm becomes paralyzed. And when the limb is amputated, the phantom is similarly paralyzed, sometimes painfully so.

The suffering caused by painful paralyzed phantom limbs is what prompted Ramachandran, in 1996, to invent the mirror box now being used to treat other central pain conditions and stroke. If you can learn paralysis, he says, you should be able to unlearn it. Patients place their

In mirror box therapy, a vertical mirror is used to superimpose an image of the patient's healthy, good limb over the felt position of the damaged or missing limb. The visual-proprioceptive feedback from this experience can often reset the body map representation of the compromised limb.

good arm into the box and are told to imagine that its reflection is really their missing limb, as if their phantom has been brought back to life. When patients wave their good arms around, their brains get fooled into thinking that their phantoms are moving the same way. Voluntary control is thereby restored to the paralyzed phantoms, and the pain goes away!

Imagining Recovery

Scott Frey has a mission in life. Raised by a single mother suffering from multiple sclerosis, he watched her spend the last fourteen years of her life in a wheelchair, paralyzed from the neck down. "Here I was, the neuroscientist son, helpless to do anything," Frey says.

But not anymore. Changing gears in his career as an experimental psychologist, Frey moved in 2004 from Dartmouth College to the University of Oregon, where he is devoting his energies to creating a center for rehabilitative neuroscience. That means using the latest knowledge about how the brain works to get people up and moving after a stroke, spinal cord injury, or amputation, to free thousands of individuals from life in a wheelchair. He says his goal "is to do things that kick me out of bed in the morning."

Frey started with stroke patients. A stroke occurs when the blood supply to one or another part of the brain is interrupted, either by a clot in an artery or if an artery bursts. The brain region nourished by that artery no longer receives oxygen, leaving it destroyed or damaged. The standard of care is "wait and see"—after a few days or weeks, the extent of damage is assessed. Depending on the brain region or regions affected, people may be paralyzed, blind, or unable to speak or comprehend language, to use or identify tools, or to perceive the space around their bodies. They may suffer from any number of peculiar deficits related to their damaged or missing brain maps.

Of course, we now know that the adult brain is plastic. It can adaptively reconfigure itself in response to novelty, practice, or damage. Merzenich showed this in one of his other early experiments. He damaged different arm maps in monkey brains but left the corresponding limb intact. As the monkeys continued to move their arms, the maps grew back. This is why many stroke victims recover some, if not all, function. Given time, damaged maps in the brain may reorganize themselves.

In general, stroke patients spend a month in physical or occupational therapy designed to facilitate and encourage the brain's inherent plasticity to do its thing. The idea is that if you do something over and over—reach for a doorknob, pick up a cup, squeeze a ball—your brain will grow new connections that undergird what you have learned. The goal of physical therapy is to drive the mechanism of neuroplasticity and restore functional maps. All manner of new technologies and techniques are being developed to improve the remapping process, including strapping down the "good arm" so a person is forced to use the "bad arm," zapping a paralyzed limb with electrical impulses so the brain "realizes" that the limb is present, and strapping useless arms and legs into robotic devices that never tire of doing movements over and over.

But after six months have passed, stroke patients who have not partially or fully recovered are almost always advised to resign themselves to accept their limitations. Further improvement is out of the question, they are told. It is what it is—unless you know Frey, who thinks that motor imagery can be harnessed to reverse or ameliorate paralysis after a stroke. Recall that your primary motor map—the one that sends commands down your spinal cord to make your body move—is temporarily off-line during motor imagery. But your higher order motor maps are whizzing along, neatly emulating the actions you are imagining.

To see if stroke patients have intact, healthy maps in these higher motor areas, Frey designed a battery of implicit motor imagery tasks. They're implicit because subjects do not know that they are being specifically called upon to conjure images in their minds. In the task, patients look at pictures of objects, such as a handlebar, displayed in different three-dimensional orientations. They are asked to imagine how they would grasp the object in the most comfortable position. Would your hand grab the handle from over its top or from underneath? Where would you place your thumb? Where are your fingers positioned?

In a pilot study, Frey recruited three patients who had not been able to move their arm for one to five years. One of them, a seventy-six-year-old man, sat in his home in front of a large television screen that showed images of the various objects and practiced how he would grasp them using mental imagery. He did this an hour a day, five days a week, for nine weeks.

"We knew he would not get function back," Frey says, "but would his brain organization look any different?"

The answer was yes. In fact all three subjects showed that they could, in their mind's eye, accurately simulate limb movements consistent with the biomechanics of their normal hand. They imagined grasping each item in exactly the same way that they would for real. And when their brains were scanned while they imagined the movements, higher areas involved in imitating and planning movements—a human "reach circuit"—lit up.

Now recall that after a stroke, the primary motor map can be damaged, in itself or as part of a wider circuit. The brain does not talk to the limb and the limb does not send feedback to the brain. Frey wondered, What if you use motor imagery to try and drive plastic changes in the damaged primary motor map? Can imagery give the brain an opportunity to encode successful sequences of movement? Can you imagine yourself out of paralysis?

The answer is maybe. Preliminary evidence is promising, Frey says, but studies to probe the potential of such interventions are just getting under way.

A Better Prosthesis

Frey also follows the travails of military personnel home from Iraq and Afghanistan minus one or more limbs—five hundred and counting as of early 2007. While engineers strive to make materials lighter and more comfortable—the Department of Defense is funding research into a mechanical arm that has most of the properties of a biological arm—artificial arms, legs, and hands are still pretty much deadweight. Some engineering solutions, like connecting sensors to chest muscles that can flex to operate a prosthetic arm, are clever but still clumsy.

Nowadays, each veteran is released with three arms: a cosmetic arm that looks lifelike but offers little in the way of function; a myoelectric arm that, using microprocessors, picks up electric signals from remaining muscles, amplifies the signals, and turns on an electric motor to provide function; and a mechanical arm that relies on physical body movements to manipulate the prosthetic, such as cables that stretch across the user's back. Vets can order specialty arms for things like bow hunting.

Nevertheless, half of all patients fitted with prosthetic arms dump them into a closet within a year, says Frey. Amputees complain that they are difficult to control and that it's easier to use their stump and good arm for most tasks. Insurance companies delay paying for prosthetic arms, which may cost $15,000, because the retention rate is so bad.

There has to be a better way. A lot of the problems are due to mechanical things, says Frey, but engineers have overlooked the most important aspect of connecting a body to a machine: the brain. The brain reorganizes massively after limb loss, and that fact should be central in the patient's adoption of the prosthesis. The more time is allowed to elapse while passively letting the neuroplasticity process bumble and grope its way to a new ad hoc mapping of the body, the more dysfunctional that mapping will be and the harder it will be to integrate with the prosthesis.

Frey wonders, Can motor imagery tasks be used to minimize dysfunctional remapping? Right now, most patients get little or no training in how to use a new arm, he says. They're supposed to go home and figure it out themselves. But motor imagery can be used to tap higher motor maps that might be harnessed for adapting to a prosthesis.

"We can use what we know about motor learning and translate that into

AIMEE MULLINS

Aimee Mullins was born in 1976 without fibula bones, which are the smaller of the two leg bones between knee and ankle. When she was one year old, both of her legs were amputated below the knee. Thus Mullins learned to walk—and run and jump and dance—with prosthetic legs. They were incorporated into her body maps from the start.

Today Mullins is a model, an actress, an athlete, and the current president of the Women's Sports Foundation, which was founded by Billie Jean King to encourage female participation in sports. Mullins was the first woman with a disability to compete in the NCAA at Georgetown University, where she set world records in 1996 for leg amputees in track and field. Strapping on her legs in the morning, she says, is like putting in contact lenses. In 2000, Mullins sprinted on the beach wearing her carbon-graphite cheetah legs—prosthetic limbs in the form of sickle-shaped springs.

rehabilitation," says Frey. "It would be a very good idea to fit people with an artificial limb immediately after amputation, before abnormal plasticity gets a chance to scramble body maps. People can practice movements using imagery circuits and use those higher order maps for prosthesis control."

Frey is now studying thirty upper limb amputees to find out how well they retain the ability to simulate movements using imagery. Unlike stroke patients, they cannot see a real arm while they imagine movements. So Frey gives them a mirror box to take home, with these instructions: Put your good hand into the box, wave it around, and imagine that the reflected image is really your missing hand. The research team will study the amputees' motor maps over time to see if or how they change in response to such vivid imagery.

The Power of Mirror Boxes

Jennifer Stevens, a cognitive scientist at the College of William and Mary, is conducting similar experiments with stroke patients using the mirror box. After a stroke, people often have uncoordinated movements, as if they have only partial access to their arm maps, Stevens says. Simulations of movement using the mirror box or motor imagery provide the brain with examples of what it needs to recruit movements; if you cannot fully extend your hand physically, your brain will never have the chance to practice the movement. Simulation using imagery is a way around the problem.

If you're a stroke patient, you place your good arm into the box and lay your paralyzed arm behind the mirror. Again, your good arm is reflected in such a way that you see two limbs. As you flap your good arm around, an amazing thing happens. Suddenly your paralyzed arm seems to be moving. It seems to be intact, uninjured, not paralyzed. The visual feedback is convincing enough to percolate downward through your body mandala and drive proprioceptive sensations in your dormant arm and hand map.

In a pilot experiment, Stevens brought five chronic stroke patients into her lab and had them sit in front of a computer, with both hands on the desk in front of them, palms facing down. They watched a movie of a wrist making twisting movements and then imagined what it would feel like to make the same motions with their bad wrist. They watched, then imagined, watched and imagined, for twenty-five-minute sessions over four weeks. They also practiced wrist movements with a mirror box for three one-hour sessions a week for four weeks. By placing their good arm into the box and making fluid wrist movements, their brains were fooled into thinking their bad arm could do the same. Meanwhile, another five patients with similar levels of paralysis underwent conventional occupational therapy.

Both groups made similar improvements, such as being able to place light objects on a shelf. But, Stevens says, this is absolutely amazing when you think about it. The imagery group improved without making any attempts to actually use their impaired arms. In standard occupational therapy, people practice holding and releasing a cup for hours at a time with the paralyzed hand. The imagery group did as well without moving a muscle. Injured neurons are just looking for someplace to reconnect, she says, and imagery plus a mirror makes it possible.

This kind of intervention is perfect for home use, Stevens says, which is why she is giving mirror boxes to a select group of stroke patients soon after they return from the hospital. With four patients having completed the home program already, it seems performance improves even when people do the imagery protocol on their own. And why not? They have nothing to lose by it and everything to gain.

Other scientists are exploiting virtual reality, a technology that allows you to interact with a computer-simulated environment, to remap the brains of stroke patients. Immersed in a virtual world, the patients imagine making normal movements in ways that prime recovery. When feedback is delivered via devices attached to a paralyzed limb, the brain can sometimes relearn the movement.

CHAPTER 6

BROKEN BODY MAPS
or, Why Dr. Strangelove Couldn't Keep His Hand Down

O ne of the immortal pop culture images from the Cold War is of the wheelchair-bound ex-Nazi scientist Dr. Strangelove, played by Peter Sellers, his right arm wholeheartedly *sieg-heil*ing just a split second before his left arm darts up and desperately wrestles it back to his side. This is a movie version of a real condition called alien hand syndrome. The problem, which usually results from damage to your frontal cortex and the connections between your two hemispheres, is pretty much what it sounds like: Your hand and arm do seemingly purposeful things without, or even in spite of, your intentions. You have a broken body map.

For example, your hand may grasp at passing doorknobs or even the crotch of a passing stranger. You may sometimes wake up to find your hand strangling you by the throat, and need to pry it away with your "good" hand, à la Strangelove. You may try to feed yourself with two hands simultaneously—or struggle to feed yourself as one hand brings food to your mouth while the other hand pushes it away. Or you may find your "bad" hand actively unbuttoning your shirt while your "good" hand tries to button it up.

Depending on the extent of damage to your body maps and other brain structures, you may feel differing degrees of continued ownership of your antic limb. You might see your hand as still belonging to you and simply be amused by its willfulness. Or you may feel possessed and even disavow that your hand belongs to you. Some people demand that their alien hand be amputated because they cannot tolerate the feelings of having a limb acting on its own, working against them.

Alien hand syndrome is among a diverse group of disorders stemming from broken body maps or defective connections between various brain maps. While each is a distinct medical condition, they are similar in that each causes bizarre behaviors and weird perceptions in the afflicted—things so strange that you, having an intact body mandala, could never imagine them in your wildest dreams. Fortunately, these disorders are rare. On the other hand, they can happen to anyone. To shed further light on the importance of intact body maps, let's take a closer look at some of them.

Amputee Wannabes

What would you say to an old friend who confided in you a long-hidden but passionately felt need to be an amputee? Moreover, she does not wish to lose just any old limb; she yearns to be rid of her left leg exactly two inches below her knee. Ever since she can remember, from around the age of four, she has known that her leg, from that point down, is "wrong." It feels wrong, looks wrong, is wrong. The shame and fear of being regarded as a kook have kept her silent all these years, but she has always fantasized about being rid of part of her left leg.

Bewildered, you quiz her about it, looking for an explanation you can understand.

"Does it hurt?" you ask.

"No," she says, "there's no pain, but it's torment living with this thing attached to my real body."

"Is your leg unhealthy in any way?"

"No," she says, "it works fine."

You rack your brain and finally ask, "Did you have some sort of early trauma involving the leg?"

"Nope," she says. "I can't remember anything like that. I just know it doesn't belong on me. And it's driving me crazy."

Your friend is among an increasingly visible group of people who call themselves "amputee wannabes." Wannabes desperately want to have their perfectly healthy limbs removed by a surgeon so that they can feel "whole." Called body integrity identity disorder, the condition does not respond to any kind of psychological intervention, psychiatric treatment, or drug therapy. The obsession, which arises in early childhood, usually after the person sees an amputee, lasts a lifetime. And it is extraordinarily specific, down to the fraction of an inch. Your hypothetical friend, assuming she is able to find a surgeon who will take her leg off, will not be satisfied if the cut is not exactly the right distance below her knee. If the cut is too high, she will be aware of the missing piece of herself—though she'll also tell you it was a small price to pay. If the cut is too low, she will remain uncomfortably aware of a small amount of "not-me" still attached to her.

Amputee wannabes sometimes go to great pains to get rid of the offending limb. One fellow froze his leg in dry ice until it was irreversibly damaged and a surgeon had to cut it off. Another man blasted his own leg off with a shotgun. Others use chain saws and homemade guillotines to do the amputation themselves. Many have been successful in this; others have died, of infection, of blood loss, of fatal miscalculation. But those who do succeed are not disappointed; quite the opposite. They say it is like the silencing of a grating, incessant noise that's gone on for so long you stopped thinking about it but has still been driving you crazy. With their limb gone, they say they experience a similar feeling of relief and release. By lopping off part of themselves, they have become whole.

Research on amputee wannabes is almost nonexistent, but it does not seem to entail any known mental disorders. Wannabes are, to all other appearances, rational, likable, intelligent, articulate people. In a 2003 documentary called *Whole*, by the filmmaker Melody Gilbert, wannabes speak out, explaining their compulsion matter-of-factly. "This is the way I should feel," declares Baz, a fifty-plus-year-old man from Liverpool. After his leg was removed, he says, "All my torment had disappeared."

"It's obviously peculiar," says Kevin, a university lecturer who had his leg amputated by Robert Smith, a surgeon in Scotland. "But knowing it's peculiar and saying it is weird does not do away with the problem."

Explanations for body integrity identity disorder run the usual gamut of Freudian just-so stories. People want to cut off their leg because they were not loved as babies, they have an unresolved internal conflict, they want sympathy, or they imprinted the body image of an amputee at a vulnerable age. A much more plausible explanation lies in some sort of miswiring within the brain's parietal circuits and primary body maps. How this occurs has yet to be discovered. Stay tuned.

Supernumerary Limbs

"Eeva," a thirty-seven-year-old worker in a paper products factory in Finland, was a perfectly healthy young woman until a day in January 2004 when a blood vessel in her brain burst, damaging her right frontal lobe. As she recovered slowly in the hospital, a brain scan revealed an additional small lesion, probably there from before or just after she was born, in the band of fibers connecting her left and right hemispheres. It had never caused her any problems that she knew of.

In the months after the brain injury, Ritva Hanninen, a neuropsychologist in the local hospital, and Riitta Hari, a neuroscientist at the Helsinki University of Technology, tested Eeva, who was showing a number of odd behaviors. For example, when Eeva met someone she wanted to greet, both of her hands flew up. She had difficulty changing her mind; faced with a simple choice—say, go inside or keep walking outside—she was effectively paralyzed. Eeva had alien hand syndrome: While reading a newspaper and turning the page with her right hand, her left hand turned back the same page; to be able to read the newspaper, Eeva had to sit on her left hand. While swimming, Eeva was afraid that her left hand wanted to drown her. Fortunately, these symptoms improved with time.

But Eeva's strangest problem, still with her to this day, is the vivid experience of having a third hand, a third arm, and a third leg. You see, Eeva's body map is fragmented with so-called supernumerary limbs. Several times a day she senses the third arm. The third leg crops up less often. The extra hand is a constant companion.

Hanninen says that Eeva is completely conscious of her ghost limbs and can analyze them. They are always on the left side of her body. They feel so real, Eeva has trouble distin-

Eeva's self-portrait.

guishing them from her real arms and legs. Once when shopping, she felt that she had accidentally taken bags from other people because her third arm made her feel as if she were carrying three bags. But, happily, if Eeva looks directly at or touches her real limb, the ghost disappears.

But Eeva's ghost hand is stranger still. It plays copycat with her real hand in the most vexing manner. When Eeva moves her left hand, say, from a table to the arm of a chair, the ghost appears on the table, in the same place vacated by her real hand, thirty to sixty seconds later. If she then moves her real hand from the chair back to the table, the ghost disappears for a while and then reappears on the armrest. If Eeva remains still, the ghost's copycat position lasts tens of minutes.

Sometimes Eeva's whole body splits. When she rises from a bench, she may feel as if only the right side of her body has started walking, while her left side stays on the bench. Repetitive and monotonous movements, such as tapping her fingers, will bring this on. Dancing prevents it.

Hari says it is likely that after the damage of the frontal motor areas, Eeva's brain has two body schemas for her left limbs, and unfortunately these schemas cannot be updated simultaneously. The lifelong small damage of the fibers connecting the two halves of Eeva's brain may still worsen the situation. Until her brain injury, Eeva enjoyed the sense of corporeal unity that most of us take for granted. But now the body maps of her left limbs are fragmented and act in two different time frames, one lagging the other by as much as a minute. Eeva dwells in a fractured world—but she is not alone.

For instance, another woman in England, whose legs were paralyzed after surgery to remove a brain tumor, reported having four legs. As she looked down in bed, she saw and felt two right legs and two left legs. When seated, she felt the hip and knee joints of all four legs to be flexed alike. After two weeks of this bizarre sensation, her body maps returned to normal.

Fading Limbs and Other Weird Body Sensations

Some conditions serve to remind us of the huge amount of complicated and counterintuitive information processing that occurs "under the hood" of the embodied, conscious mind.

P.J., an English woman now in her early sixties, was some years ago in a serious accident that knocked her out cold for half an hour. For the next couple of years P.J. felt fine, counting herself lucky that her concussion had left no lasting effects. But then, out of nowhere, her right arm went numb and began to jerk. P.J.'s doctors found a small cyst in her left parietal lobe at the site of her brain injury. The cyst, they said, was causing the problem, but it could be controlled with medication.

That worked for two more years, whereupon, in 1998, P.J. went back to her doctors complaining of odd sensations. When she lay in bed at night, she suddenly realized that her right arm was missing. It was gone, vanished. With mounting panic, she rustled the covers until suddenly it was back, but only if her eyes locked firmly onto it. It happened elsewhere, too. In fact, whenever P.J. took her eyes off her right arm, it slowly drifted away and disappeared. Only when she looked at it did she know where it was. The same thing happened with her right leg. If she took her eyes off of it, it faded from sight and consciousness.

One day, sitting on a bus, P.J. was startled when another passenger tripped over her right foot. When she looked, she realized that her foot was planted in the middle of the aisle.

The following week, P.J.'s physician put an object on the back of P.J.'s right hand. She felt it okay, but then, over tens of seconds, the sense of touch, the sensation that something weighed on her hand, faded. Lighter objects disappeared in three seconds. Heavier ones lasted more than ten.

The problem: The cyst in P.J.'s brain had grown to the size of a small egg. With pressure on her left parietal lobe, P.J. could no longer keep track of her body. It would not stop fading away.

Strokes can also disable your body maps. "Bob," a retired stockbroker, suffered a stroke in the portion of his parietal lobe that specializes in touch and personal body parts. If you ask Bob to point to his shoe, he does so easily; but ask him to point to his foot and he balks. Ask him what time it is and he glances at his watch without a second thought; but ask him to look at his wrist and he gets confused. He thinks for a moment and then points to his shoulder. Pin cardboard cutouts of animals to Bob's clothes: a giraffe to his shoulder, a frog to his knee, a lion to his elbow. Ask him to point to each animal you name and he does it, no problem. But ask him the name of the body part under each animal, and he's lost.

Another stroke patient insisted that her left hand belonged to her niece. She did not respond to touch on her own hand, but rather she detected it on her niece's real hand—but only when she could see it. Her body maps were projected to another person.

Rarely, heart attacks can leave in their wake weird bodily sensations. "Carol," a thirty-year-old teacher, had a cardiac arrest accompanied by shock, brain damage, and coma during childbirth. The baby did not

Carol's self-portrait.

survive. Three months later, as Carol gradually recovered, she reported seeing her image about three feet in front of her body, as though she were gazing in a mirror. If she moved her arm or face, the image moved the same way with familiar mirror reversal. If she looked up, the image of herself was on the ceiling. Looking down, it was on the floor. This sensation, called autoscopy, is unlike an out-of-body experience in that people don't think it's real. It lasts a few seconds at a time and then, thankfully, it gradually disappears.

A patient's depiction of Alice in Wonderland syndrome.

Some people, following brain damage, have hallucinations that distort their body schema. They say "My hands and feet are melting down" or "My abdomen is twisting and attaching to my back." Some migraine headache sufferers develop what is called Alice in Wonderland syndrome. They experience an aura accompanied by a distorted sense of their face and hand.

Finally, a condition called finger agnosia results from damage to the left parietal lobe. Your finger maps become fused, undifferentiated. If someone touches one of your fingers, you will not be able to tell which one. You can no longer count or do simple arithmetic.

Affordances

"Carter" was a master chef at a well-known New York restaurant when, in late 1994, a blood clot in his brain almost cost him his livelihood. Rushed to the hospital in time to receive state-of-the-art clot dissolving care, Carter was left with a potentially devastating problem: He could no longer recognize fruits and vegetables. He couldn't tell a banana from a leek, though he could still tell a bread knife from a butcher knife and a hawk from a handsaw. He could use English fluently, and his senses were all intact. He had no discernible problems naming or thinking about any other categories of object—just fruits and veggies.

It sounds like a career-killer for a chef, but Carter managed to get by. You see, his body mandala still knew what to do with each item. There was nothing wrong with the body maps containing his visual-motor templates for how to manipulate objects. And there was nothing wrong with the body maps that storehoused his library of well-practiced motor sequences involved in food prep. He could still peel a carrot, slice a tomato, or dice an onion—but first he had to be told what each thing was. He would simply query the kitchen staff: "Hey, Jane, is this a cucumber? Yeah? Thanks." Chop chop chop.

If Carter's clot had hit a different part of his brain, he would have been left with an opposite problem, called apraxia. He would know what a cucumber is. He could look at one and tell you all about its culinary properties, only Carter's hand would not be able to assume the correct posture for gripping the cucumber. He would hold it awkwardly and incorrectly, as a Neanderthal might handle a telephone.

Apraxias are related to the theory of affordances, which is worth exploring in some detail since it is intimately tied in with the properties of your body mandala. The theory was put forth in the 1960s by an unorthodox psychologist named James Jerome Gibson at Cornell University. Gibson, who died in 1979, said animals and people view their environments not in terms of objectively defined shapes and volumes but in terms of their own behavioral potential. In other words, you immediately apprehend what you see in terms of how you think you can interact with what you see. You see affordances. Affordances make possible and facilitate certain actions. So, handles afford grasping. Stairs afford stepping. Knobs afford turning. Doors afford passage. Hammers afford smashing.

Think of a still lakeside inlet fringed with rushes and dotted with lily pads. Consider how this scene looks very different to different kinds of animal—say, a frog, a hippo, and a sparrow. Each takes in the scene instantly as an array of affordances. Both the frog and the hippo see it as something they can swim through and submerge themselves in; but the affordances of swimmability and submersibility do not even occur to the sparrow. The frog and the sparrow see the lily pads as potential platforms—that is, as things that afford sitting; the hippo sees them only in terms of their swallowability, with sittability not entering its mind for a nanosecond.

You also perceive the world through an automatic filter of affordances. Your perception of a scene is not just the sum of its geometry, spatial relations, light, shadow, and color. Perception streams not just through your eyes, ears, nose, and skin, but is automatically processed through your body mandala to render your perceptions in terms of their affordances. This is generally true of primates, whose body mandalas have grown so rich with hand and arm and fine manipulation mapping, and even more so for you, a human animal.

Consider a blue jay perched on your windowsill, looking in at your workspace. In one sense you and the bird see the identical scene. The bird has extremely keen vision, probably even keener than yours. But despite this, in a crucial sense, the bird doesn't see the same chair or coffee mug or keyboard that you see, and the reason comes down to affordances. We tend to think of visual understanding of an object to be all about edges, angles, textures, colors, shadows, and so forth. That's the basic part of vision; but there's a lot more that goes on in your brain after those low-level features are analyzed. As visual information makes its way up the cortical visual hierarchy, more abstract or complex features are inferred from it, such as detecting motion, identifying body parts or faces, and knowing what objects belong where. At even higher stages, it gets handled by multisensory areas including, crucially, the body maps of the posterior parietal and frontal motor cortex. We are less directly aware of this higher visual processing, but it is extremely important. When you see a chair, you "see" its sittability, its stand-upon-to-reach-the-high-shelf-ability, and other uses that your human body can make of it. And when you see a coffee cup, you "see" its graspability, its volumetric capacity, its drink-holding-ness. These are body- and action-based concepts, but they are automatically evoked by the sight of the chair and coffee cup. The blue jay, meanwhile, does not see any of these affordances, though it may see different ones. It may see the coffee cup as affording head-insertability, where it could conceivably find something worth eating. It certainly sees the top of your chair's backrest as an affordance for perching, which isn't something that occurs naturally to you.

A region of your premotor cortex has several indispensable functions. One of them is transforming visual and semantic information (knowledge based on something's meaning or general use) about an object directly into a motor command that shapes your hand appropriately. For example, as you reach for a coffee cup, your hand pivots to vertical and your fingers hook just right so that you can pick it up in a way that affords drinking. When you reach for a fork, your hand assumes a different shape en route to making contact with it, so that you end up with a perfect grip for scooping pasta into your mouth. In short, some of the neural circuitry in your frontal lobe, along with a similar region in the parietal lobe, contributes to your ability to perceive and use tools correctly. Graspability, pushability, typability, pokeability, steppability, climbability, cursor controllability—all kinds of usability are perceived automatically at a preconscious level through these higher-order body and space maps. And damage, whether to this map itself or immediately upstream or downstream from it in the cortical processing chain, is behind many forms of apraxia.

Martial artists see a different set of affordances than people untrained in hand-to-hand combat. Lapels and shoulder fabric are gripping points that afford all sorts of leverage. Elbows and wrists afford a variety of locks and twists. Highly trained martial artists see these affordances directly, as inherent parts of the concept of the body, just as an accomplished pianist sees not just individual keys but whole interrelated harmonic complexes brimming with possible melodies that can be extracted from it as wholes, not as individual finger and hand movements.

You also see the world in terms of conserving energy and protecting yourself from harm. According to Dennis Proffitt, a psychologist at the University of Virginia, you have a natural tendency to view hills as steeper when you are tired, less physically able, or carrying a heavy load. If you think you could hurt yourself, inclines appear greater. The distance to the ground seems farther. Your perceptions of the world are modulated by your brain to keep you from danger.

CHAPTER 7

THE BUBBLE AROUND THE BODY

or, Why You Seek Elbow Room

Margaret Wertheim was promoting her book *The Pearly Gates of Cyberspace: A History of Space from Dante to the Internet* when an anthropologist in the audience stood up to tell a remarkable story.

There is a tribe in Namibia wherein each person is born with a kind of self-space around the body. This self-space is like a bubble that extends beyond the body and, being attached to the body, moves as the person moves. And because this envelope of self-space constantly intermingles with other people's self-spaces, individuals in the tribe are never alone. They wonder, the anthropologist said, how we in the West can possibly see ourselves as isolated points in space. They feel infinite pity for us. They wonder how we bear it.

The tribe, it turns out, are the Himba, a nomadic people who live in Kaokoland, a harsh desert in northwestern Namibia adjacent to the aptly named Skeleton Coast, where they tend cattle and goats. For tourists on safari, they are an exotic spectacle. Himba women cream their bodies twice a day with a mixture of rancid butterfat and ground ocher scented with the aromatic resin of a local shrub. The cream gives their bodies an intense reddish glow. They are beautiful.

But for scientists who study the brain, the Himba are a window into one of the more wondrous ways that human beings perceive the world around them. Here is a culture that explicitly posits the existence of personal space around the body. We in the West talk about our metaphorical "elbow room" and the like, but few people take it literally. The Himba acknowledge this bubble of personal space, navigate it, share it, mingle in it.

To grasp the nature of self-space, you need to repeat that little exercise from the Introduction: Put your arms straight out in front of your body, as far as they can reach. Keep your hands flat, fingertips extended straight ahead. Now wave your arms up and down and sideways. Make great big circles from over your head down past your sides. Pretend you're Shiva with four arms so you cover more territory.

Now imagine all the space that your arms have passed through. This is the personal space around your body—what neuroscientists call peripersonal space—and every inch of it is mapped inside your brain. In other words, your brain contains cells that keep track of everything and anything that happens within the invisible space at arm's length around your body. When you observe or otherwise sense objects entering that space, these cells start firing.

The reason is practical. As you move through the world, your brain needs to know exactly where your body is positioned in space. You need to locate objects approaching your body—like someone moving his fingers closer and closer to your belly intending to tickle you, or a low-hanging branch on a mountain trail, or a softball speeding toward your mitt. You need to move around, reach out, pull away, approach, and defend.

How this space is represented in your brain and how you use it to navigate your world is a fascinating tale that is just now emerging from laboratories around the world. But before we get to the science, consider some examples that are closer to home.

Many people swear that they see auras around other humans. Could auras be real in the Himba sense of peripersonal space? Can the perception of auras be explained in terms of brain physiology? There is evidence from a scientist in England that the answer, at least some of the time, is yes.

Have you ever been to a party when someone, most likely from another cultural or social background, stands much too close to your face? There he is, eight inches from your nose, jabbering away in a friendly tone, oblivious to the discomfort he is inflicting on you. You back away, just a little half-step, and reestablish a proper speaking distance. But then he follows, and again he's in your face. You might repeat this many times until he backs you into a wall. Your personal space comfort zone, which you learned from your own culture, is being invaded. If the parts of your brain that map your body and its bubble of near-space could talk, they would be screaming, "Get me out of here!"

In another example, great basketball players like Bill Bradley and Michael Jordan or legendary soccer players like Pelé and Mia Hamm have extraordinary physical abilities—lightning-fast reflexes, excellent peripheral vision, strength, agility, and the like, all of which have been studied scientifically. They practice harder and longer than most elite athletes, giving them the extra edge that defines each superstar.

But there is one trait they all share that has not been explained adequately. When such athletes are on the court or field, they are mapping the space around them and people in that space in ways that most of us cannot match. Their personal space and body maps, along with a newly discovered mapping system called grid cells, seem to be exquisitely developed, which may be one reason they score so many baskets and goals.

Fenway Park

Peripersonal space was first explored systematically thirty years ago by Edoardo Bisiach, an Italian neurologist who is now retired and living in the countryside between Milan and Lake Como, where he grows camellias, peonies, and tea roses. Bisiach believes that the best window we have for understanding our peripersonal space mapping is through stories of when it fails.

A relatively common failure of space mapping is called hemispatial neglect, or "neglect" for short. The condition is usually caused by a stroke in the right parietal lobe. A neglect patient is completely unaware of the left half of space, the left half of her own body, or both. The unawareness is complete. She doesn't even know that the left half of the universe and the left half of her own body are gone from consciousness and memory. Fortunately, neglect tends to fade in just a few days or weeks.

In a classic 1981 experiment, Bisiach asked neglect patients to close their eyes and imagine the famous Piazza del Duomo in the heart of Milan. The Piazza, with its magnificent basilica, palaces, and statues, is as familiar to Italians as Times Square is to Manhattanites or Piccadilly Circus is to Londoners.

DENIAL, A FORM OF NEGLECT

These symptoms sound odd, but when the right hemisphere is damaged, spectacular delusions arise out of your disorganized body schema. Listen to Dr. Anna Berti, a neuroscientist at the University of Turin in Italy, interview one of her patients, C.C., whose paralyzed left arm rests in her lap next to her good right arm.

"Can you raise your right arm?"

"Yes." C.C.'s arm goes up.

"Can you raise your left arm?"

"Yes."

There is no movement.

"Are you raising your left arm?"

"Yes."

"Can you clap your hands?"

C.C. moves her right hand to the midline of her body and waves it in a clapping motion. The left hand is motionless.

"Are you sure you're clapping?"

"Yes."

"But I can't hear a sound."

C.C. replies, "I never make noise when I do something."

Insistent denial of paralysis was long thought to be a psychological problem, Berti says. It was a defensive reaction to a stroke: *I am paralyzed, it is so horrible, I will deny it.*

"You are facing the Basilica," Bisiach tells each patient. "Tell me what you see. Describe all the buildings."

Scanning the scene with their mind's eye, the patients faithfully name all the buildings on the right side of the majestic plaza. They ignore structures to their left.

"Now you are standing at the gate of the Basilica, looking out," Bisiach instructs. "Tell me what you see."

This time the patients accurately name all the previously neglected buildings that are now on their right. They do not mention those to their left, even though they had just named them moments before.

This would be like an American viewing a familiar baseball field, say Boston's Fenway Park, from behind home plate. He could describe first base, the Red Sox dugout, and the infamous "Pesky" Pole, but everything to the left would simply not exist. Bring him around to the other

But it is not a Freudian dilemma. Rather, it is a variation on neglect, which has a different underlying brain pathology. Neglect usually involves the parietal lobe. But brain damage in denial patients tends to occur in the supplementary motor area, which is involved in the mental simulation of movements. When you close your eyes and simply imagine a golf swing or skiing maneuver, you activate this part of your brain.

When Berti asks C.C. to raise her left arm or clap her hands, the region that imagines such movements produces a familiar pattern of activity in her brain. But the regions that maintain awareness of and carry out movements are not working.

The conflict is overwhelming. C.C.'s sense of having moved via simulation is powerful. Awareness is absent. Paralysis is complete. Her brain's solution: Confabulate.

If prodded for hours, patients make up stories to explain their lack of action, Berti says. One woman said her arm "went for a walk." A man claimed that his motionless arm did not belong to him. When it was placed in his right visual field, he insisted it was not his.

"Whose arm is it?" Berti asked.

"Yours."

"Are you sure? Look here, I only have two hands."

The patient replied, "What can I say? You have three wrists. You should have three hands."

side of the stadium, facing toward home plate, and he will now see third base, the scoreboard, the famous outfield wall called the Green Monster, and the "monster seats" above it, that he previously neglected on that side of the field.

Not long after Bisiach led his patients through the Piazza experiment, he visited a lawyer who was also suffering from neglect. Facing the man, Bisiach asks him to describe his office while seated at his desk. No problem, the lawyer says, and proceeds to mention, in rich detail, his reading light, a painting, and every object on the right side of the room. Bisiach brings him around the other side of the desk and asks him to again describe the office. Now the lawyer describes his favorite piano, old tapestries, and other objects that were previously on his left. In the lawyer's world, space on the left side of his body has vanished. It has vanished so completely, he isn't even aware that it should be there. Meanwhile, his awareness of space on the right side has expanded.

Imagine how this feels. You wake up in the hospital and you're told you've had a stroke. You have lost awareness of the space on the left side of your body. Everything and anything that takes place in that space escapes your notice. You ignore people on the left side of the room, eat only the food on the right side of your plate, read only the right side of the newspaper page. If you shave, you just scrape or buzz the right side of your face. If you put on lipstick, you apply it to the right side of your mouth only. You neglect all sights, sounds, touches, and even smells on the left side of space.

Your neurologist gives you a pencil and paper with a horizontal line drawn on it and asks you to bisect the line with an *X*. You mark the mid-

---

TREATMENTS FOR NEGLECT

Is there any treatment for these dreadful body delusions? Not much, unless you want to count putting ice-cold water in one ear or tingling the back of your neck with a vibrator.

Pretend you are a neglect patient. You are comfortably lying down on a couch with your head nestled to one side on a pillow. A doctor pours a few ounces of ice water into your left ear for one minute. This strongly stimulates a region in your inner ear, the semicircular canals, that contributes to your sense of balance. Your eyes gyrate involuntarily toward your left side as your subjective sense shifts toward the colder ear. You feel vertigo. And your sense of denial evaporates.

Or, while you are seated, looking straight ahead, the doctor applies the tip of a vibrator to the left side of the back of your neck. This alters the balance of left and right input from your vestibular system and throws your neck proprioception out of kilter. Your egocentric perception of space is upset. Your denial vanishes.

If the doctor puts ice water in your ear and vibrates your neck muscles, both on the same side, you get double the effect. But if he applies each stimulus on opposite sides, the effect is canceled out.

Both ice water and neck vibration work by biasing vestibular signals that are involved in spatial awareness, Dr. Edoardo Bisiach says. The effects are temporary. One patient who insisted that the left side of his body was evil and controlled by the devil was helped by the ice water treatment—for ten minutes.

Other treatments include training the visual system to attend to the neglected space, mental imagery training, wearing prisms to reorient space, and video feedback.

point way off to the right. Next he asks you to draw a daisy. You make a nice stem and fat round center. But you only draw petals on the right side. When you draw a clock, all the numbers, one through twelve, are bunched on the right side of its face.

But you are not blind. Your memory is fine. Your doctor can draw your attention to the left side of space by making you look more carefully: "Woo hoo, over here!" You'll say "Oh my!" as you see things you had neglected.

So what does all this have to do with peripersonal space? It turns out there are subtypes of neglect that provide elegant proof that your brain maintains a distinction between peripersonal space and the space beyond it, what is called extrapersonal space—the space that is farther away from your body, out past your fingertips. Some stroke patients show purely extrapersonal neglect. When asked to bisect a line past arm's reach using a laser pointer, they mark the midline far off to the right; but when asked to do the same thing with a pencil on a sheet of paper within their bubble of peripersonal space, they do it correctly. Their perceptions within peripersonal space are normal.

Multisensory Connections

Scientists used to think of the parietal region—a region, as you'll recall from chapter 3, crammed with maps of your body and the space around it—as being a purely multisensory hub. In the old view, touch information flowed in through the primary touch cortex, visual information flowed in through the primary visual cortex, sound information flowed in through the primary auditory cortex. An orgy of cross-talk occurred, and the integrated information was then passed forward to the motor network, where it served as the basis for plans and actions.

But this is a vast oversimplification. It turns out the sensory maps of your parietal lobe are also de facto motor centers, with massive direct interlinkage to the frontal motor system. They don't simply pass information to the motor system, they participate directly in action. They actively transform vision, sound, touch, balance, and other sensory information into motor intentions and actual movements. And by the same token, the maps of the motor system play a fundamental role in interpreting the sensations from your body. Your parietal lobe is not purely sensory, and your frontal lobe is not purely motor. Physical sensation and action are best seen as a single sense that, like a coin, has two inseparable faces with different appearances. Consider the fact that people who have a body part paralyzed from damage to their primary motor map complain that the part also feels numb. Yet their sensory maps are all intact. So shouldn't they be able to feel normal sensations? They are not, because their sensory and motor maps, while spatially separate, are functionally one.

Multisensory cells and systems are all the rage in neuroscience these days. If you think about it, ordinary perception almost always involves multiple senses. It turns out the senses interact with one another profoundly. You will see something faster if it also makes a noise. A sudden touch on one hand can improve your vision near that hand. Seeing a friend speak across a crowded room can help you hear what she is saying. A picture of a snake or spider shown near your hand draws your attention to your hand far faster than, say, a picture of a rope or flower.

What you hear influences what you feel. In one dramatic example, called the parchment skin illusion, you rub your palms together while listening to different sounds. Higher frequencies make you feel as if your hands are rough. Lower frequencies give the impression of your hands being smooth, although nothing about your hands has changed. Similarly, all else being equal, an electric toothbrush will feel more pleasant and less rough on your gums and teeth when the overall sound level is reduced.

The next time you go to a movie theater, take a moment to consider that speech is not coming from the actors' lips. The sound of their voices is being piped into speakers far removed from their celluloid actions. Your brain creates the illusion of actors talking to one another, thanks to your multisensory cells. Of course, a badly dubbed foreign movie doesn't fool you a bit. It's just annoying.

If you have a computer handy, you can check out the McGurk effect (www.media.uio.no/personer/arntm/McGurk_english.html). In this auditory-visual illusion you will see a film clip of a person saying "da, da, da, da." But if you close your eyes, you will hear him really saying "ba, ba, ba, ba." Then if you mute the sound and just watch his lips, you will clearly see that he is saying "ga, ga, ga, ga." The effect is quite astonishing. It happens because your brain does its best to reconcile mismatching information whenever it can. Bimodal vision-and-hearing cells chatter to one another about it and settle on the "da, da, da, da" interpretation.

Multisensory neurons are also at work when you recognize a type of music from its beat. Jessica Phillips-Silver, who recently earned her Ph.D. at McMaster University in Hamilton, Ontario, can demonstrate this by holding your hands and asking you to bounce, knees bent, in synchrony with her. In the background she plays an ambiguous rhythm with no strong accents. When the two of you bounce to every second beat, you will say you are hearing a march. But if you bounce on every third beat, you will say you are hearing a waltz. The movement of your upper body and vestibular activation are critical for the effect. What you feel with your body literally shapes what you hear, thanks to multisensory neurons.

Probing the Bubble

So now you know that your brain maps the space around your body. But what is that space like? Is it a universal space, like one huge bubble enveloping your whole body? Or does it exist in segments, like Penfield's homunculi?

Two Princeton University neuroscientists, Michael Graziano and Charles Gross, helped find the answer in 1994 when they inserted electrodes into monkey brains and explored an important body map known as the premotor cortex. They were curious about some cells there that respond to both touch and vision, even though it is a "classic" motor area. When they touched a monkey on, say, the back of its hand, one or more of these cells in the map's hand region would fire. They also found that if they moved an object to within eight inches of the same spot—provided the monkey could see it, of course—the same cells would fire. In other words, these cells were mapping not just touch, but the nearby bubble of space around the body. When the seen object moves closer to the monkey's hand, the cells fire faster. When the object moves away, the cells slow down.

These cells focus your attention on the body part being approached and automatically prepare motor plans you can take in response, whether it's to move out of the way, reach out to intercept the thing, or stay still and let it touch you. Beyond that, such cells can even induce physical sensations before you actually get touched. As every parent knows, you only need to wiggle your fingers above your child's rib cage to elicit gales of laughter. It isn't uncommon for people to feel a tingling in their skin as something with emotional significance—whether a hypodermic needle or a lover's caress—approaches. This is the result of these touch-vision cells going into overdrive.

WHY YOU CAN'T TICKLE YOURSELF

If cells that respond to touch and vision are so exquisitely sensitive, why can't you tickle yourself? You can wiggle all ten of your fingers and draw them close to your belly, yet you won't feel a flutter of anticipation or mirthful desire to pull away. You're a zombie when it comes to self-inflicted tickling.

The reason has to do with the fact that your brain is in the business of predicting your interactions with the world. When someone else tickles you, there is a sense of surprise and panic. Those other fingers feel like creepy crawlies, making you howl in protest. But they aren't dangerous creepy crawlies, and so you laugh with relief.

When your own fingers are involved, though, there is no surprise. You are in control. Your touch is familiar. You brain predicts the force, location, and speed of your movements and, this being ho-hum, cancels out or attenuates the sensation of self-touch.

Your brain carries out this feat by generating a carbon copy of your movements along with the actual motor command. The duplicate, called an efference copy, predicts the effects of your action, such as bringing your wiggly fingers toward your body. The predicted effect of the efference copy and the actual sensation from your motor command are compared. If there's a mismatch, you know the sensation came from the outside world (someone else's fingers). But if there is no mismatch, your prediction is deemed accurate. You do not feel a tickling sensation.

Incidentally, the reason you can't tickle yourself also explains why shoving matches tend to escalate into fistfights. In a study called "Two Eyes for an Eye: The Neuroscience of Force Escalation," people held out their left index finger, which was given a slight push by a motor. Then they were asked to match the force by pressing a force transducer that delivered a second push to the same finger.

People consistently pushed back harder with the transducer. Just as when you try to tickle yourself, your brain predicts the consequences of your movements and reduces the sensation. So when somebody hits you, you will hit back with greater force because your brain overestimates how hard you were hit. This is one way that street brawls spiral out of control. Or children take up the refrain: *But she hit me harder!*

Graziano and Gross's experiments reveal that each part of your body has its very own spatial map attached to it. When your arm moves, the bubble of personal space around your arm moves along with it. When your foot moves, its peripersonal space map moves, too. These maps are body-centered or ego-centered representations of visual space.

The same goes for sounds. You have multisensory cells that keep track of your body parts and the sounds around your body parts. When you sit in the dining room reading your paper and you hear a family member approaching from behind in the kitchen, the cells fire more rapidly. When the sounds grow fainter, the cells slow down. Blind people are aces at tracking sounds around their bodies using such cells.

Seeing Auras

"Gloria" did not realize she was different from other people until shortly after her seventh birthday. She remembers thinking, Surely everyone sees colored auras around the heads and faces of people they know. It seemed perfectly natural to her to see the exact same colors associated with the face or spoken name of each person. It was not until Gloria was studying psychology a decade or so later that she discovered the oddity of her experiences.

How odd? When Gloria gets to know new people, they each acquire a colored aura. These halos can be blue, pink, purple, any color. If she knows two Alexes, each will have a different hue. Unlike the temporary auras associated with migraine headaches or certain forms of epilepsy, Gloria's auras are constant, invariable, distinct.

And so it was that Gloria in 2003 found herself in the laboratory of Dr. Jamie Ward, a psychologist at the University College of London, who figured out the cause of her bizarre perceptual world.

Gloria has emotion-color synesthesia. She genuinely sees auras, says Ward. She is not confabulating.

Synesthesia is a condition affecting up to five percent of the population in which normally separate sensations are joined. The awareness of one sense produces a response in one or more other senses. Thus tastes can have shapes. Numbers or letters have colors. Red has a smell. Voices have flavors. Certain sounds look like glass shards.

The Russian-born artist Wassily Kandinsky said that when he saw colors he also heard music, which is why he developed his style of abstract painting. Kandinsky was capturing music on canvas. Some synesthetes can "hear" his music by looking at his paintings.

Other people—more are turning up in Ward's lab all the time—have vision-touch synesthesia. When they see another person being touched, say, on the cheek, they feel it on their own cheek. If they see an actor being stabbed in the stomach during a movie, they feel a sensation in their own belly, but without pain, as if anesthetized. Like Gloria, they are astonished to learn that not everyone in the world has these experiences.

While all people link senses in a metaphorical way—"feelin' blue," "hot chick," "sour face"—synesthetes do so to a greater degree, Ward says. The reason may be that sensory areas of their brains are abnormally cross-wired. The infant brain is born with a huge number of redundant neural connections, which undergo a pruning process as the baby grows up and acquires skills. One theory of synesthesia is that sometimes some of these redundant connections remain in place, linking two or more senses at a lower level than normal. In effect, multisensory cells are created lower down in the sensory processing stream of a synesthete.

The mark of a true synesthete is that their perceptions do not change over time. Most experience their blended sensations in space; they see colored letters floating outside their body. For some, the colors appear only in the mind's eye. In any case, each synesthete is unique, based on individual brain wiring, as to which senses are crossed and to what degree.

When Ward tested Gloria in his laboratory, he first showed her eighty-three words and asked her to report any colors. She repeated the test a week later and again four months later. Her matches were consistent through time, a feat that would be very hard to fake. On another test, Gloria was slower in naming colors that conflicted with her automatic synesthesia. That is, if she always saw pink around a name and it was shown in blue, it would take her longer to read the name out loud. Finally, she did not see colors around unfamiliar names and faces but did see them around highly emotional words.

Gloria's emotion-color synesthesia raises a tantalizing question. Many people around the world, in all cultures, claim to see auras. Science has been forced to reject the idea that our bodies are surrounded by mystical energy fields, but could some people's experience of them be as real as looking up into the sky and seeing a rainbow? Could auras be a natural construct of the parietal lobe?

One thing is certain, Ward says. People who claim it is possible to *learn* how to detect auras are not talking about synesthesia. Auras in the sense of a parietal blending of peripersonal space and color, or any other human sense, could never be taught. It is a natural product of a cross-wired brain. Gloria does not believe she has mystical powers. She does not think that what she does is remarkable. She just sees colors around people and cannot suppress it. But many other people who genuinely see auras are tempted by paranormal explanations. They attribute auras not to labile body maps but to supernatural forces, astral planes, leaky chakras, or energy fields of pure life force that emanate from all living things.

Scientists have never been able to detect with advanced instruments the kind of energy field that allegedly gives rise to auras in the paranormal sense. When the philosopher Sir John Eccles talked about a "field of psychons" as creating a unity of subjective experience, he did not base his claims on any experimental evidence or designs for empirical testing. When New Age gurus invoke the mysteries of quantum physics to explain the mysterious nature of energy fields and human consciousness, they are essentially explaining one mystery with another mystery.

But the fact that our body and peripersonal space maps are tremendously flexible provides a new scientific window into understanding many strange experiences. Jet fighter pilots sometimes say they enter an altered state when flying for long periods in monotonous conditions—uniform clouds, engine noise, vibrations. In this condition, they sometimes "leave" the aircraft and float outside the cockpit, looking back in at themselves. Eventually they force themselves to snap to and get back into their bodies. Mountaineers trekking at high altitude and sailors crossing the ocean alone also report losing their bodies.

Michael Murphy tells anecdotes of transcendent experiences in sports in his book *In the Zone*. Athletes leave their bodies or see other bodies change shape on the playing field. A well-known distance swimmer described how, whenever his physical body was exhausted during a competition, he would relax by floating overhead while his body continued to swim, until he felt refreshed, at which point he would reenter his body. Another swimmer says he can see the entire pool from a larger raised-up perspective and anticipate the moves of the other swimmers.

You can have weird experiences falling into and waking up from sleep. Have you ever awoken to the feeling of an ominous presence in the darkness pressing down on your body? Odds are it wasn't a dream. People have been reporting these encounters for millennia, which surely lent credence to the existence of otherworldly beings like ghosts and incubi. Or have you ever felt yourself leave your body as you fall asleep? Both phenomena, which are surprisingly common, are created when your brain shifts its state of arousal in the transition from sleep to wakefulness or vice versa. Every night while you're dreaming, your body is totally paralyzed from the neck down via inhibitory circuits in your brain stem (failures of this system are involved in sleep violence and sleepwalking). Your brain does this to keep your body from jumping out of bed and acting out your dreams. But sometimes you stay paralyzed after you have awoken, and your body mandala's best-fit interpretation is that a crushing weight is pinning you down. It can be terrifying. But rest assured, when it ends it's because your brain has reestablished the connection with your muscles, not because the incubus has vanished back to Hell.

When people enter deep meditation or trance, they say that their bodies and minds expand out into space. Body awareness fades, and they are left with a unitary yet diffused and nonlocalized sense of themselves. Along with it come feelings of joy, clarity, and empathy. When Buddhist lamas meditate in brain scanners, activity in their parietal lobes plummets. It can't be a coincidence that the dissolution of the bodily self accompanies the shutting down of the body and space maps that create it.

Shadowy Illusory Persons

Ever had the creepy feeling, while you are wide awake, that another person is lurking behind your back, only when you turn around, no one is there? What about an out-of-body experience? Have you ever felt yourself floating up near the ceiling, looking down at your corporeal self?

Such experiences, which may be more common than is generally acknowledged, are almost always explained in terms of paranormal forces—an encounter with ghosts or crossing to another realm of reality.

But according to Olaf Blanke, a neurologist at the Ecole Polytechnique Fédérale de Lausanne in Switzerland, the feeling of an illusory shadow person or the sensation of leaving one's body can be induced, in mentally healthy persons, by delivering a mild electric current to specific spots in the brain.

A zap to one spot, the right angular gyrus, recently gave one woman the palpable sensation that she was hanging from the ceiling, looking down at her body. Current to the left angular gyrus gave another woman the uncanny feeling that a shadowy person was behind her back and that he was intent on interfering with her actions.

Both women were being evaluated for epilepsy surgery at University Hospital in Geneva, Switzerland. Physicians implanted dozens of electrodes directly into their brains to pinpoint the abnormal tissue causing their seizures and to identify adjacent areas involved in language, hearing, or other essential functions, so as not to excise them inadvertently. When each electrode activated a different patch of brain tissue, the women said what, if anything, they experienced.

Despite their epilepsy, both women had normal psychiatric histories, Blanke said. The women were stunned by the bizarre nature of their experiences.

One patient was a twenty-two-year-old pharmacy student who had electrodes implanted into the left side of her brain in 2004. "We were checking language areas," Blanke said, when the woman turned her head to the right. That made no sense because the electrode was nowhere near areas involved in movement control. It was in a multisensory area where the parietal and temporal lobes meet.

Blanke applied more current. Again, the woman turned her head to the right.

"Why are you doing this?" he asked.

The woman replied that she had the weird sensation that another person was lying directly beneath her body on the bed. It was not in the mattress, but rather stretched out behind. It felt like a "shadow" that did not speak or move; it was young, more like a man than a woman, and it wanted to interfere with her.

When Blanke turned off the current, the woman stopped looking to the right. The strange presence went away. Each time he reapplied the current, she turned her head to try and see it.

The woman sat up, leaned forward, and hugged her knees. Now when the current flowed, she noted that the "man" was also sitting and that he was clasping her in his arms. She said it felt unpleasant. When she held a card in her right hand, the person tried to take it from her. "He doesn't want me to read," she said.

Because the illusory person closely mimicked the woman's body posture and position, Blanke concluded that she was experiencing a perception of her own body—a felt double or doppelganger. She did not recognize that the person was an illusion of her own body.

Out-of-Body Experiences

"Heidi" suddenly felt herself lifted out of her body. Floating near the ceiling, she looked down, aghast. Seated around her real body were three people, one of whom held an electrode over the exposed right side of her brain. Blanke was applying small amounts of current to different areas of her cortex to find the locus of her seizures.

When Blanke stimulated Heidi's right angular gyrus, she felt herself rise up, as if she were the gauzy apparition in a Tim Burton movie.

"I am at the ceiling," she exclaimed. "I am looking down at my legs." This had never happened before. She was stunned.

"What?" Blanke was equally astonished, and removed the electrode.

"Wait," said Heidi. "I'm back on the table now. What happened?"

"I'm not sure," he said, "Let's try again."

Blanke stimulated the same spot in Heidi's brain for another two seconds. Because the electrode is silent, she had no way of knowing when to expect anything. But while the current flowed, she found herself back at the ceiling, outside her body, floating, with her ghostly legs dangling below her ghostly self. She gasped again.

"What do you see?" Blanke asked Heidi-on-high.

"My back is touching the ceiling. My legs are hanging down a little. I can see the three of you."

"Do you have arms?"

"I'm not so sure about my arms," Heidi said. "But I have a head and a body. I see the bed and the side table. I'm lighter than usual, not moving."

Blanke was fascinated. From the ceiling Heidi saw only the lower part of her body. But why would she tell him that? Why not her whole body? Then it occurred to him to consider the position of her real body— propped up in bed, arms straight down at her sides. From her vantage near the ceiling, she saw those same body parts—feet, pajamas, trunk, and legs—that she would see looking at herself from the bed.

Blanke decided that Heidi was not making this up. Given that, he struggled to find an explanation. "Try looking at your limbs," he said, applying the current for the third time. "Tell me what you see."

Again she gasped. Now, when she looked at her outstretched arms, the left arm seemed to shorten to half its normal size. As in a Tom and Jerry cartoon, it grew shorter and shorter, and then, when the current stopped, it popped back out to its normal size.

Heidi had never read a neurology textbook, Blanke says, and had no way of knowing that stimulation to her right brain would affect the left side of her body, specifically her left arm.

Oddly, though, both legs appeared to shorten by a third during the stimulation. Blanke decided to bend her legs in the bed and see what would happen.

Again the current flowed; this time Heidi screamed. Both legs seemed to fly up and were about to hit her in the face, even though her real legs remained motionless. When she closed her eyes, she had the sensation of doing sit-ups, with her upper body approaching her legs.

Heidi's uncanny adventure, which took place in December 2000, is the first recorded case of an out-of-body experience induced by electrical stimulation of the brain. As long as her body maps were synchronous, her experience and behavior were fluent, holistic, and integrated. But when Heidi's maps went briefly out of sync, her felt position in space and her seen position in space did not match. Her mind cast about for the best-fit way to turn her confusion into a coherent experience, and concluded that she must be floating up and away with a view downward.

But what if you have an out-of-body experience without someone zapping your right angular gyrus? Plenty of people report briefly perceiving the world from a location outside their bodies, often during a near-death experience. One explanation for the phenomenon is alterations in blood flow. Large arteries converge near the angular gyrus inside your brain. If anything constricts the flow of blood to that area, your felt body sense can become disoriented. You might get the feeling that you are floating above an operating table or the scene of a car accident. At the same time, your field of vision might have what is called a scotoma—a big blank spot, like a black splotch at the bottom of a well—that your brain fills in with images of what it expects or would like to see.

Peripersonal Space in Culture

In the late 1990s, Richard Nisbett, a professor of social psychology at the University of Michigan, met a Chinese student, Kaiping Peng, who told him, "You know, the difference between you and me is that I think the world is a circle and you think it's a line."

Nisbett was startled. He strongly believed that all human groups perceive and reason in the same way, that people everywhere rely on the same tools for perception, memory, causal analysis, categorization, and inference. How could one culture think in circles, another in lines?

Unfazed, Peng continued, "We Chinese believe in constant change, but with things always moving back to some prior state. We pay attention to a wide range of events, we search for relationships between things, and we think you can't understand the part without understanding the whole. You Westerners live in a simpler, more deterministic world. You focus on salient objects or people instead of the larger picture. You even think you can control events because you know the rules that govern the behavior of objects."

Nisbett was intrigued. Is it possible, he wondered, that your culture shapes not only your speech and attitudes and judgments but even your basic patterns of perception? Is it possible that how you experience your senses, your body, and the space around your body is largely defined by your culture? After all, your brain is constructed by an interplay of genes and experience, with culture providing much of the input. So it was worth investigating.

Nisbett and Peng, now a professor at the University of California at Berkeley, have conducted numerous experiments showing the extent to which culture shapes perception. For example, when American students are shown an animated underwater scene, they describe a big fish swimming among smaller fish. Japanese students looking at the same scene describe the background and the scene in general and pay less attention to the big fish.

This result is intriguing, but the difference might stem from how people from each culture use language; it does not necessarily prove that they perceive the same scene differently. So in another experiment the scientists have their subjects look at pictures while their gaze is tracked with a device called an eye tracker. What they find is pretty sensational. When Americans look at a photograph of a tiger in a jungle, for example, their eyes fixate first and primarily on the animal. When East Asians look at the photograph, their eyes fixate on objects in the background with occasional fixations on the big cat itself. In other words, Americans focus their attention on a central object, while East Asians take in the whole scene. And this difference shows up at the level of how their eyes scan an image, which is a function carried out well below the level of conscious control.

So at least in some areas, you do perceive the world differently depending on what culture you grew up in. How you allocate your visual attention, how you use your eyes to parse a visual scene, varies as a function of culture. This example is of visual mapping, not body mapping, but it is a potent illustration of how deeply culture can penetrate into faculties we generally assume are hardwired into us as a species. Significant hardwiring is there, to be sure, but it can be molded by early experience more than we tend to appreciate. You are a child of plasticity as writ by your culture. How you use and conceive of your body is no different.

A new academic discipline called sensory anthropology focuses on how cultures stress different ways of knowing through the body maps and the senses. Notions of sight, sound, touch, taste, smell, balance, proprioception, and personal space are all conceived or even mapped differently in people from various cultures. Culture deeply modulates perception.

The Anlo of Ghana hold that balance is a powerful sense, important in the way that vision is to Westerners. Their language contains more than fifty terms for different kinesthetic styles, and each way of walking says something about a person's moral character. The worst thing that can happen to an Anlo is loss of the vestibular sense, because balance is the most important sense of all. Personal space is defined by balance. And dance is an essential part of life. During ritual dances they can independently move eight or nine parts of their bodies.

The Paluti of Papua New Guinea believe personal space is defined by sound. The Ongee of the Andaman Islands believe personal space is defined by smell. The Dogon of West Africa speak of "hearing a smell."

They classify words by smell: Good speech smells sweet, bad or impetuous speech smells rotten—indeed, the "mouth too ready to speak" is likened to the rectum.

Americans protect the bubble of space around their bodies and think of it as a comfort zone, which other people may not enter uninvited. Thus the cultural anthropologist Edward T. Hall divides space around the body into zones, like concentric sectors on a dartboard, with you as the bull's-eye, and argues that these zones have different dimensions in different cultures. Mediterranean and Asian cultures have relatively closer personal space zones, while Northern Europeans have more distant zones. In particular, Hall says, Americans have four zones. Intimate space extends six to eighteen inches from your body. It is the space you use for embracing a lover, comforting a child, or whispering. Personal space extends from eighteen inches to four feet from your body—about the same volume as your peripersonal space (coincidence?). It is the distance you adopt when talking to a friend. Social space, four to twelve feet from your body, is used for talking to acquaintances, strangers, or your boss. And when you address an assembled group, you will stand twelve or more feet away from your audience to create public space.

In each social context, Hall says, you choose your comfort zone and broadcast it to others with body language—with gestures, eye contact, posture, facial expression, and how you listen. If your space is violated you may feel uncomfortable, threatened, or upset. Hall first observed this when he worked for the State Department in the 1950s and watched an American diplomat back into a wall while talking to an Arab diplomat.

On a subway, you make yourself as small as possible and try to avoid body contact with strangers. On an elevator, you avoid eye contact, emotion-laden expressions, and loud speech. But at a sporting event or music concert, you may feel intimate with the crowd and bask in the collective sensorium.

A Sense of Where You Are

It was positively spooky the way Bill Bradley played basketball. He seemed to know the location, velocity, and direction of every player on the court at every given moment and effortlessly threw the ball to where he expected teammates to be. Playing for Princeton and later for the

Knicks, he was always a little bit ahead of everyone on the court, knowing where there was an open shot, when to jump for it, when to pass, when to feint. With his back to the hoop, he could toss the ball over his shoulder and sink the shot every time.

As Bradley once told the writer John McPhee, "When you have played ball for a while, you don't need to look at the basket when you are close in like this. You develop a sense of where you are."

Much has been written about the makings of superstar athletes. As noted earlier, the most important fact seems to be that they practice harder and longer than most other elite athletes. Sure, they are born with physical advantages—fast-twitch muscles (the kind of muscle you rely on in sprinting and boxing), long limbs, high anabolic thresholds, extraordinary hand-eye coordination, lightning-fast reflexes, and the like—but so are other elite players. The best of the best simply work at it more.

All that practice early in life leads to deeply ingrained motor patterns that help the athlete excel. Bradley shifts his feet in the same patterns tens of thousands of times until the moves are unconscious. Brazilian soccer superstar Ronaldinho uses his eye-foot coordination to encode the position of the soccer ball relative to his head, knee, and foot. Red Sox pitcher Daisuke "Dice-K" Matsuzaka can control precisely how and where a variety of pitches, including his ninety-six-mile-an-hour fastball, whiz through the strike zone.

Top athletes also tend to have superb vision. Hitters see the baseball as it leaves the pitcher's hand. A quarterback can pick out receivers on the fly. Bradley has a reputation for seeing out the back of his head. His peripheral vision is off the charts. He could stare at the floor and see a pass coming in from way over his head. According to McPhee, he could look at everything, focusing on nothing, until the last moment of commitment.

But there is one trait among great athletes, especially those whose game is played on open courts or fields (like soccer, basketball, American football, rugby, lacrosse, and hockey), that has not been described on ESPN or elsewhere. It explains why some people have an extraordinary sense of where their bodies are located in space, as well as the fast-moving bodies of all their teammates and opponents. Namely, the very best athletes have really great "place cells." And maybe even more important, they have spectacular "grid cells."

Place cells and grid cells are space-mapping neurons linked to a memory-forming region called the hippocampus. The hippocampus is evolutionarily much older than the cortex. So despite the amazing power and flexibility of our cortical space and body maps, this ancient system of place and grid cells is still very much with us—you could say it was "grandfathered in." Instead of mapping personal space from an egocentric point of view, as your parietal and premotor circuits do, place cells and grid cells are what scientists call geocentric.

They are different: Place cells are context-sensitive, while grid cells are context-independent. Place cells map the space around your body in terms of whatever environment you happen to be in—a room, a city street, a basketball court. They tell you where you are relative to the specific landmarks around you. They are what enable you to plan your route through a restaurant full of tables, keep track of where you are in a Wal-Mart, and help you decide where to go next while you're picking your way through a crowded room.

Grid cells are similar, but they do not attune themselves to landmarks. They map space independently from your environment. They are your dead reckoning cells. The point two feet in front of your nose is the point two feet in front of your nose regardless of whether you're in a cocktail bar or lying in bed or standing in the middle of a featureless plain.

Place cells were discovered in 1971 when two neuroscientists, John O'Keefe and John Dostrovsky, implanted electrodes into the brains of mice in an effort to study memory. Their target was the hippocampus. As the animals moved around their familiar enclosure, the scientists noticed that some cells fired when a mouse was in the southwest region of its home enclosure. Other cells fired when the animal moved to the northwest region. The same thing happened in different areas of the east half of the enclosure. In fact, it was possible to tell where an animal was inside its enclosure simply by looking at which cells were active. Each time an animal moved, a different population of hippocampal cells marked its place in space. If the animal moved back to the same location, the same cells became active again.

The researchers named these cells "place cells." They went on to learn that a rodent has many thousands of place cells, each tuned to a different region of space, called a place field. Even though there are only thousands of cells, a rat can learn many more locations than it has individual place cells through the power of combinatorics—the same principle that allows ten buttons on a telephone to represent all the phone numbers of an entire nation. The place cells can be active in millions of combinations to map all place fields in a given environment, whether it's a cage, a ship's hold, a barn, a wide-open pasture, or any other place a rodent might find itself. Moreover, some place cells fire in response to edges in an environment, like walls. And when a mouse or rat enters a new environment, a new place map is formed in minutes.

You have place cells too. When you walk into your kitchen, certain place cells fire when you are standing in front of your refrigerator. As you move toward the sink, a different set of place cells will mark your new position in the room. If you walk into your dining room or living room, another combination of place cells will mark your spot in space.

Your place cells have, in a sense, memorized the contents of each room, helping you know where you are in each zone of space. Thus in the dark you can move around any room in your house or apartment and not bump into things because your place cells have mapped where each piece of furniture is located, where the doorknobs are, and how far the light switch is from the doorframe. You have an internal map of where objects are located in relation to one another and in relation to your body as you move through space. Your place cells also take information from other parts of your self-motion system, including cells that keep track of where your head is turned, and constantly help update you about your balance and your body schema.

Spin yourself around a few times in the middle of a room. Then try to reach a door. You won't know which direction to go until you locate an object you recognize. Only with this cue can you work out where the door is located. This means that your place fields are calibrated according to fixed reference points—sofa, chair, table, window, door—that do not usually change. If you move your furniture around, your place fields reconfigure to update your map.

When you enter a place you've never been before—say, a ballroom—new combinations of place cells rapidly come to map the new space. Just like for the rat in its enclosure, one group of cells comes to represent the foyer, another set represents the area around the buffet table, still another set represents the dance floor under the chandelier. Every time you return to any of these regions, the same group of cells fires as a unit to give you a sense of where you are.

Incidentally, place cells explain why some people always seem to know which way is east, west, south, or north. You ask them, "Which direction are you facing," and they are usually right. This is because they have place cells that always fire when they face south, others for north, and others for east and west. If you're confused about cardinal directions, you'll always be confused, because your place cells are confused.

Grid cells, first described in 2005, map space differently. They supply you with your sense of dead reckoning, your ability to navigate without landmarks. The scientists who found them, in Edvard Moser's research group at the Norwegian University of Science and Technology in Trondheim, say it makes sense that the brain would have some way of keeping track of the body in space independently of details in the environment. There should be some way to calculate where you are based solely on your own movements, not on where the furniture is placed.

Grid cells do the job. Located just one step higher in the cortical hierarchy from place cells, in a region called the entorhinal cortex, each grid cell acts as though the surface of your local environment had a triangular grid painted all over it. (Grid cells have only been demonstrated thus far in rodents, but scientists who study navigation are extremely confident that humans have them, too.) A grid cell is active when you are at the vertex of any of the triangles in the field in front of you but inactive for locations between the vertices. The grid persists like graph paper spread as far as you can see, or like the Holodeck on *Star Trek* before scenes are projected onto it. When you move through space, grid cells mark your position independent of context. Place cells "say" *I am in the store, I am in my house, I am in a strange plaza.* Grid cells keep track of where you are in all contexts, in all kinds of places, as if they were a property of the environment itself and not cells in your brain.

"Grid cells came as a big surprise," Moser says, "but now that we have seen them, they make sense. I strongly believe you are born with them or they develop very early in life. There are many reasons to believe that place cells are sums of grid cells," he adds, but that research is just getting under way.

Nevertheless, Moser, when asked, is willing to venture a guess that great athletes have highly developed place cells and grid cells. Yes, they need fast reflexes, trained muscles, great eyesight, and developed brain networks to compare different trajectories; but when Ronaldinho looks down a soccer field, he is mapping the entire field in his brain. He has an effortless, innate sense of where he is in space and time, thanks to how well his brain maps that space. Every time he takes a step, an entire new geometry of action is created within his brain. In ten seconds, Ronaldinho will see at least one hundred alternatives and will make choices that draw on his body mandala, place cells, and grid cells.

Using and Blending Personal Space

The Himba imagine that a bubble of personal space literally surrounds your body, the same way a magnetic field surrounds an atom or a planet. While science can't quite yet sign on to this interpretation, the evidence makes clear that your peripersonal space bubble is, psychologically speaking, as real as anything. This space is part of you, no less than your limbs and head. Without it you would still have a body, but your isolation from the physical and social world would be profound.

For the next few days, try thinking about your personal space as you move about and do your normal activities. Take a walk by yourself, go for a run, sit at your desk, cook a meal. Try to appreciate the myriad ways that you use the space unconsciously.

If you are a solo dance performer, your personal space is your medium for expression. By extending the lines of your body into space, by arching and bending, you are setting your space into motion, shaping it for others to admire. Indeed, you can make a small room seem enormous by the quality of your movements. You know when there is or is not enough room to make certain movements based on your body maps. You know how to use shadows to change perceptions of your personal space. Professional dancers say that dance is a spatial extension of the body that reaches out and touches other bodies. It involves "leaking into space," unveiling the invisible.

The martial art tai chi is a graceful and elegant way to explore your personal space. Learning the structured movements or forms is like learning a foreign language, only it is the language of body and space in motion. The goal is total unification of mind, body, and intention. Barbara

Davis, editor of the *Taijiquan Journal*, says that some students have difficulty finding the boundaries of their personal space, some are too rigid
about holding their space, and others are all too ready to "fall down and
be a doormat." To learn tai chi, or any martial art, Davis says you have to
retrain your body and your relationship with your personal space.

When you're threading your way through a subway station or standing
in a crowded elevator, your personal space rubs against and slides past
the space of others. But there are other conditions in which personal
spaces can merge. As you think about your personal space, see if you feel
anything when you come into close contact with friends and family. The
Himba say they are never alone because their space maps fuse with others' throughout the day. Do you feel blended personal space? Do you
sense the creation of "we-centric" space?

If you are a mom or dad, hold your child close and think about your
body maps. When your child sits on your lap, are you palpably sensing
each other in shared space? It is likely, but not yet proved, that your brain
contains spatial mapping cells that specialize in "affiliative behavior,"
which is a clinical term for cooperation and intimacy. When you hug
someone you love, these cells, dedicated to making you feel safe in the
envelope of shared personal space, are likely buzzing.

The reason to think there might be such "hug" cells is that neuroscientists have found "flinch" cells in the monkey brain used for thwarting
threats within personal space. Flinch cells fire when objects approach the
face or body. The monkey will squint and blink, lift its upper lip, turn its
head away, shrug its shoulders, or lift a hand into the space near its head.

Michael Graziano, the Princeton University neuroscientist who discovered flinch cells, says, "Your brain needs a system to keep you from
bumping into furniture and staying a healthy distance from a cliff, to help
you run through a twiggy forest without poking out your eye, brush away
an insect, reach safely around a prickly object, or sit at a desk without
bruising your arms and elbows as you work. Your life would be impossible without protective mechanisms operating out of consciousness."

So might you also need a system for allowing others to come close inside your mapped body spaces. Life is full of joint actions in which personal space is shared and movements are coordinated—a fast pass in
basketball, a piano duet, martial arts combat, acrobats, a cheek-to-cheek

dance, dressing a child, carrying a heavy piece of furniture with another person.

In one experiment of joint action, pairs of people were asked to lift wooden planks off a conveyor belt. You could only touch the planks, which varied in length, at the ends. Thus you could carry short planks by yourself, but at some point you would have to seek help from the other person. This transition point is interesting because it reveals how you take your partner's action capabilities (remember affordances?) into account. If both of you have long arms, you'll wait longer than a pair that has shorter arms. You will also adjust your action to the exact arm length of your partner.

When two people juggle together, they plan and execute their actions in relation to what they predict the other person will do—in shared space mapped by each brain. In fencing, each person controls personal space via fancy footwork. When one person penetrates the personal space of the other, the attack is on.

Horses and riders blend personal space. Good riders know how to give up their center to a cantering horse while the horse gives up its center to the rider. With each step, the horse and rider react to mutual feedback of blended personal space. The horse gives cues and the rider gives cues. Novice riders tense up because they do not know how to respond to the horse's space and body maps in motion. Horses sense stiffness in inexperienced riders and may, if they're feeling ornery, try to toss them off their back.

In traditions of healing touch—shamanic healing, energy healing, universal life energy, Reiki, and scores of other healing practices from around the world—practitioners use a combination of visual imagery, motor imagery, and gestures to merge their own peripersonal space sense with that of their patients. It might involve laying on hands, manipulating the vitalistic "energy fields" believed to suffuse and surround the body, or passing magnets or crystals over special body points called chakras. The experience, both for the healers and their patients, is quite real: Both can often literally feel the shifting of the energetic currents or fields they believe are there.

The scientific method has never been able to confirm that chi flows or other mystical vital energies are real and present in the mind and body.

Yet the experiences of these things are so palpable for so many people that it would be a cop-out to dismiss them out of hand as "nothing more than" wishful thinking. Perhaps science, having banished these energies from its account of reality, can nonetheless explain the sensory awareness that people have of them. The brain's touch, movement, and peripersonal space maps go far in explaining many key elements of these beliefs and experiences.

Peripersonal space is physically, literally mapped in your brain's parietal and frontal lobes. So are your motor intentions within that space. Your sense of owning this space is so real and encompassing that you may be tempted to feel that you can direct or otherwise manipulate the space as if it had substance or intrinsic energy. This is because your experience is of your brain's representation of that space, rather than of the space itself. In your higher-order action and peripersonal space maps, your body mandala is constantly blending the objective with the subjective. The objective constitutes your physical movements and the feedback sensations you receive by interacting with the things around you. The subjective constitutes your motor plans, both real and potential; the possibilities for action, including affordances, which you subconsciously perceive and automatically simulate; and the actions of other people, which you also simulate in your body mandala.

Because of this seamless subjective-objective blending, it is easy to perceive the subjective component as having objective reality. And because the many maps of the body mandala share information back and forth, these beliefs can even percolate down to the primary touch map and generate phantom sensations—tingles and gentle forces—that the mind interprets as perceptions. This establishes a feedback loop, reinforcing the belief in mystical energy fields all the more. Have you ever had a Reiki practitioner hold her hands over your chest? Even skeptics are likely to feel an anticipatory tingle. Have you ever played with a Ouija board? The forces you seem to feel on the pointer are coming from your and your partner's muscles—but the illusion of outside agency is incredibly convincing.

The idea that peripersonal space can be harnessed to treat and cure human ills is widely accepted in cultures around the world. The fact that metaphysical healing practices endure says something important about their efficacy, for indeed they do very often work. But the reason they work is not, in the scientific account at least, metaphysical. Rather, they work because people expect them to work, and because the body mandala is flexible and creative. You have already seen the power of expectation and belief in creating your reality. In the same way, expectation and belief are primary engines in health and disease. Placebos are a potent form of medicine. For people who are drawn to spiritual beliefs, healing touch works wonders.

Musicians strive for joint action that transcends each individual. Watch your favorite band in a live jam session. And have you ever gone to a reggae or rock concert where thousands of people move in unison to the music? If you stand back and watch the crowd, you may get a vivid sense of One Big Body Map. Seriously, try it. The same goes for being at a gospel service or for when a batter hits a home run in a baseball stadium. As the crowd leaps to its feet, you can feel the unity of the experience not just in your eyes and ears but in your expanded body map.

And lovers? Have you ever noticed the way lovers hold hands, with fingers interlaced? Children and friends hold hands, but with palms touching. By intertwining their hands, are lovers mingling their body maps? It seems obvious that lovemaking is the ultimate instance of blended personal space. The act brings two bodies and their bubbles of space into one body, one space. They are a unit. Some might say it is entanglement, as when subatomic particles have partners, but you don't need to invoke the mysteries of quantum mechanics to explain the phenomenon.

CHAPTER 8

STICKS AND STONES AND CYBERBONES

or, The End of the Body as We Know It?

In a third-story lab of the Brain Science Institute building, located deep inside the sprawling campus of Japan's RIKEN Institute near Tokyo, Takezo sits uncomplaining in his monkey chair. His furry little butt rests on a padded platform. At waist height a broad black table stretches before him. His arms and hands are free; in one of them he has a small rake, its handle just a couple of feet long, which he's using to pull raisins from far points on the table to within reaching distance of his other hand. He's very focused. Few things are as motivating to a Japanese macaque as fruit—though a near contender might be a hot tub. These monkeys are famous for lounging through long stretches of winter in Japan's natural volcanic hot springs.

In an ordinary human chair next to Takezo's steel-and-plastic monkey chair sits a smiling young scientist who is just as active as he is. Every time he rakes in a raisin, she places a new one somewhere else on the table. She also interacts with him. She smiles at him, talks to him in sweet, encouraging tones, and gives him frequent caresses and supportive pats. There is an ulterior motive in all the touching: In somatosensory experiments with animals it is vital to establish a high level of trust and familiarity. When the time comes to implant recording electrodes in Takezo's brain, so that his body and action-space maps can be probed and charted, he must be willing to permit lots of touch and manipulation of his limbs. It also keeps him calm and happy.

When Dr. Atsushi Iriki and his guest enter the room, Takezo stops and stares; he knows Iriki, the senior scientist whose lab this is, but he sees few unfamiliar faces, and even fewer of them belong to gaijin (foreigners). The younger scientist bows and smiles to let Takezo know everything is fine. She coos gentle words to him in Japanese and coaxes his attention back to the raisins.

"Takezo has mastered the rake now," says Iriki. "We're going to start him on the joystick tomorrow."

Takezo can boast an achievement that very few other monkeys in the world ever will: He can wield a tool, deftly and with full intention. If this fails to strike you as a real achievement, that's because you are a tool-wielding primate of the highest order. Your body mandala is several stages more sophisticated than Takezo's, which in evolutionary terms is about thirty million years behind yours. Unless you are disabled by stroke or brain injury, you take a great deal for granted. Simple rake wielding is quite a victory for Takezo, for Iriki's lab, and for the science of body maps.

The idea of training monkeys to use tools came to Iriki while vacationing one summer in Okinawa. He began thinking about rakes as he watched a casino employee dressed in a Playboy bunny outfit who was using a hand rake to gather in chips from the card table. The work he was on vacation from involved probing some of the more sophisticated body maps in the parietal cortex of monkeys. One body map in particular had been puzzling him. Some of the cells in this map responded to images of sticks pointed toward the body, while others responded to sticks oriented crosswise to the body. Inspiration hit him as he watched the bunny wielding her rake. Here was one of the simplest possible tools, and she was using it to augment her body's capabilities. Iriki imagined what must be happening in her parietal lobe to extend her arms' dexterity with such ease and grace using a stick fitted with a wedge of plastic.

"I thought: Here's a stick aligning to the body axis," says Iriki. "She's using it to alter her body schema. So why couldn't we train a monkey to use a rake, and see if that's what these neurons are involved in?"

And so in 1996 Iriki began a landmark series of experiments to see what happens in the parietal lobes of monkeys who are trained to use tools. He was motivated by the intuition—shared with quite a few other scientists, psychologists, and philosophers—that tool use expands the body schema. Many people have speculated about this, and everybody on earth has seen plenty of examples that seem to corroborate it. Iriki recalls sitting at the counter in a sushi restaurant one night, watching a chef carve up a fish. When the knife unexpectedly bit into the fish's spine, the chef yanked his hand away and cried "Ouch!"

"There is a story about a master Chinese painter," says Iriki, "who is said to have told his students: To be a true master of the brush, if someone were to cut the brush while you were writing, the brush must bleed."

But as a scientist Iriki wanted to find out whether people are being purely metaphorical when they talk like this, or whether they are drawing their metaphors from a deeply, neurally real experience. With this sort of big picture in mind, he went back to his lab, back to his macaques, hoping that a tool-training experiment would shed some light on the neural basis of body schema.

Remember, the posterior parietal lobe is like a major river where tributaries of multiple senses and actions converge and integrate. It was already known that there is a body map (one of several multimodal maps) in the deep fold at the back of the parietal lobe that combines information about vision and touch. You'll recall that these cells have bimodal receptive fields—that is, they respond equally well when the body part they represent is touched or when the eyes see something in the space near the body part. For example, a cell in the hand region of this map will fire with the same vigor to something touching the hand as it will to the sight of an object close to the hand. This bubble of near-space that (from the parietal neuron's perspective) enhaloes the hand is the hand's peripersonal space. This map cell represents both the hand itself and the region of space surrounding it—the region where the hand's potential to act or be acted upon by nearby objects is high. In contrast, the sight of an object far beyond the hand, in extrapersonal space, doesn't trigger a response in these cells. The cell deems the object too far away from the hand to be included in peripersonal space, and doesn't fire in response to it. Other cells in this map respond to objects near the face and head. And surely other cells do the same thing for the knee, foot, tail (in primates who happen to have them), and so on. Together they map the space around your body as belonging to your body.

These cells were certainly interesting, but as Iriki began studying them with his rake-wielding monkeys, no one had a good idea how they contributed to the body schema, to reaching, grasping, and manipulating things, and certainly not what, if anything, they were contributing to your ability to wield a rake, a pen, a pool cue, a cursor, or a joystick.

Monkey See, Monkey Rake

It took a long time to develop a protocol to effectively train a monkey to use a rake. (In fact, Dr. Iriki's first great challenge was to prove that monkeys, unlike apes, are even capable of learning to use tools, since they demonstrate virtually no natural inclination to do so either in the wild or in captivity.) After many months, Iriki's team developed and refined a training process that can turn a naïve monkey into a tool user in as little as ten days to two weeks of daily training.

As soon as he had his first brood of fully trained rake-wielding monkeys, Iriki installed tiny hatches in their skulls, implanted dozens of microelectrodes into their posterior parietal neurons, and measured the neurons' activity while the monkeys raked in the goodies. What he found amazed him. The visual receptive fields of these visual-tactile cells no longer extended to just beyond each monkey's fingertips. Now they extended to the tip of the rake! The hand's peripersonal space, which for the monkey's entire life prior to rake training had never extended to more

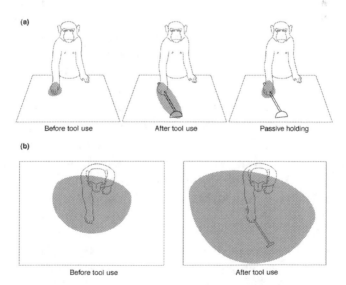

(a) Before learning to use a rake (left) or while passively holding the rake (right) without the intention of using it as a tool, the monkey's hand-centered visual-tactile receptive fields stay confined to the hand's immediate vicinity. But while the monkey is actively wielding the rake (center), the cells' visual receptive fields expand along its length. (b) The visual-tactile receptive field expansion of one of the monkey's shoulder-centered neurons.

than a few inches beyond its fingertips, had now billowed out like an amoeba's pseudopod to include a lifeless foreign object. In other words, the monkey's parietal lobe was literally incorporating the tool into the animal's body schema. Here, apparently, was the neural correlate of the body schema's powerful flexibility.

What Iriki measured was the morphing of these cells' visual receptive fields, but as a tool user yourself, you know that the touch aspect of the tool-using experience is equally, if not more, profound. Imagine you lose your sight and need to learn to walk with a cane. At first you are bad at it. You stumble into things, and your flailing cane is as much a menace to your surroundings as it is a sensory aid to you. You are slow to assemble a mental model of the terrain before you, using nothing but the patterns of scraping and resistance the cane's tip meets as you swing it. As you tap and sweep the cane, at first you are conscious mainly of the sensations in your hand and arm—which, after all, are the true physical locations of the feedback the cane is giving you. But after some practice, a remarkable illusion takes hold: The fact that you're actually sensing all those forces and vibrations through your hand and arm fades from consciousness, and your awareness of those sensations moves out to the tip of the cane. Appreciate that for a moment. Your perceptual experience literally feels located at the tip of the lifeless stick in your hand.

This amazing flexibility in your body schema relies heavily on the body maps in your parietal lobe (with major cooperation from your frontal motor system, of course). Cells like the ones Iriki studies lie at the crux of your ability to sense the texture of your food through forks and knives or chopsticks. They allow you to pick up a bat or a racket and instantly convert your naked, inadequate primate arms into a formidable ball-slugging force to be reckoned with. They're behind people's deft ability with tools like drills, whisks, chain saws, and keys; with bodywear like hats, helmets, knee pads, skirts, and skis; even with vehicles, from skateboards and surfboards and bicycles to cars and boats and airplanes and space shuttles. Again, these cells are also at the heart of why you hunch down your neck when you drive your car into a parking garage with low clearance, and why you have an intimate sense of the road's texture based on the vibrations in your seat and the handling of the steering wheel, and why a good driver can confidently estimate to within an inch whether the corner of her bumper can clear another car while making a U-turn. Your body mandala incorporates your car, your bat, your racket, your pen, your chopsticks, your clothes—anything you don, wield, or guide—into your body's personal sense of self.

So Iriki's sushi chef wasn't just on hair-trigger alert against slicing his finger off; hands, knife, and fish were, as far as his higher order body maps were concerned, all truly part of him. And the Chinese calligrapher who spoke of the bleeding brush was using a poetic metaphor to describe the very real experience of tool-body unification that a skilled master enjoys. And so it isn't pure wishy-washy mysticism to strive to "become one with" your putter, your racket, your brush, your video avatar, or whatever tool it is you seek mastery with: It has a solid experiential and neuroscientific underpinning.

Takezo is part of a long line of experiments Iriki has carried out since his original study. Over that time he has performed several variations on basic rake use. He has given the monkeys a short rake, which they had to use to retrieve a longer rake in order to reach the raisins placed out of the short rake's reach. He has put up vision-blocking mounds (like speed bumps) and surrounded the table with mirrors, forcing the monkeys to map the locations of the raisins in a new way, using their reflections rather than direct-line sight. He has put mirrors on the rakes themselves.

One day while watching his children play a Nintendo go-kart racing game, Iriki realized he should test whether his monkeys could learn to reconstitute their peripersonal space maps correctly using a variety of modified video feeds. Several subsequent experiments involved blocking the monkeys' view of the table and their own arms using an opaque barrier at neck level, forcing them to watch and guide their own actions on a video monitor. At first he gave them direct, unaltered video feeds, but later he also gave them abstract representations to work with, such as a minimalist version in which a phosphorescent line segment represented the rake tip and a white dot represented the raisin on an otherwise black screen. In another experiment he put backward-facing mini cameras on the underside of the rakes.

In each case, the purpose is to see whether and how the monkeys are able to make the required mental transformations in body and action space to keep successfully raking in the raisins. In all cases so far, the monkeys have learned the skill, and their body schemas have morphed appropriately. It's all an attempt to figure out how flexible these periper-

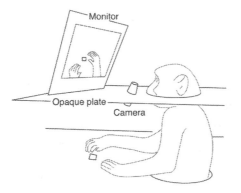

The monkey must learn to use its body maps in a novel fashion in order to retrieve the food it wants.

sonal space maps are. By understanding how they adapt with training, scientists like Iriki think they will gain important insights into the even greater tool-using ability of the ape lineage and the almost godlike flexibility of the human body schema.

Cyborgs of the Stone Age

One fact that intrigued Iriki was the unbreakable training period barrier he ran up against in every monkey he trained: ten to fourteen days. No matter how intensively they drilled, no matter how well they streamlined the training protocol, not even the most gifted macaque could be rake-trained in under ten days. This fact provided a strong clue as to what was going on.

So Iriki rake-trained a new cohort of monkeys and this time removed some of their parietal neurons and did a genetic analysis on them. Specifically, he measured the expression patterns of certain genes involved in brain growth and learning. He found these growth factors concentrated in the arm and elbow region of the parietal body map where the bimodal tool-use neurons were found. Many of the neurons in this map had grown long-distance connections (up to a few millimeters) to forge new synapses in other nearby body and body-centered space maps—connections that don't normally exist in the Japanese macaque brain. Rake learning, for a monkey, evidently involves more than ordinary learning; it engages full-blown neuroplasticity, which requires a complex cascade of gene expression. This cascade can't happen overnight, but needs several days to play out—ten to fourteen days, to be exact.

Iriki says there is an evolutionary insight in all this. It seems that this kind of enriched transwiring of parietal body-action maps has been steadily selected for in the primate line over the past twenty-five or so million years as monkeys became apes and then apes became human beings. It exists only as latent potential in monkeys, who don't face the right combination of evolutionary pressure and opportunity to turn this tool-using circuitry into the developmental default. Still, being primates, their body mandalas are complex enough that it exists as realizable potential: With rigorous artificial training it can be coaxed from mere potential into behavioral reality.

In contrast, our nearest cousins, the subhuman apes, have a genuine instinct for tool use. It may pale beside ours, but it's distinctly there. The reason is that the maps in their body mandalas are more richly interconnected from birth. The map enrichment Iriki managed to induce painstakingly in monkeys develops as a matter of course in the brains of apes. And so chimps and bonobos routinely fish for termites using peeled twigs, use rocks to crack nuts, prop up fallen branches to use as ladders, and so on. The other great apes, gorillas and orangutans, are generally less toolish, but they are certainly capable. For example, a wading gorilla will systematically poke a stick into a murky riverbed, searching for a ford. Humans have enriched their body mandalas even further, to the extent that we require—and even seek out with insatiable, instinctive hunger—rich sensorimotor interaction with tools starting in infancy.

Let's take a quick look at human evolution. What web of circumstance led us to develop from a species of chimplike apes into a race of upright, spacefaring philosophers with aspirations to godhood? It didn't begin with improved brains. For quite some time after our ancestors split with the ancestors of today's chimpanzees, our brains and theirs remained pretty much the same size. What seems to have really jump-started it was a radical change to the body: our assumption of a permanently upright posture. No other primate does this. The rest of our primate kin are all inveterate knuckle-draggers.

We gave up a lot in the bargain. Our knees and spines are ill suited to bear the full force of our weight, and to this day these remain among the most vulnerable and poorly engineered parts of our anatomy. We also came away with a much higher center of mass, making us slow and

· WHEN PLASTICITY MASQUERADES AS EVOLUTION

Penfield never learned this, but the primary touch homunculus is actually four homunculi laid out in parallel. Two deal with touch, and two specialize in proprioception—your felt sense of limb positions and movements. In the best-studied proprioceptive submap (neuroscientists call it Area 3a), the hand maps of different primate species contain a different number of finger maps.

Marmosets, which lack opposable thumbs and tend to use all their fingers together as a unit, don't have separate finger maps. Their proprioceptive map looks like a mitten. Macaques, which have fully opposable thumbs and a larger repertoire of grips, possess distinct proprioceptive maps for the thumb and index finger. But their middle, ring, and little fingers are mapped together as one. Moving up the evolutionary ladder, the great apes (bonobos, chimpanzees, gorillas, and orangutans) have distinct proprioceptive maps for the thumb, index finger, and middle finger, and only their ring finger and pinky maps are blurred. We humans—known for our penchant for touch typing and pianism—have distinct maps for all five fingers.

How to explain this variation? One possibility is sheer genetics. Such differences in proprioceptive maps may be a product of brain evolution: As primate hands and fingers evolved freer, more mobile joints and new muscle attachments, the primate brain evolved specialized circuits to perceive and control its more versatile hand maps.

But there is another explanation: plasticity masquerading as evolution. Perhaps the genetic program responsible for creating this primary proprioceptive map in the brain changed little over the millions of years that separate monkeys from apes. Maybe the only things that evolved to a significant degree were the arms, hands, and fingers. Each species has its own set of mechanical and structural properties for limbs—the shape of bones and joints, the pattern of muscle and tendon attachments. Maybe the proprioceptive hand maps of monkeys are fingerless not because their genes decree it, but simply because anatomical limitations force the monkeys to use their hands as a unit.

Thus neuroplasticity might play a larger role than is generally appreciated in creating the "species-typical" organization of at least some brain maps. Evolution may craft anatomical improvements in body parts, and then the brain gerrymanders its body maps to capitalize on those improvements. Many unique features of the human mind and brain may be due to hidden, emergent processes like this one.

topple-prone. If you've ever tried to catch a dog who would rather play keep-away than fetch, you'll appreciate how much speed and maneuverability we sacrificed.

But the great benefit was hand freedom. Apes' hands have to do double duty as fine manipulators and part-time forepaws. This subjects them to considerable engineering compromises. But by standing upright we cast off this limitation, and evolution could optimize our hands as hands proper. They became not only more delicate but a lot more nimble, dexterous, and clever. Our arms were also modified, especially at the shoulders. Aside from the gibbons—the so-called "lesser apes," who hurtle arm-over-arm through the jungle canopy like Spider-Man—we are the only mammals that can pivot our forelimbs upward past our heads. The primate body mandala was already far richer than that of any other mammal, thanks mainly to our heavy reliance on our arms and hands and thumbs. We simply continued the trend.

Permanent two-legged walking coincided with the very first stone tools: sharp-edged shards of intentionally broken larger stones that were selected for their suitability as throwing weapons and butchery tools. Of course these tools were primitive compared with the precisely chipped, symmetrical, fire-hardened stone hand axes that their descendants—our ancestors—would be making several hundred thousand years down the line. But they were certainly tools, and they quickly became central to the bipedal apes' way of life. (They certainly must have used sticks as well—as spears, clubs, staffs, and prods—but only their stone tools have survived into the present for archaeologists to find. In fact, chimps recently shocked primatologists by sharpening sticks and spearing bush babies for meat.) The craft of stone tool making improved through the ages in parallel with the remarkable ballooning of our brains. Our network of body maps grew richer and richer, and at the same time—and not just coincidentally—our brains ramified out into other realms of advanced mentation such as language, abstract thought, and a degree of moral and emotional sophistication never before seen on this earth.

In this view, the backbone of the story of human evolution has been the story of perfecting our knack for incorporating an increasingly sophisticated assortment of physical tools into our increasingly flexible body schemas. We evolved from apehood to personhood by developing a deep-seated cybernetic nature. Tool use went from a supplementary survival

GRUNT, TWO, THREE . . . INFINITY!

Some body maps seem to have veered from their earlier functions. Consider two brain regions that seem to have their origins in ordinary homuncular body maps but bootstrapped their ways into a realm of infinity.

The first is a patch of cortex known as Broca's area, which is critical for language processing. Damage to this area compromises the ability to apply the rules of grammar. Speech becomes "telegraphic": It consists mostly of nouns and verbs, and it lacks the complex sequencing and embedding of words and clauses that separates Tarzan-speak from Ciceronian eloquence.

Broca's area is acknowledged as the brain's engine of grammatical fluency, but exactly what it does within the larger semantic economy of the human mind remains unclear. Though ensconced solidly in the frontal motor cortex, it doesn't seem to be a motor area per se. But the location of Broca's area is intriguing. First, its adjacency to the hand and mouth portion of the primary motor cortex is suggestive, given that the mouth and hands are the only two motor channels people use to spew forth the rat-a-tat patterns of spoken and sign language. Second, Broca's area lies right next to the frontal mirror neuron system, which serves as a bridge linking your own body awareness and intentionality with those of others through an automatic process of mental action simulation (more on this in chapter 9). This Broca's area–mirror neuron connection, though circumstantial, suggests a tantalizing fit with the gestural origin of language hypothesis, which holds that our

skill to an innate drive—what can be called the cybernetic instinct. We are able to fluidly and creatively reconfigure our body schema with ease; for us, it's as simple as picking up a stick, or a pair of scissors, or a keychain. The impulse to augment our bodies with artifacts was bred into us over tens of thousands of generations on the African savanna. It turned us into tool-wielding savants who mastered fire, conquered the seven continents of the world, and eventually plunged a stick with a flag on it into the surface of the moon.

Not only can the human body mandala learn to incorporate tools—it needs exposure to tools for normal development to occur. A human is not the only animal with culture, just as an elephant is not the only animal that is deft with its nose. Culture is not just an important part of our survival kit; it is the essence of it. We are born in an absurdly immature state and spend many years utterly dependent on the physically and mentally protohuman ancestors began languagelike communication through a kind of sign language, then started augmenting it with vocalizations, and then, as our vocal tracts became more sophisticated, eventually supplanted the gestures like a cast-off scaffold.

The second body-map-derived area to consider is basically a counting region—a math region—and if it is damaged you may suffer acalculia (an inability to manipulate numbers). Located in the parietal cortex, it seems to have connections with the finger regions of the nearby primary touch map. Some scientists propose that this region forms while young children learn to count using their fingers; counting, adding, and subtracting become internalized and automated. If this view is correct, the region's link to the fingers of the homunculus attests to math's digital (*digit* is Greek for "finger") origin.

The theme here, then, is body maps that outgrew their bodily origin and became something new. An area specializing in the control of our early grunts and the intention-reading system became one of the main hubs of language, which opened the human mind to an infinite scape of apprehension, from herbology to astrology to theology to Shakespeare. Meanwhile, back in the parietal lobe, the laborious finger-folding arithmeticking of preschoolers lays the foundation for their eventual entry into the timeless realms of Pythagoras, Euclid, and Sir Isaac Newton. Oh, what a body map can do! It's no exaggeration to say that body maps played a key role in raising our minds from the limited sphere of our bodies into contemplations of infinity.

---

mature adults around us. Our immature brains are culture sponges. We can afford to be born with such a relatively blank slate because our genes take it on faith, as it were, that we will be surrounded by a culture that is worth absorbing. The two main elements of human culture are a spoken language, and at least a minimal set of tools plus a matching set of tool-related skills. Even stone-age technology is a neurally highly advanced ability, requiring an extremely sophisticated body mandala. If it weren't, other animals would have developed it too.

Cavemen in the Cyber Age

Jaron Lanier smiles as he recalls what it was like to have lobster legs sprouting from his body. He thinks all the way back to the early 1980s, when he and his friends were pioneering the technology of virtual reality.

VIRTUAL REALITY 101

Virtual reality, or VR, uses a special headset connected to a computer to immerse you in an illusory three-dimensional environment. The headset covers each of your eyes with a miniature TV screen. The computer keeps track of where your head is in space and uses this information to calculate what you should see. Each eye is shown a slightly different view of the scene, so you perceive depth. Motion trackers tell the computer whenever your head swivels, pitches, tilts, or moves in any direction, and the viewpoint presented to each eye is updated accordingly. Thus, you have the convincing impression of being somewhere else—in a different room, inside a maze, on top of a mountain . . . anywhere, provided the computer running the simulation is fast enough.

The digital representation of your body in virtual reality is called an avatar. When two people interact face-to-face in a virtual environment, they are actually interacting avatar-to-avatar. An avatar may resemble the user who is "wearing" it, but it can be anything—a supermodel, a Zulu warrior, a space suit, a stick figure, a giant bowling pin, whatever. Virtual mirrors can be placed in a virtual environment so that users can "see themselves"—view their own avatars.

More advanced virtual reality setups give you some sort of interface device, commonly a cyberglove. The glove fits over your real hand, and just like your headset it sends position and motion information to the computer. The computer then adds the illusion of a hand to the virtual scene. The hand may be attached to your avatar or may seem to float in space, depending on how the simulation is programmed. You can use this cyberhand to interact with virtual objects in the scene. Common examples: pushing around virtual blocks, throwing virtual balls, firing virtual weapons, and pressing virtual buttons.

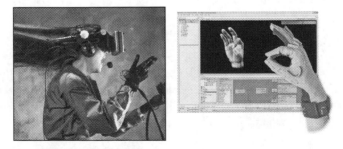

Left: One of NASA's VR interface systems. The head-mounted display provides both stereo vision and stereo sound, and two cybergloves give the wearer many options for interacting with the virtual environment. The wearer's streaming hair was done for humor's sake, but it illustrates VR's potential for even deeper immersion using wind tunnels or fans, treadmills, smells, and more. Right: A cyberglove.

Of course the objects in a virtual reality simulation are weightless, and although they present visual surfaces to the eye, they offer no physical resistance to your hand. This is a major limitation. In the future, virtual reality researchers hope to develop a good "haptic instrumentation" for virtual reality, meaning cybergloves or even cyberbodysuits that create artificial touch and force feedback to lend virtual objects qualities of solidity, texture, and heft. Current-generation virtual reality systems are limited to head-mounted displays, cybergloves, and variations such as the cybermouse, for controlling a three-dimensional floating cursor, and the cybergun, for war training simulation or video gaming.

Another challenge: Immersion into a virtual environment will need to emulate natural forces on the body, such as those that occur whenever you rotate your body and reach for an object. If the virtual environment is not extremely true to your normal body maps, you are prone to aftereffects such as reaching errors, motion sickness, and flashbacks. In other words, you could suffer cybersickness.

As he had done hundreds of times before, Lanier snugged the virtual headset over his eyes and found himself standing in a virtual room. But this time his avatar (his virtual body, programmed by his colleague Ann Lasko) was new, and not quite human. He held out his arms, and as usual, his avatar's arms did the same thing. But looking down at his rib cage he could see six segmented legs, twitching gently like reeds being tousled by a breeze. He set about figuring out how to control them.

As Lanier experimentally moved different parts of his body (his real body), the lobster legs bent and waved in ways that seemed random at first. But in fact there was a formula to it. The computer that was rendering his avatar was also tracking the bending of his joints (his real joints) and feeding that information into a composite control signal for the lobster legs. The recipe was complex. A subtle combination of the angles of the left wrist, right knee, and right shoulder, for example, might contribute to the flexion of the "elbow" joint of the lower right lobster leg. It was much too complex and subtle for his rational mind to grasp. But the inherent sensorimotor intelligence of his body map network was able to learn the patterns involved at a gestalt level and acquire the knack for controlling the new appendages. He soon mapped the lobster avatar into his own body schema.

The system did impose some moderate limitations on Lanier's movements. So long as he wanted to retain control of the lobster arms, he had to move his real body according to certain patterns and postures that weren't exactly the ones he would have chosen naturally. (An engineer would say that the lobster arms were robbing some of the "degrees of freedom" from Lanier's movements.) But he was still able to navigate decently well and use his hands and arms to do other things. And in exchange, he was able to learn to control a new set of limbs.

"After a bit of practice I was able to move around and make the extra arms wag individually and make patterns of motion," he says. "I was actually controlling them. It was a really interesting feeling."

This was just one of many small informal experiments Lanier and his team ran in those days. They toyed with a variety of altered avatars to see how much distortion, reformation, augmentation, and general weirdness they could impose and still get the mind to accept the avatars as "my body." They tried lengthened limbs, they tried shoulders at midtorso, they tried giant hands and stretchy arms like the superhero Plastic Man—and the mind would accept most of it. Just as Heidi's body mandala had done on the operating table during her electrically induced out-of-body experience, the cybernaut's body maps negotiated a new set of best-fit interpretations for the unnatural sensory input.

Consider one more of these experiments, which also involved a virtual, alien appendage with no analog on Lanier's real body. But unlike the lobster arms, in this case the appendage actually seemed to have a sense of touch. Lanier explains:

You can put buzzers on different positions on your body, and if you adjust them within a given range of frequencies and phases you can generate phantom sensations between the buzzers. Now a very interesting variation on this is to put a buzzer in each hand and play with their frequencies and whatnot until you get the feeling of a sensation out there in thin air between your hands. It's a weird, off-body tactile sensation. It's a truly strange experience.

What we did was combine that illusion with an avatar that had a visual element that you could control using the lobster arm technique. The avatar had a short tentacle sticking out of your belly button that you could learn to wriggle around. Then with the buzzers going, it felt like the sensation was in the tip of this appendage. When you get the visual and tactile experiences going together, it becomes just astonishingly convincing. When you combine somatic illusions with visual feedback like that, you just get to this whole new level. It's like your homunculus is maximally stretched at that point.

Lanier has a flair for naming things, most famously the term "virtual reality" itself. More recently he has begun popularizing a new catchphrase that encapsulates virtual reality's ability to radically reorganize the body schema: He calls it "homuncular flexibility."

When you think of homuncular flexibility, think lobster arms. Think umbilical tentacle. Think of the illusions presented in chapter 3—the rubber hand, the shrinking waist, Pinocchio, the rubber neck—and imagine their analogues in virtual reality. When you first read about those illusions, you would have been within your rights to think, "Yes, it's all very cool . . . but so what? Are these illusions anything more than just parlor tricks?" It is clear why a neuroscientist would be excited by them, but do they have any potential application outside the lab?

Yes, they do—or at least, they will. Not so much in the physical world, but in the virtual. In virtual reality, where your visual-spatial environment can be totally controlled, these illusions go from mere gee-whizzery to usefully exploitable properties of the body mandala, especially when supplemented by well-chosen touch and auditory inputs. The body sense you grew up with and have taken for granted your whole life is a lot more mutable than you ever suspected. Virtual reality is a powerful way to tap into that flexibility. Drastically altered bodies are going to be useful someday soon in video gaming, psychotherapy, rehabilitation medicine, and computer interface generally.

As for the umbilical tentacle and lobster arm experiments, Lanier says he and his pals were simply messing around with the technology. They were like the pilots of the first biplanes a century ago, doing the first loop-the-loops just for the thrill of it, just to see if they could. They didn't do controlled experiments; they were just doing proof-of-concept work.

"But what a concept!" Lanier says. "I don't know how far it can go, but I suspect that if we really play with it we can come up with some quite spectacular applications."

VIRTUAL REALITY, FROM THEORY INTO PRACTICE

Most people's intuition about VR's usefulness is along conventional lines. Imagine immersive versions of video games like "The Sims," "Second Life," and "World of Warcraft"; virtual conventions where professionals mill about and wheel and deal face-to-face through their avatars; realistic urban warfare zones where U.S. marines can hone their tactics, including how to interact with civilians. VR is going to make all of these possible. They are obvious and inevitable.

Aside from applications in the training of surgeons, soldiers, and other professionals, virtual reality is a promising tool for certain kinds of learning related to body maps. Lanier offers the example of juggling:

"If you build a particular motor skill in a slowed-down environment, you learn it much faster," he says. "I did the first experiment on that with juggling. I programmed in extra-slow juggling balls and slowly sped them up. People really responded with accelerated learning. This is now being offered as a rehab tool, by the way. And it works, if not for all motor skills, then at least for a subset of them that involve fast, ballistic types of motion."

Virtual reality is also finding increased use in treating phobias. In traditional exposure therapy, patients are increasingly exposed to the things they fear—snakes, heights, spiders, and so on—and gradually grow inured to the things that once drove them to irrational heights of terror. But this kind of therapy can be expensive, dangerous, or impractical. In contrast, virtual exposure therapy has the virtue of immersing the patient in a full three-dimensional, interactive world that's safe and programmable. Consider the difference between a still photo showing two shoes on the ledge of a skyscraper and the street below and a simulated experience in VR. Immersion is far more powerful than a photograph. VR fully engages a person's parietal body and space maps, creating a sense of presence within the situation rather than glimpsing the scene inside a static frame. The same goes for exposure to spiders and other objects of phobia, as well as for re-creating war zones for the treatment of post-traumatic stress disorder.

Finally, the pornography and sex industries are sure to drive a lot of innovation and demand for VR, as they have been doing with new technology for decades (e.g., videotape, pagers, and the Web). The intersection of porn and virtual reality is known as teledildonics. Not only will people be able to change how their partners' and their own avatars appear, they'll be able to alter the felt size and configuration of their body parts. If the touch delivered by a sexual interface device moves, say, one inch on your skin while its virtual counterpart moves two inches, your body schema will believe in the doubled dimensions of whatever it is you want to double in size. Without a doubt, this will have great commercial appeal.

Bending the Homunculus Till It Breaks

Ever since those early forays into homuncular flexibility, Lanier says he's been deeply impressed by the brain's willingness to let its sense of embodiment be warped by artificial sensory input. Unfortunately, he wasn't able to pursue it very far due to hardware and software limitations. After an initial spike of interest during the 1980s, the public and much of the business world grew disillusioned with the hype surrounding virtual reality. The budding digerati recognized virtual reality's revolutionary potential, but the technology of the day was simply inadequate to do more than reveal a rough outline of the future. But today with faster computers, advances in three-dimensional rendering, and cheaper components, there is a revival in virtual reality research, notably in fields relating to psychology. This includes the study of human-machine interfaces, where the power of homuncular flexibility holds great promise.

There's no question the body schema is incredibly labile. The really interesting question then is, How flexible? Where does it all break down? How far can you stretch the homunculus before it revolts? How far can your body schema bend before the illusion is spoiled?

Enter Dr. Jeremy Bailenson, an assistant professor of communication at Stanford University who recently teamed up with Lanier to repeat and extend some of those early shoestring experiments. Bailenson's research explores the intersections between virtual reality, body schema, homuncular flexibility, and social psychology.

His lab is a small room in one of Stanford's old brick buildings crammed full of computer equipment and workstations. Adjoining it is a much larger and completely empty room where people decked out in virtual reality headsets can wander without fear of tripping over any peskily nonvirtual obstacles.

"We have a bunch of projects going," says Bailenson, looking around the room considering which ones to demonstrate. "Ah, yes, here's one that's related to homuncular flexibility."

He indicates a computer workstation with a Web camera perched atop the monitor. The camera tracks your facial expressions and transforms them into control signals for a robot hand. The hand, which is wearing a red woolen mitten, juts out from beside the monitor as though offering a handshake. Raising or crinkling your brow opens and closes the hand's grip. Moving your head up and down controls the hand's angle in a vertical plane. After a bit of practice you can learn to use your face and neck to deliver a handshake. This prototype works fine, says Bailenson. But his lab will need to acquire a more fully articulated robot hand before he can see how much manual dexterity a person can exert with face muscles.

At a nearby workstation Bailenson indicates another face-tracking camera. This one uses your expressions to alter a shape floating on the screen. A neutral expression elicits a green cube. An angry face transforms it into a red octahedron. A smile turns it into a yellow pyramid. Bailenson says he wants to see if you can learn to use this interface to read emotions as easily as you can from faces.

Bailenson also wants to see how people's avatars affect their social interactions. For example, in one study he randomly assigned avatars of different heights to volunteers. Imagine you are a subject in the study. Your avatar might be taller or shorter than your real body, or it might be close to your true height. In the first phase of the experiment you are allowed to "see yourself" in a virtual mirror in an otherwise empty virtual room. Bailenson tells you to walk around the room and get used to the headgear. Subconsciously you also register your new height (assuming it has changed).

For phase two you go through a virtual door into another room where you meet face-to-face with a volunteer "wearing" a different avatar. Both of you are then required to play a simple negotiation game in which you must come to a mutual decision about how to split up a sum of money. The game ends and the money is assigned to each player only when both of you agree to the terms you've negotiated.

You probably think you wouldn't be a pushover just because you happened to get a shorter avatar. You probably think the height of your avatar would have no influence on your negotiation skills. And you may be right—but don't be too sure. Bailenson found a dramatic correlation: The majority of players, regardless of whether they are tall, short, or of gender-typical height in real life, will negotiate much less effectively and less aggressively if they receive a shorter avatar. Bailenson says the finding floored him.

"If your avatar is just six inches shorter than your negotiating partner, you're twice as likely to end up accepting really, really unfair terms at the end of the transaction," he says. He is running similar experiments that vary race and gender. The interplay between your body schema and body image is as slippery and as complex as ever.

Bailenson is also running experiments in which he measures people's heart rate and skin conductance—the autonomic signals measured in lie detector tests—and uses that information to modulate certain features of their avatars. For example, he makes people's heart rates control their avatars' heights within a certain range. If your heart is beating fast, your avatar is four inches taller than when your heart rate is slow. Or your skin conductance—basically, the sweatiness of your palms—determines your avatar's translucency. The more uncomfortable or nervous you are, the more you sweat, and the more see-through you become. The more confident you feel, or the better you start to perform, the more solid-looking you are.

Bailenson expects these methods will inject a new dimension into social psychology—the study of how people interact, negotiate, influence, perceive, and judge one another (and themselves). In real-life interaction people's body images and schemas are relatively stable. But with virtual reality your body schema and image, which are integral to how you see yourself and treat others, are as flexible as your wardrobe. Results from these studies may impact how people end up using virtual reality as more and more social and business interactions migrate into shared virtual environments.

What will happen in a world where you can strike up friendships from opposite ends of the earth without ever actually seeing other people's real faces and body language? What will it do to the business world if everyone is hyperconscious of avatars' heights, races, and gender? How might autonomic changes to your avatar affect communication between you and your online friends, or with your therapist, or in multiplayer games where negotiation and dialogue are important elements of play? Only time and further research will tell.

Through the Looking Glass

Dr. Iriki also has an interest in the body schema's interface with cyberspace. While he watched his children play their Nintendo road racing game, he was impressed by how absorbed they were. They not only had an emotional investment in winning, they seemed to be embodied in the game world itself. As their insane cartoon go-karts screeched around corners, the kids leaned their weight into the couch as though it would help balance their turns. When their carts jumped or dodged, the kids mimicked or responded to the motions with their whole bodies. The kids' enthusiastic body movements got Iriki thinking about his monkeys again, and convinced him that he should start them on video displays and joysticks. Physical tools like rakes may be one thing, but can monkeys make the next leap, into the use of virtual tools? Indeed they can.

Takezo is again sitting in his monkey chair, but now he is adept with the joystick. He fiddles with it as intently as any twelve-year-old Nintendo addict fighting his showdown with the end-of-level boss monster. With his right hand, Takezo sweeps his viewfinder around in search of the next raisin. He spots it. His left hand darts out with its rake and pulls in the treat. Just like the rake, the joystick and the camera it controls have been added to his bodily sense of self; they aren't lifeless foreign objects anymore, but honorary eye and neck muscles. Takezo can use the correlation between his hand movements on the joystick and the shifting view it creates on his monitor to map the table space in front of him. The instant he spots the raisin, his parietal space maps talk to his frontal motor maps to create a precisely targeted rake-reaching motor program. The actual table is invisible, but he is no longer dependent on "real," unmediated seeing and reaching. Thanks to the plasticity-driven changes in his brain, his interconnected body maps create an intuitive link in his mind between screen space, table space, and reach space.

Looking back, maybe it isn't too surprising that monkeys are able to use cybertools such as joysticks and shifting camera views. The primate body mandala is formidably flexible. In an earlier experiment, Iriki got curious to see what would happen if he showed the monkeys images of their hands greatly enlarged, like a Mickey Mouse glove. As expected, their parietal hand maps expanded to accommodate the altered visual input. Their body schemas willingly accepted the illusion of a supersized hand.

Your body schema will also readily accept changes in scale and magnitude, of course. Not only in size, but in distance. For example, if your virtual hand moves five times as far and as fast as your actual hand does, you will experience that directly. In fact, if the distance multiplier isn't insanely large, you won't even notice!

Nor do kids (of all ages) notice the degree to which their own body schemas absorb the characters in the games they love to play. Homuncular flexibility explains why. Their deep captivation occurs not just because of the graphics, the fast pace, the bells and whistles, but also because their body maps are infused with the cybernetic instinct.

It is worth noting that Nintendo's latest gaming console, the Wii (pronounced "we"), absorbs the player's body schema more deeply than any other system on the market. It does this through a novel control device—a small wireless wand that keeps track of how it is moved and rotated in space. Every swoosh, twist, and jerk of the wand translates into a related move in the video game. Swords, baseball bats, golf clubs, boat tillers, you name it, faithfully mirror the player's actions. The wand also emits sound effects and vibrations, deepening the illusion by engaging the body mandala through additional senses.

In the early weeks following the Wii's commercial release at the end of 2006, Nintendo had to recall and strengthen the wrist straps looped to the control wands because they kept breaking and flying from players' sweaty hands, shattering windows, cracking television screens, and bruising foreheads. Many players say that after a few minutes of play the illusion can become so convincing that it is hard not to get overenthusiastic. They forget they are not truly wielding a sword. They become heedless of the sofas and coffee tables in the living room. Think of the Wii as an intermediate step between "traditional" console games like the Xbox and future VR-based gaming systems, which seem destined to make the Wii as tame and passé as "Tetris." Consider what the Canadian educator, philosopher, and scholar Marshall McLuhan wrote about in the 1960s. Television, he argued, represents a technological extension of your ability to see and hear. In a similar vein, video games and VR games on the horizon represent a technological extension of your body schema into a constructed world of pure fantasy.

It is an area of gleeful geek speculation as to what's going to happen in another generation or two once virtual reality technology gets both cheap enough and high-quality enough to penetrate the consumer electronics market. What, if anything, will it do for (or to) our homuncularly flexible children? Will it benefit them? Might it harm them, socially or neurally, in unforeseeable ways? These questions are wide open.

On the negative side is the litany of problems surrounding today's video games and online allures. Kids ignore homework and chores, according to critics. They isolate themselves from flesh-and-blood peers and family, entrenching antisocial habits. They sit for hour after hour, day after day, moving nothing but fingers and eyeballs and growing fat and flabby from inactivity.

As video games and virtual communities are scaled up beyond the confines of today's relatively small, flat-screen monitors into the total-immersion experience of virtual reality, these trends may amplify. Already some hard-core players of massively multiplayer games like "The Sims," "Second Life," and "Ultima Online" value their virtual relationships and their avatars' well-being more than their own. When virtual reality becomes ubiquitous, will such people recede even further from the real world? Will their ranks multiply?

Another issue is whether violent video games increase aggression in chronic gamers. There is abundant controversy over the effects of games such as "Quake," "Doom," and the infamous "Grand Theft Auto" on young people's behavior. Evidence that video games may be harmful is found in a recent study where teenagers were randomly selected to play either a violent video game or a nonviolent video game for thirty minutes. Then their brains were scanned to see what areas had been engaged by the games. Compared with teens who played nonviolent games, those who were immersed in violence showed less activity in the prefrontal cortex—an area involved in inhibition, concentration, and self-control—and increased activity in the amygdala, which corresponds to heightened emotion. However, as the video game industry and many civil libertarians were quick to point out, the study did not show that these differences were long-term, or even harmful while they lasted. When you read the literature on this controversy it quickly takes on the flavor of a he-said, she-said squabble, with neither side able to soundly refute the other.

Whichever side you take in today's debate, it is legitimate to ask whether tomorrow's fully immersive blood-drenched, morality-free games will be patently harmful. Expect a lot more controversy over these issues through the 2010s and '20s.

Lanier is in the optimists' camp. He thinks the "genuine weirdness" of VR-turbocharged homuncular flexibility will have many uses and benefits, but first people will have to go through a less imaginative phase of treating virtual reality as essentially just a three-dimensional interactive movie—that is, you simply "don" an avatar and walk around in it like a Halloween costume. The avatar might be of a different gender, it might be taller or shorter than your real body, it might look like an elven knight or a Confederate soldier, but basically you participate in the virtual world on the terms of your natural body schema. But Lanier sees that as merely the entry point. "The future application of virtual reality, and the real art of it," he says, "will be to change your sensorimotor loops, to change the nature of your own body perception through the avatar."

Thus imagine you are a child learning about dinosaurs. Your virtual-reality-assisted lesson will not merely take you back to the late Cretaceous like a time-traveling field zoologist sent to observe *Tyrannosaurus rex* in its natural habitat; you will actually become the dinosaur. Your *T. rex* avatar's arms are foreshortened and two-clawed, and, like Lanier's lobster arms, are much less dexterous than your real hands. But this dexterity isn't being lost, it's just being rerouted and translated to other parts of your body. Some of your hand and arm movements are fed into greatly enhanced mobility for your huge and powerful neck and jaws, and the rest is fed into a control signal for a giant tail you can swoosh to and fro. After a while of playing around in this avatar, your primate-style body schema fades into the background and is supplanted by a saurian one.

Lanier expounds on avatar educational possibilities. "In learning trigonometry, you could become the triangle," he says. With the right interface, being isosceles or right-angled or congruent could have muscular, sensory, physically intuitive consequences that reinforce many of the important trig concepts that kids struggle to grasp when they are taught solely using chalk-scrawled figures and Greek terminology.

"In learning biology," he continues, "you become a molecule with a specific shape that only docks onto certain receptors. Suddenly the lessons are not so abstract. From early in life, every child has the experience of being a triangle, a molecule, a *T. rex*, an octopus, and God knows what. So in addition to learning how to control their own bodies, they learn from early childhood how to control other bodies."

The interesting question then is, Does that mean anything? How does that affect development, how does that affect cognition, how does that affect culture, how does that affect society?

"It's going to be a very interesting experiment," Lanier says. "It won't be systematic. It will be commercial and it will be driven by a lot of user interest. It will be like the World Wide Web was ten years ago and like MySpace is today. Twenty years from now, give or take, the tools for this will be everywhere, and then a generation of kids will grow up with it."

Lanier thinks the outcome will be positive overall. He predicts that early, lifelong experience with homuncular flexibility will be similar to growing up multilingual. Kids who grow up speaking more than one language get slight but measurable cognitive advantages that last a lifetime.

"In the same way, being multihomuncular"—he chuckles—"will be a lifelong enhancement."

CHAPTER 9

MIRROR, MIRROR

or, Why Yawning Is Contagious

I t was a hot summer day in 1991 on the wonderfully medieval campus of Parma University in Italy. In a modern neuroscience laboratory, a monkey sat upright in a special primate chair, waiting for researchers to return from lunch. Electrodes had been implanted into the part of its brain involved in planning and carrying out movements.

Every time the monkey grasped and moved an object, some cells in that brain region would fire, and a monitor, connected via thin wires to the electrodes, would register a sound: *brrrrip, brrrrip, brrrrip.*

The scientist in charge of the experiments, Giacomo Rizzolatti, was interested in the act of grasping. When you reach out for your morning cup of coffee, which cells plan and guide the movements that culminate in your latching on to the cup? How do your fingers know how to form the correct shape for lifting the cup's handle? How do you bring the cup to your mouth and not your nose? Rizzolatti hoped to find the cellular circuits behind such actions—reaching out the arm, curling the fingers, grasping the cup—by eavesdropping on neurons in different parts of the premotor cortex.

On this day, a graduate student sauntered into the lab with an ice cream cone in his hand. The monkey stared at him from across the room. The student glanced at the monkey. Nothing out of the ordinary. But when the student raised the cone to his lips to take a lick, something surprising happened. The monitor sounded: *brrrrip, brrrrip, brrrrip.*

But the monkey had not moved! It had simply observed the student grasping the cone and moving it to his mouth. It seemed like quite a strange thing for a cell in its motor map to be doing.

The same thing happened with peanuts. When the monkey picked up a peanut or when it saw a human or another monkey pick up a peanut, a particular group of cells fired. Soon the researchers found other cells that fired when the monkey broke open a peanut, saw someone else break open a peanut, or heard a peanut being opened. It happened with bananas, raisins, cups, indeed all kinds of objects. Most of the cells in the premotor cortex seemed to have "pure" motor functions, consistent with the traditional understanding of that region. But as soon as the Italians started probing deeper, they discovered that a sizable subset of the neurons in this map also represented the perception of the same actions they encoded.

Rizzolatti, an elegant Italian with a mop of soft silvery hair and a mustache shaped like a smile, immediately saw the implications of what he was witnessing. "We were studying canonical neurons involved in grasping objects of different shapes and then we observed this strange thing," he recalls. "Of course, we decided to study this in a more formal way."

Three years and scores of experiments later, Rizzolatti and his team published their first scientific papers on these "mirror neurons." Mirror neurons comprise a previously unrecognized element of certain body maps. The Italians found them in two areas of monkey brains—the premotor and parietal cortexes—and also discovered that these mirror regions had important links to another region called the STS (shorthand for superior temporal sulcus, located above the ear toward the back of the head), which helps process facial and body movements and hand actions. Other researchers would soon find mirror neurons in three other sectors of the cortex called the insula, the cingulate, and the secondary touch cortex.

The mirror neurons in the premotor cortex are active only while the monkey is acting or perceiving an action. They are silent when the animal looks at its hand alone or an object alone. In other words, they are not attuned to hands or mouths or peanuts or cups as such, but to intentional and purposeful behaviors involving those things. Some cells are tightly coupled to exact movements. Some respond to the general goal of the action.

The Italians also found mirror neurons in the touch and movement maps in the parietal lobe, a region thought previously to deal only with space perception. For example, in one monkey they found 165 parietal neurons that were involved in both the act and the perception of grasping food or putting food into a container. Some fired with the act of grasping, no matter what happened next. Others fired when food came to the mouth but not when it went to the container. Another subset of the neurons fired when food went to the container and not to the mouth.

They also found mirrorlike properties in neurons that track body movements like walking and arm swinging. Located in the STS, these neurons are not interested in the monkey's own movements. Rather, they are dedicated to detecting biological motion: Is that thing moving in the bushes a creature, or is it just a bobbing branch or shadow? This is pretty important for survival in the jungle or, if you are a human, walking down a dark city street late at night. Is that shape behind the trees a mugger or a mailbox?

Biological motion detection was first described in the 1970s by a Swedish psychophysicist from the University of Uppsala, Gunnar Johansson. Johansson put small lightbulbs on an actor's head and joints—shoulders, elbows, wrists, hips, knees, and ankles—and turned out the lights. When the actor sat still in a chair, all you could see was a random jumble of lights. But as soon as the actor moved, the form of a person became instantly apparent. The impressive part isn't simply that you can see how each point corresponds to a part of the actor's body; it's how vivid and robust the perception is. Johansson found that it took a minimum of just seven lights to trigger this perception of human biological motion.

Since then, countless such experiments show that you can tell, by the way bodies move in the dark with little lights attached, whether a person is male or female, foreign or familiar, happy or sad, afraid, disgusted, embarrassed, putting out the body language of any strong emotion, or preparing to make a next move. All that, from just seven points of light. Your visual system is exquisitely tuned to biological motion, and neuroscientists have finally figured out how it works. The STS is one of the main inputs to your mirror circuits. It contains body maps for biological motion, operating as a kind of "life detector," especially when complex behaviors are involved.

Telepathy

As with many big new findings in science, it took a few more years for the research community at large to grasp the significance of Rizzolatti's findings. But grasp it they did.

In 2001, V. S. Ramachandran, the neurologist who figured out the nature of phantom limbs, declared, "Without a doubt it is one of the most important discoveries ever made about the brain. Mirror neurons will do for psychology what DNA did for biology: They will provide a unifying framework and help explain a host of mental abilities that have hitherto remained mysterious and inaccessible to experiments."

Using a variety of brain imaging techniques, scientists went on to discover, in humans, many more elaborate mirror circuits that, cognitively speaking, leave monkeys in the dust. You can think of mirror neurons as body maps that run simulations of what others people's body maps are up to. In this way, they serve to link our body schemas together across the otherwise tremendous gulf that separates one person's subjective world from another's. They allow you to grasp the minds of others, not through conceptual reasoning, but by modeling their actions, intentions, and emotions in the matrix of your own body mandala.

For instance, when you watch someone else perform an action—say, using a broom—you automatically simulate the action in your own brain. You understand the sweeper's action because you have a template for that action in your own motor maps. When you see someone pull back his arm, as if to throw a ball, you have a copy of what he is doing in your brain that helps you understand his goal. You can read his intentions. You know what he is most likely to do next.

"When you see me doing something, you understand because you have a copy of the action in your brain," says Rizzolatti. "It's so strange. You become me. When I see you grasping an object, it is as if I, Giacomo, were grasping it."

The same principle applies to perceiving and understanding other people's emotions. When you see a friend choke up in emotional distress, your brain automatically simulates that distress. You empathize. Actors, who can make you laugh or cry, are very good at reading the felt states of their own bodies and transmitting those feelings via mirror system communication.

SPEAKING OF DOGS

Your mirror neuron system may possibly even jump species. Think about domestic dogs. Dogs are highly social, intelligent animals. We have been able to integrate these deadly carnivores into our homes because evolution has endowed them with instincts for fitting into a socially stratified yet cohesive and cooperative pack. Now, if you look at one of the prick-eared breeds such as the German shepherd, it is amazing how much emotional expressiveness there is in those fuzz-covered triangular ears. Whether they are erect, relaxed, swiveled forward, tilted out or pulled flat against the skull, they are eloquent advertisers of the dog's mood and inclination. A dog's ear posture combines with its other facial and body language—mouth "smiling" or snarling; eyebrow nubs set to convey helplessness, confidence, or innocence; neck high or low; tail wagging, up, flat, or between the haunches—to express an impressive range of moods (even a floppy-eared beagle can tell you what it's thinking). Remarkably, we are able to read this alien body language with ease. After all, we are primates; our ears are totally immobile and purely ornamental. But thanks to our mirror neurons and homuncular flexibility, we easily become "bilingual," if you will, in canine body language.

"We are exquisitely social creatures," says Rizzolatti. "Our survival depends on understanding the actions, intentions, and emotions of others. We simulate these automatically, without logic, thinking, analyzing."

Luckily, he says, when you observe an action you do not automatically act it out, and when you observe an emotion you do not automatically experience it in full. Your mirror neuron system cordons off the simulations in much the same way it inhibits you from acting out while you scheme or plan an action before you're ready to execute it.

There may be no such thing as telepathy, but mirror neurons are the next best thing.

Shall We Dance?

How do lowly neurons carry off such a sophisticated feat? How can brain cells, even working together in a circuit, be so incredibly smart? Most sensory neurons are rather pedestrian. They devote themselves to ordinary features of the outside world. For example, some fire when they detect a horizontal line, while others are dedicated to vertical lines. Others detect a single frequency of sound or a direction of movement. Moving to higher levels of the brain, scientists find neurons that detect far more complex features such as specific body parts, or flowers, or letters of the alphabet. As you've already seen, you have neurons in your higher motor maps that help your body plan complex movements and postures. For example, some neurons fire when you bring your hand to your mouth from any starting point around your body—that is, they represent the goal of moving hand to mouth.

Mirror neurons make these complex cells look like nincompoops. They seem uncannily smart in the way they link perception, action, and intention. Say you are trying to learn French. You can hear the sounds but you don't know how to repeat them accurately. Somehow you have to form your mouth into the right shape and right nasal resonance to produce those new sounds. You need to bring two complex properties together: sensory detection and motor planning. This is exactly what mirror neurons do. When you learn French or any new language, they map sounds and, using the same circuitry, produce those sounds.

Now apply this transformation—perception to action and vice versa—to the things you know and do every day.

Are you a NASCAR fan? Seventy-five million Americans are enraptured by the sight of stock cars racing endlessly around in circles on banked speedways. Many a NASCAR widow has wondered just how it could be quite so riveting. Think about each fan's mirror neurons, how their brain circuits resonate when drivers accelerate out of 90-degree corners, brake with the engine, downshift with both heel and toe, and pass one another at 150 miles per hour. Anyone who has mirror neurons and drives a car can relate to the sport of NASCAR racing.

The same goes for golf, tennis, soccer, and all the rest. Seeing is doing, and vice versa. Go to any sports bar on any day of the week and watch the spectators whoop and howl at the TV set. Their mirror neurons are a big part of why they watch so raptly and why they react so personally to each score, block, and fumble. And increasingly, many athletes hone their skills by playing video games. For example, race car drivers who "practice" screeching turns in a virtual rendition of the Indianapolis 500 track develop miniaturized mental maps of the course. They gain a genuine edge during a real event.

Your mirror neuron system becomes more active the more expert you are at an observed skill. When pianists listen to someone else's piano performance, the finger areas in their primary and premotor cortex increase above their baseline activity. Their mirror neuron systems are automatically running the performer's keystroking in emulation. The same thing does not happen in the brains of nonmusicians. While they can certainly appreciate the music deeply, their experience is inevitably shallower than the pianist's in at least one way, because they are not experiencing what it is like to actually produce it.

The same goes for sports: The better your own skills, the more deeply you understand the skilled performances you witness. For example, when classical ballet dancers and experts at a Brazilian martial art called capoeira watched video clips of each kind of performance, the dancers' brains showed distinct patterns. The movements in ballet and capoeira are equally athletic and difficult, with similar limb movements. Yet ballet dancers have weaker mirror responses when watching capoeira, and vice versa. Male ballet dancers have a weaker mirror response when they watch videotapes of moves typically made by female dancers, even though both sexes train together. The same goes for ballerinas watching male ballet movements. The actions you mirror most strongly are the ones you know best.

But what if you don't play an instrument or sport? What if you watch a kid flip over backward on a skateboard and you have never been near a skateboard? No way could you do those moves. Will your mirror neurons flip along with the skateboarder? The answer is yes and no. To the extent that you relate in a basic sense to the act of balancing and moving forward, your mirror neurons will resonate. But your mirror system activity will pale next to that of an expert skateboarder watching the same acrobatics. His understanding of another thrasher's hotdogging is much deeper than yours.

A recent experiment illustrated the tight link between action and perception. You are blindfolded and taught to move your arms in an unfamiliar pattern—a bit like a sign language version of John Cleese's silly walks. You practice the moves without the benefit of sight. Later you are shown a biological motion display of various arm movements and are asked to identify the unusual ones you practiced while blindfolded. The better you learned the moves, the better you are at this biological motion test. When you learn a new motor skill, you see the world differently. You understand actions differently.

Thus athletes who make fast movements, as in martial arts or fencing, might come to experience time and space differently from those who play slower-moving sports like surfing or archery. Your body maps the world according to what you have learned how to do with your muscles, which affects how you see the world.

Do you like to watch dance performances? Your mirror neurons make dance appreciation possible. Again, your biological motion detectors, via mirror mapping, are charged up. As you watch dancers move, your mirror neurons make predictions of the trajectory and dynamics of those moves. Movements can be fast, slow, or intertwined, with no clear beginning or end. Limbs are temporarily occluded so that your brain has to interpolate where they are going. At any moment the movement might stop, expand, contract, or continue in another direction. When dance steps are predictable and unimaginative, the performance is boring. But if the movements violate your predictions and keep you guessing, you feel exhilarated.

"Dance is a spatial extension of the body that reaches out and touches other bodies, just as a voice is an aural extension," says choreographer Ivar Hagendoorn. Watching dance, you have the feeling of movement without actually moving yourself. Indeed, dance demands an agility of perception equal to the agility of the dancer. It requires good mirror neurons. When you watch dance, your brain dances.

Do you like listening to news and feature reports on National Public Radio? Next time you tune in, pay attention to how the reporters capture your interest. When you hear feet crunching on gravel or a doorknob being turned, your auditory mirror neurons kick in and lead to motor and visual imagery of those same actions. A knock at the door produces the same brain response whether you see it, hear it, or do it yourself, which gives insight into why radio sound effects are so evocative.

Do you like art? When you see baroque sculptor Gian Lorenzo Bernini's hand of divinity grasping marble, you see the hand as if it were grasping flesh. Experiments show that when you read a novel, you memorize positions of objects from the narrator's point of view. And as you watch the movie *The Good, the Bad, and the Ugly*, mirror neurons that involve your hand movements start to fire whenever Clint Eastwood grabs a gun.

Parenting

In trying to understand human behavior, evolutionary psychologists suggest that all through the Stone Age, the human brain evolved modules for language and other uniquely human traits. Just as you have eyes for seeing and ears for hearing, the claim goes, you are born with a hardwired set of specialized brain modules for absorbing language, detecting cheaters of the social contract, calculating sexual attractiveness in others, and so on. In other words, the brain is the computational version of a Swiss Army knife.

Mirror neurons provide an alternative explanation for human brain design. Your brain is unique not because it has evolved highly specialized modules, but because it is parasitic with culture, says Ramachandran. Mirror neurons absorb culture the way a sponge sucks up water. "You can learn much more easily how to shoot an arrow or skin a bear by watching your mom and dad [do it] than by listening to them describe it," he says.

According to Ramachandran and others, mirror neurons are a major factor in the great leap forward in human evolution one to two hundred thousand years ago, answering the question "What made *Homo sapiens* so darned sapient?" Unique human abilities like protolanguage (in which sounds were mapped to lip and tongue movements), empathy, theory of mind (attributing thoughts and motives to other people), and the ability to adopt another person's point of view arguably arose at this time. Mirror neurons set the stage for the horizontal transmission of culture. As science writer Matt Ridley says, nature occurs via nurture.

Mirror neurons do not negate the fact that there are special areas for language in the human brain, Ramachandran says. But these regions do not have to be performed at the moment of birth to explain how they develop. An alternative theory holds that language areas are shaped by mirror neurons as a baby learns to speak by miming and understanding the lip and tongue movements of others. Think of a mother saying "mama" to her infant son. Mirror neurons are active when the baby sees and hears someone say "mama" and when he utters those twin syllables himself. They are the same neurons. The same brain structures that produce language participate in comprehending it. In other words, mirror neurons serve as a bridge for decoding and internalizing the meanings of other people's actions by processing them directly within the child's own body maps.

Language can often seem abstract and transcendent of the body, the world, and even time itself. But language is more closely tied to your body mandala than you may realize, especially where its acquisition during childhood is concerned. If you read the verb "lick," your tongue area will light up. If you hear someone say "kick," it activates your leg areas. Christian Keysers, a mirror neuron researcher at the University Medical Center Groningen in the Netherlands, says that mirror neurons may very well be a key precursor to abstract thought and language. For example, he explains, you use the word "break" as a verb as in "I see you break the peanut, I hear you break the peanut, and I break the peanut." The constant is the mental simulation of breaking even though the context varies in each case. So your body is the foundational source of meaning—not just of words and actions but even the meanings of things you learn about through your eyes, ears, and bodily experience.

Newborns do not talk, but their mirror neurons kick in within minutes of birth. If you stick out your tongue at a newborn infant, he may stick his tongue back out at you. Scientists take this to mean that newborns have an innate sense of a general body plan, but the only muscle they have much control over is the tongue (it is exercised in utero when the fetus sucks its thumb). Newborns cry more when they hear another newborn crying than when they hear white noise, their own cry, the cry of an older baby, or an adult faking a cry. Two-week-old infants sometimes imitate lip protrusion, mouth opening, tongue protrusion, and finger movement.

As the baby matures, his brain receives sensations of touch, proprioception, balance, and the like to build up a model of the world with itself at the center. By the time they are two, children learn quickly and primarily through imitation, which lets them absorb far more knowledge and skill than could ever possibly be explained to them verbally. They then spend years practicing what they have learned. When you realize that children have a system of neurons that is capable of learning by simply seeing, hearing, touching, then you begin to see that the world itself is the teacher, with you, as the parent, in a starring role. Your child's mirror neurons resonate with your words, intentions, and moods. How you react to adversity or happiness is absorbed by your children through their mirror neuron system as they watch you from moment to moment.

In fact, it has been shown that the imitation instinct in human children is so strong they tend to "overimitate." Imagine an experiment in which a scientist shows a simple puzzle box to a young child. She watches with interest as the researcher performs a series of simple steps that result in the box opening and a treat being revealed. Some of these steps are mechanically necessary to get the box open, but a few of them are blatantly inessential. He resets the box and hands it to her. As you might expect, it's monkey see, monkey do: She repeats his actions as faithfully as she can, including the "filler" steps.

Now imagine that the scientist performs the same experiment with a young chimpanzee who is at a roughly comparable stage of cognitive development. The ape wants the treat. He watches and learns how the box is opened. And when he gets hold of it, he opens it in as efficient a manner as possible, omitting the inessential steps. The human child has the same basic ability to analyze and understand the box as the ape child did, but her human mirror system is a much stronger force behind her actions. It may seem counterproductive for her to be such a slavish imitator, but this is only a temporary phase while her mind is immature. Her highly developed mirror system will serve her well as she gets older. She is the one who will go on to absorb the vast array of complex skills and understandings that human culture affords.

Interestingly, says Dr. Iriki, even though monkeys have mirror neurons, they don't actually imitate each other. This may come as a shock, because we tend to imagine monkeys as the quintessential copycat mischief-makers. This isn't to say monkeys are oblivious to each other. Far from it. They watch each other constantly. Newborns imitate lip smacking and tongue protrusion. Older monkeys take cues from each other, follow each other's examples, exploit each other's discoveries. If one monkey sees another lift the lid of a box and pull out a banana, she will quickly run over and take a peek inside the box herself.

You could argue that this qualifies as imitation, but that misses the point. True imitation is of the "aping" variety—mimicking specific gestures that can include arbitrary action sequences. Apes and humans can learn detailed action sequences, like opening a puzzle box to extract a goodie, based on just one viewing. Monkeys can be taught complex action sequences too, but it typically takes a period of patient training in a laboratory setting. In the wild, monkeys imitate each other only at the level of the basic primate repertoire of simple grips and gestures: poking, picking, lifting, pulling, and so on. But for apes and humans, these basic actions can serve as building blocks in long, complicated, and arbitrary action sequences.

Consider a young chimpanzee who watches while an elder snaps a twig off a bush, strips it of leaves and twiglets, pokes it into a termite mound, and comes up with a highly nutritious insect kabob. The young chimp runs off into the bushes to find his own twig and attempts to replicate the same feat. That's true imitation, and monkeys virtually never approach this level.

So if monkeys don't use their mirror neurons for imitative learning, what *do* they use them for? Remember, imitation is not the only function of mirror neurons. They still give monkeys insight into each other's goals and intentions based on action observation. Even if their mirror neurons aren't developed enough to generate precise imitation, in the soap opera world of primate society, action understanding and intention reading are essential abilities.

Shared Manifolds of Space

Many actions are ambiguous. Someone lifting a key may be about to open a door, hand it to another person, or stuff it in a pocket. Mirror neurons allow you not only to understand the action, but to apprehend the intentions behind it.

In an experiment conducted in 2005, Dr. Marco Iacoboni, a mirror neuron researcher at UCLA, scanned the brains of twenty-three people as they watched video clips of scenes before and after a mock tea party. The hand grasping the cup was the same. But the background in each scene was different—neat versus messy. Mirror neurons in the right premotor cortex registered a difference, Iacoboni says. Mirror cells that respond to hand movements were more active when the scene was neat, which implied that someone was about to drink tea. They were less active when the scene was messy, which implied that the tea party was over. These neurons are interested not only in the motion but also in the motivation behind it, he says. They predict intentions as well as define actions. They not only know what is happening—hand grasps cup—but why it is happening—hand grasps cup in order to drink.

Mirror neurons also create what are called "shared manifolds of space," similar to the "blended peripersonal space" mentioned earlier. Watch a fast pass in hockey, listen to a piano duet, or watch two people dance the tango. Mirror neurons help people coordinate joint actions swiftly and accurately, providing a kind of "we-centric" space for doing things together.

You engage in joint action all the time. You do it when you dress a child, shake hands with a client, or wash dishes with your spouse. If you are holding up one end of a couch and negotiating your way down a corridor, you adjust your actions to those of the person carrying the other end.

When you engage in any cooperative task, your body maps and mirror neurons help you anticipate the actions of the other person. Subconsciously you begin to mimic the other, synchronizing your movements, postures, and mannerisms. You are in shared peripersonal space with mirror neurons mapping the interaction. Did you ever see a movie with Ginger Rogers and Fred Astaire? She matches all his moves, only she does them backward and in high heels.

Think about an orchestra conductor and the gestural form of communication he has mastered. He raises an eyebrow and the cellos charge in. He crooks his index finger and the trumpets roar. He makes a tiny patting motion and the violins fall silent. Conductors transmit an enormous amount of musical information instantly, without words. Musicians follow each cue, locked by mutual gaze and transmissions of pacing, tempo, energy, and body-map synchrony.

But unless you are schizophrenic, you do not actually lose yourself in group embodiment. When you read a novel or play a video game, you may get engrossed in an imaginary world, but you don't confuse real with imaginary life. You don't confuse self and others. You do not hallucinate. When you perceive the actions and emotions of others, you use many of the same neural mechanisms as when you produce those same actions and emotions. This is the bridge between first-person and third-person agency.

Thus, when you perceive events that are the product of your own actions, like hearing or watching yourself play the piano, you recognize yourself via a close match in mirror neuron activity. You can identify the sound of your own hands clapping or the stance you take while throwing darts. To understand others you need to map yourself, your own body.

Persuasion

Mirror neurons are not without a dark side. Nearly all character-centered video games, violent or otherwise, engage mirror neurons with vigor. If violent video games do indeed make chronic players more aggressive, the mirror neuron system is surely one of the main channels for this effect. Noxious celebrities like gangsta rappers who extol murder, rape, and mayhem are engaging the mirror neurons of their fans, who want to emulate them.

Mirror neurons, which operate largely outside consciousness, also play a role in hidden persuasion; you may not be surprised that subliminal influence can be slipped into your mind through them. Marketers, charmers, and con artists intuitively know this. The trick is to subtly mimic someone's gestures and body language after a small delay. On average it will increase the social influence of the imitator on the imitatee. The imitatee is likely to pay better attention, consider the imitator's claims and positions more positively, and come away with a better liking for the imitator. It's a far cry from mind control, perhaps, but unlike many techniques that supposedly exert subliminal influence on people, this one really works.

Dr. Bailenson from Stanford University is also looking into this effect. In virtual reality simulations he can precisely measure and control the extent to which computer-controlled avatars mimic the head movements of volunteers in the simulator. Swayed by their mirror neurons, people are much more receptive to avatars that subliminally mimic them. This confirms the basic effect. With a setup like this, Bailenson explores the phenomenon in more detail than real-world experiments ever could.

How long can the avatar wait to mimic your body language and still have it influence you—half a second, two seconds, ten seconds? Are some aspects of body language more effective than others at beguiling an imitatee? How loose can the imitations get before the subject's mirror neuron system stops recognizing them as such? Bailenson hopes answers will shed light on, among other things, human gullibility and resistance to common social pressures.

Of course, not all covert influence is malicious. Psychologists and psychotherapists are beginning to exploit mirror neurons in their clinical practice. Therapists can now help clients realize how their beliefs and emotional states came into being and how their mirroring of the world is causing them grief or psychic pain. Clinicians can help people understand how they "know" things without conscious thought. Moreover, mirror neurons provide a neurobiological basis for transference and countertransference—how therapist and patient become deeply attuned to each other in the healing process. Indeed, therapists can use their own mirror system to understand the client's problems and generate empathy. They can help clients understand that many of their problems stem from what other people say and do.

I Feel Your Pain, I Feel Your Pleasure

In the 1962 film *Dr. No*, James Bond opens his eyes to find a tarantula in bed with him. As it creeps ever so slowly up his arm, you can just *feel* the hairy, spidery legs, because your mirror neurons are in overdrive.

You have mirror neurons for emotion reading and empathy in two areas folded deep inside your cortex, called the insula and the anterior cingulate cortex. When you see a look of disgust on someone's face, mirror neurons in your insula give rise to feelings of disgust in your own body. When you see joy, you feel joy. When you see sadness, you feel sadness. When you see pain, you feel pain. When you see someone's upper arm being jabbed with a needle, the same muscle in your arm tenses up and you start breathing faster.

Tania Singer, a neuroscientist at University College London, illustrated this phenomenon by recruiting lovers and putting one of them (the woman) into a brain scanner and then zapping each person with painful electric shocks. Each woman in the scanner registered a pain response in her anterior cingulate when she received a shock—and also when she witnessed her beloved being shocked. Women who scored higher on an empathy questionnaire showed greater activity in this brain region. This means that when you empathize with someone's pain, including a stranger's, at some level you actually feel it. Just as frontal and parietal mirror neurons represent both the observation and execution of actions, these emotional mirror neurons represent both the witnessing and the experience of certain feelings and emotions. (Women tend to have more active mirror neuron responses and to be more empathetic than men, although the reasons for this are not yet clear. It may be that high levels

AUTISM

Mirror neurons are currently a prime suspect in the hunt for the causes of autism. The cardinal features of autism, a congenital brain disorder, are lack of empathy, imitation, language skills, and an internal model of other people's mental states—in other words, the very functions that mirror neurons specialize in. Recently, V. S. Ramachandran confirmed that the mirror neuron systems of autistic children are feeble or absent. (They also have scrambled cortical body maps, a fact whose significance isn't yet understood but is likely related to the mirror neuron deficits in some way. They are also hypersensitive to touch.) Their mental aloneness, lack of play, poor eye contact, and disinterest in the animate world are all consistent with a mirror neuron system that is not properly engaged. When an autistic child tries to mimic a facial expression, he does not get the feeling and meaning of it. He does not connect what it feels like to be sad, angry, disgusted, or surprised with the minds of the people around him. He does not appear to feel the emotional significance of faces or bodies. He cannot learn by seeing and doing.

of testosterone limit empathy in some way. In general, women are stronger empathizers, while men are stronger systematizers.)

When someone yawns, you yawn, thanks to mirror activity. When you see someone scratch his chin, you may feel an itch on your own chin. When you see someone afraid, you feel a visceral flutter of fear. This sensation can initiate a fight-or-flight motor preparation in your own body. When danger lurks, fear spreads through the crowd. Everyone gets emotionally aroused and ready to run.

Being touched and seeing someone else touched activates the same neural circuits. For example, Dr. Keysers put people in a brain scanner and brushed their bare legs to see which of their body maps "lit up." As expected, they showed activity in primary touch areas, especially in the secondary touch map. Then he had them observe an actor being touched in the same spots. Again, the secondary touch map lit up. When he replaced the legs of the actors in a video clip with rolls of paper towel, the circuit lit up weakly. If the brush merely approached the actor's leg and did not make contact, the touch region was not activated. According to Keysers, touch has a privileged status in our social world, allowing us to confirm that other people are alive. Hence, "Let's keep in touch."

And pornography? An estimated nine million people, or about 15 percent of Internet users in the United States, visit one of the top adult websites each month. Think about it. Mirror neurons allow you to put yourself into somebody else's shoes. In fact, they automatically put you in those shoes; you can't turn off your mirror neuron system at will. This adds an extra kick to the titillation of pornography. You understand touch on others by virtue of your own experiences of being touched. When you witness touch, you simulate the same kind of touch in your mind's body.

If you watch sadistic pornography, you will not share any pleasure unless you are a sadist too. It will make you uncomfortable. One study of sadomasochists looking at sexually explicit S&M images revealed that their insulas lit up not from feelings of disgust but from pleasurable sensations in the body.

Also consider homophobia. Undoubtedly hatred or disgust toward gays arises from a number of factors, and mirror neurons may be one of them. When men and women see sexually aroused genitals of the preferred sex (opposite for heterosexuals, same for homosexuals), their mirror neurons and reward centers fire away. Mirror neurons play a key role in sexual response. Thus when a man sees two other men in sexual congress, he can't help but experience it, even if it's at a subconscious level, in his mind's body. In effect he feels the "unnatural" act is being forced upon him. Not being gay, he finds the prospect of sex with other men unappetizing. This may make a "live and let live" attitude just that much harder to adopt.

CHAPTER 10

HEART OF THE MANDALA

or, My Insula Made Me Do It

D o you consider yourself to be emotionally intelligent? Are you empathic, able to read other people's feelings even when they try to hide or swallow them? Or do friends rib you about your social cluelessness? Do people see you as spiritually grounded, emotionally balanced, a rock? Or do they say you're repressed, tactless, juvenile? If you weren't in good touch with your own emotional inner world, how would you ever know?

Several years ago, nine women and eight men came to Dr. Hugo Critchley's laboratory at the Institute for Cognitive Neuroscience at University College London to explore their level of emotional sensitivity. Critchley, an expert on brain mapping who is now at the University of Sussex, was interested in the relationship between emotional intelligence and a brain function called interoception—your ability to read and interpret sensations arising from within your own body.

Pretend you are a participant in such an experiment You lie down in a brain scanner, put on headphones, and place your left middle finger on a pad that monitors your heart rate. Your right hand rests on another pad with two buttons. As the scanner monitors your brain activity, you listen through the headphone to several series of ten beeps. After each ten-beep sequence there is a pause and you are asked to make a choice: Press one button if you think the beeps were in time with your own heartbeats, or press the other button if you think the beeps were slightly out of sync with your heart. Critchley repeats these sequences, sometimes in sync, sometimes not. Can you tell the difference?

Four of Critchley's subjects were supremely confident about when the pulse was synchronous or asynchronous with their hearts. They could feel the difference, accurately, every time. Two subjects were veritably heart-blind. They never had a clue about whether the pulses were in or out of sync, and could only guess at random. The others fell in between.

The brain scans revealed significant activity in several brain regions, notably the insula and anterior cingulate cortex. Both these regions are crucial centers of emotional cognition, and as this study makes clear, they are also necessary for attending to feelings that arise from your body.

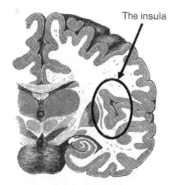

The insula

But the most significant finding in Critchley's study involved just one brain region, the right frontal insula. This area showed the greatest activity in those who were best at following their heartbeats. Moreover, these were the people who scored highest on a standardized questionnaire to probe their empathy levels. So the better you are at tracking your own heartbeats, Critchley says, the better you are at experiencing the full gamut of human

A cross-section through the middle of the brain reveals the insula.

emotions and feelings. The more viscerally aware, the more emotionally attuned you are.

In a follow-up study, Critchley found that people with greater empathy have more gray matter in their right frontal insulas. That is, the thicker this part of your insula, the better you are at reading feelings in yourself and in others. The fact that some people are more emotionally aware than others has a neural, physical basis.

These experiments are a window into some of your most important and fascinating body maps—those that deal in interoception and emotion. Most of this book has been about exteroception, or externally oriented perception. The main goal of exteroception is to create maps and models of your body, the world around your body, and your body's relationship to the world. You have read about the many ways your brain creates and maintains maps of your skin surface, limb position, joint movement, and musculoskeletal system so that you can move about and interact with objects

THE OTHER HALF OF THE NERVOUS SYSTEM

Your nervous system has two major divisions. One is the central nervous system—your brain and spinal cord. The other, called the peripheral nervous system, which suffuses the body, also has two major divisions. One is the somatic nervous system, which relays motor commands from your brain to your muscles and sends feedback information, including touch and proprioception, back up to your brain. The other division is the autonomic nervous system, which regulates your body in important ways. Its nerves connect your brain to your internal organs. One of its most important jobs is to maintain homeostasis, or balance of your body's basic functions and energy usage. It keeps your heart rate, body temperature, blood pressure, blood sugar levels, nutrient levels, water content, and other vital parameters within a healthy range.

The autonomic nervous system itself has two halves, called the sympathetic and parasympathetic nervous systems. (Whoever bestowed these names should be shot.) The sympathetic side is your "fight or flight" system. When you feel threatened, it kicks into high gear: Your heart beats faster, your breathing quickens, blood is diverted to your muscles and lungs, your mouth dries up, your pupils contract, your senses focus outward. Your body is prepared to expend every erg of energy it can muster to survive and prevail in battle.

The parasympathetic side is your "rest and digest" system. When you feel safe and at ease, your heart and breathing slow down, blood is diverted to your gut to absorb nutrients, you salivate freely, your bladder and sphincter muscles loosen up, and your mind can focus on internal needs like elimination, eating, drinking, socializing, and sex.

Some functions, like sweating, are under the control of both halves of your autonomic nervous system. Another exception is sex, which taps both

and people. You have distinct fibers in your spinal cord that carry such information in both directions: up from your body to your sensory maps, and back down from your motor maps to your muscles.

Interoception is a separate realm of somatic sensation that is oriented inward. It has two sources. The first is the internally mapped state of your body. Bring your attention to the sensations these maps are generating in you right at this moment. Think about your heart, lungs, stomach, intestines, rectum, larynx, throat. Try to feel their activity if you can. All your innards have receptors that send information up to your brain for mapping your "gut" feelings of hunger, thirst, air hunger, and other visceral sensations. In other words, just as your parietal and frontal lobes

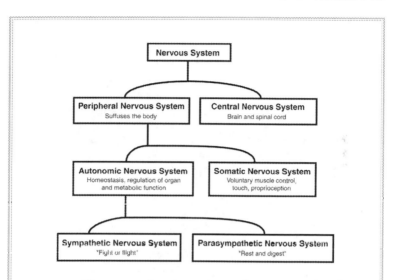

systems at different times. Sexual arousal is mainly a parasympathetic function: There's a reason romance often involves a nice full meal, a bit of wine, and a quiet, relaxing space. But during orgasm and ejaculation, the rhythmic contractions of the genital muscles require a jolt from the sympathetic nervous system.

When you're thrust into fight-or-flight mode, the surge of nervous energy coursing through your sympathetic system will sometimes spill into your parasympathetic system, inadvertently activating functions that have no value in a life-or-death struggle. It's why, for example, you may empty your bladder, bowels, or stomach in a moment of terror.

have a patchwork of sensorimotor homunculi, your insulas contain a quilt of visceral homunculi.

The second source of your interoceptive maps consists of a different class of receptors found on your body's surface, including your teeth, gums, and tongue. Unlike the touch receptors that deal in pressure and vibration and are tied mainly to deliberate touch and action, these other receptors carry information about the "homeostatic" condition of your body—temperature, pain, itch, muscle ache, sexual arousal, crude touch, and sensual touch. Homeostasis refers to your body's ability to maintain internal balance. Your spinal cord contains an evolutionarily older set of fibers that carries this information to and from your brain.

THE POWER OF TOUCH

Itch, tickle, pain, temperature . . . sensual touch? Sensual touch seems like the odd man out on this list of sensations. It seems that emotionally significant touch should simply be a form of light touch, which, as you'll recall, travels up the much newer tract in the spinal cord along with proprioception and high-resolution touch information. But sensual touch flows into the brain through the much more ancient spinal tract along with pain, itch, tickle, and temperature. What is sensual touch doing in that company?

Affectionate and playful touching is a key part of mammalian body awareness and brain development. Even mammals that grow up to lead solitary adult lives start out in close, affectionate contact with their mothers and siblings. Mammals are the animals that nurse, that lick and nuzzle one another as a way to reinforce bonds of intimacy and that engage in re-strained rough-and-tumble play to hone their body maps for whatever life throws at them. In short, early and frequent exposure to sensual touch is es-sential to normal, healthy brain development in mammals. The same was certainly true of our premammalian, postreptilian ancestors hundreds of mil-lions of years ago, back when we were evolving our close-knit family style of survival in the shadows of the dinosaurs. This feature goes back a long way in our line, and that is why it remains part of the older sensory tract, not the newer one.

Mother rats lick their young to calm them. Baby rats that do not receive fre-quent sensual touch in the form of such licking grow up to be more anxious and neurotic than those that do. And the cycle can be self-reinforcing: When these emotionally scarred rats grow up to become mothers they lick their pups less than normal, passing the emotional baggage down through the genera-tions. In a landmark study a few years ago, Michael Meaney, director of the Program for the Study of Behavior, Genes and Environment at McGill Univer-sity in Montreal, worked out the exact neural and genetic mechanisms behind this pattern.

Sensual touch is especially critical for primates and humans. It's not just that children deprived of physical affection often have emotional problems later in life—though that is very important. It goes even deeper, to the level of physi-cal growth, health, and homeostasis. Consider what sensual touch does for premature infants: Frequent, gentle massage causes them to gain weight up to 50 percent faster than if they receive minimal handling. It also makes their breathing and heartbeats healthier, and makes them more alert, less fussy, and better at sleeping. These benefits follow them all through infancy and toddler-hood.

Affectionate touch may not seem as if it belongs on a par with nutrition, lis-tening to music, and playing with toys, but it does.

This may seem strange at first, since many of your body parts end up being mapped by both systems. If someone pinches your arm, the pressure and pain will be represented in your primary touch map. But the pain will be re-represented in your insula. Why is pain from one pinch mapped in two places? Because your insular maps serve a different function from your primary touch and motor maps. They are the command center for homeostatic self-regulation. For example, to run your body's thermostat properly—to keep your body temperature constant—your brain needs to know not just your core temperature but also about air touching your skin. Pain in your muscles, lungs, and joints is important for marshaling your body's resources during exertion, but so are sensations of strain and movement and resistance in your joints and skin. So the primary brain maps for homeostatic signals from your body surface—about itch, sharp pain, dull pain, burning pain, tickle, sensual touch, heat, and cold—as well as the sensations arising from your body's interior, are mapped in your insula, not your primary touch cortex. You use these feelings less to deal with the outside world than to seek balance within your body and put your internal sensations in context.

And as Critchley's results imply, interoception does far more for you than just letting you know you are hungry or exhausted or sexually sated. It is also a crucial ingredient in some of the most important aspects of human beingness: sentiment, sentience, and emotional awareness.

The Sting of a Bee and the Sting of Rebuke

Like the mirror neuron system, your interoceptive maps are a souped-up version of neural circuitry that had already become highly advanced in the primate line.

In lower vertebrates—a frog, say—sensory information is integrated in the primitive base of the brain. These animals do not have a cortex, the mantle of higher thought and awareness. So a frog's vision is extremely primitive and robotic in function. It is keyed to buglike motions made by small dark dotlike objects. When the frog "sees" such a stimulus, a targeted tongue attack reflex is triggered. This is just about the only way the frog has to visually identify its food. When a frog is placed in a terrarium and surrounded by dead insects suspended on strings, it will starve to death. Its cortex-free vision just doesn't have the power to recognize individual features of its prey, like legs or wings.

The greatest evolutionary innovation of mammals was to expand the cortex to tremendous size. The cortex imbues the mammalian mind with the capacity to form highly detailed and versatile representations of sights, sounds, and actions. So a rat, for example, has a rich understanding of the space around its head, thanks to its sensitive whiskers and well-developed body and whisker maps. And even though rats don't have particularly good vision, they can still tell an insect from a wad of used dental floss at a glance, because they have cortical vision maps.

But in the rat—and for that matter, in all other mammals aside from primates—the homeostatic information from the body does *not* form a rich interoceptive map in the insula. Rats do have insular maps, to be sure, but they are rudimentary. In a rat, pain, itch, sensual touch, and that whole ancient group of somatic senses are primarily integrated in the base of the brain and in subcortical emotional centers. Their interoception, then, is more reminiscent of the frog's automaton-like vision than the primate's keen, knowing eye.

The same goes for cats, dogs, horses, and other four-legged animals. Because of this difference in mapping, some experts claim that their sensory experiences must be profoundly different from ours, even though we are often tempted to attribute human emotions and intentions to our pets. While a dog may show "shame" through its body language, it does not feel what you feel when you are ashamed. Dogs are clearly emotional and self-aware, but they are not in the same league with you.

In primates, interoceptive information is elaborated through a rich set of mappings in the insular cortex. And in humans it is richer still. Thus you have a little insula map for sharp pain, another for burning pain, one for itch, one for aching, one for overexerted muscles, and so on, along with visceral homunculi that represent the state of your lungs, heart, and the rest of your innards.

And even that is just the beginning of what your brain does with this information. After reading off the internal state of the body from both the left and right insulas, the human brain—and only the human brain—performs yet another level of integration. The information from both your insulas is routed to the right frontal insula, the same region Critchley found corresponding closely in size and metabolic vigor to a person's empathic talent.

INTUITION CELLS, AKA VON ECONOMO NEURONS

In all the talk about what makes humans special, you'll hear many of the same arguments. We walk upright. We have opposable thumbs. Our brains are enormous. We have language. We're top predators.

But there is one feature peculiar to humans that you've probably never heard about. You have, tucked into your anterior cingulate cortex and frontal insulas and especially in your right front insula, a special class of cell found in no other species except our cousins in consciousness, the great apes, elephants, and whales. Called Von Economo cells after the scientist who first observed them in 1925, they are big, fat, highly connected neurons that appear to be in the catbird seat for enabling you to make fast, intuitive judgments.

Intuition is your capacity for quick and ready insight. Often you know and understand things instantly, without rational thought or inference. You feel when something's fishy. You sense it when you have an instant personal bond with a stranger. You are positive that the charismatic politician on television last night is lying through his teeth.

You can make snap judgments because your brain contains Von Economo neurons, but to keep things simple, let's call them intuition cells. A very small number of intuition cells showed up in your brain a few weeks before you were born. Studies suggest that you probably had about 28,000 such cells at birth and 184,000 by the time you were four years old. By the time you reached adulthood, you had 193,000 intuition cells. An adult ape typically has 7,000.

Intuition cells are more numerous in your right brain. Your right frontal insula has 30 percent more than your left insula. Intuition cells are especially large and seem designed to relay information rapidly to other parts of the brain. They contain receptors for brain chemicals involved in social bonds, the expectation of reward under conditions of uncertainty, and for detecting danger—all ingredients of intuition. When you think your luck is about to change playing blackjack, these cells are active.

John Allman, a neuroscientist at the California Institute of Technology in Pasadena and a leading expert on comparative brain development, says that when you meet someone, you create a mental model of how that person thinks and feels. You have initial, quick intuitions about the person—calling on stereotypes, memories, and subliminal perceptions—which are followed seconds, hours, or years later by slower, more reasoned judgments.

When you make fast decisions, Allman says, your frontal insula and anterior cingulate are active. When you experience pain, guilt, or embarrassment or engage in deception, these areas are active. When you think something is funny, these same cells fire up, probably to recalibrate your intuitive judgments in changing situations. Humor serves to resolve uncertainty, relieve tension, engender trust, and promote social bonds.

All your social emotions and moral intuitions are processed in this circuit, Allman says. Oddly, they are related to food. Recall that your insulas map your visceral sensations, including gustatory experience. You feel the need to eat or eliminate, rest or run, save energy or expend energy, in this body mapping system. Recall, too, that your right frontal insula re-represents these basic bodily functions as social emotions, which are similarly expressed as polar opposites: love-hate, lust-disgust, gratitude-resentment, self-confidence–embarrassment, trust-distrust, empathy-contempt, approval-disdain, pride-humiliation, truthfulness-deceit, atonement-guilt. These emotions cause you to approach or retreat, favor social bonds or disrupt social bonds.

Allman thinks that intuition cells, like mirror neurons, may be defective in autism spectrum disorders, which feature an inability to think and interact intuitively. These cells arose late in evolution, he says, and have not had much time to become integrated with other cell populations. This may make them vulnerable to dysfunction in a manner analogous to our propensity to suffer lower back, hip, and knee disorders from adopting our bipedal posture.

Your right frontal insula "lights up" when you feel all the quintessential human emotions—love, hate, lust, disgust, gratitude, resentment, self-confidence, embarrassment, trust, distrust, empathy, contempt, approval, disdain, pride, humiliation, truthfulness, deceit, atonement, guilt. It also "lights up" when you feel strong sensations, from physical pain to a fluttery stomach to tingling loins.

If your right insula is damaged by a stroke, you will not be able to detect or feel disgust. If you look at someone who takes a bite of food, spits it out, and makes a retching sound with a disgusted look on his face, you will just smile, take a bite of the same food, and declare it delicious.

This dual physical-emotional sensitivity is not just a coincidence. The right frontal insula is where conscious physical sensation and conscious emotional awareness coemerge. Consider this amazing fact: The right frontal insula is active both when you experience literal physical pain and when you experience the psychic "pain" of rejection or the social exclusion of being shunned. It lights up when you feel someone is treating you unfairly. Scanning experiments have proven all this, and the results are profound. Welcome to one of the most important regions in the human brain.

Reason Runs Hot

Arthur "Bud" Craig is a neuroanatomist at the Barrow Neurological Institute in Phoenix, Arizona, and the first person to figure out how interoception is uniquely wired in the human brain. He is the kind of super-intense scientist who unapologetically spouts rapid-fire jargon—ventrolateral prefrontal cortex, solitary tract nucleus, posterior ventral medial nucleus. But for those who listen and translate, Craig is telling a story that drastically revises our scientific understanding of how bodily sensations are mapped in the human brain and turned into feelings, motivations, pain, and sentience.

The right frontal insula is the focal point of all this, according to Craig, because it literally connects the state of your body to the state of your brain. By "your brain," in this context, he means the sensory perceptions, abstract thoughts, linguistic processing, and motivations that occur elsewhere throughout your cortex. Your right frontal insula gives rise to the map of "the emotional me" and "the emotional now" by integrating homeostatic information from both your body and your brain. This is a profoundly important insight. You detect the state of your body and the state of your mind together in the right frontal insula. It is here that mind and body unite. It is the foundation for emotional intelligence.

If your mirror neurons are activated by another person's emotional state, your right frontal insula lights up. If you sense fear in a crowd, crave drugs, or see someone cheat, your right frontal insula lights up. If you are a schizophrenic, your right frontal insula is deformed.

Your right frontal insula integrates your mind and body through strong connections with three other brain regions. One is the amygdala, a lower brain area that plays a key role in linking strong emotions to experiences, people, and things. Another is the orbitofrontal cortex, a region that is critical for self-discipline and for setting plans and priorities in relation to rewards and punishments. And finally it is linked to the anterior cingulate cortex, which allows you to monitor your behavior for mistakes, correct and avoid errors, evaluate context, and plan and carry out actions that have emotional and motivational significance. The anterior cingulate also contains a mapping of your body, with your head at one end and your feet at the other, but so far as is known, the orbitofrontal cortex and amygdala do not.

In every brain imaging study ever done of every human emotion, the right frontal insula and anterior cingulate cortex light up together, Craig says. He takes this to mean that in humans, emotions, feelings, motivations, ideas, and intentions are combined to a unique degree, and that this is a key element of our humanity.

Actually, the idea that we sense our emotions from our bodies has been around for more than a century. Two psychologists, William James and Carl Georg Lange, long ago developed a theory that emotion arises when you perceive changes in your body. When you run from a bear in the woods, you are afraid not because of your rational assessment that you are about to be eaten, but because your heart is racing, your stomach and sphincter are clenched, and you are running as fast as you can. In the wake of an argument, as long as your heart is still racing you still feel angry. There is an aspect of this with bearing on many relationships: In women, according to the Stanford neuroscientist Dr. Robert Sapolsky, the autonomic nervous system ramps down more slowly than in men. As Sapolsky likes to say to his wife after a spat, "Honey, don't forget the half-life of the autonomic nervous system!"

This theory explains why people with whole-body paralysis often complain that their passions and emotions have become blunted. It is why psychopaths, who often have trouble feeling sensations from their body, feel no guilt, remorse, or anxiety about their actions. It is also why taking a beta blocker—a drug that quiets your sympathetic nervous system—can banish the butterflies from your stomach, still your quivering limbs, turn off your drenching stage-fright sweats, and allow you to speak or perform calmly in public. In other words, the fear is more in your body than in your mind. Dampen your interoceptive signals, and you dampen the fear.

Antonio Damasio, a neuroscientist who heads the Brain and Creativity Institute at the University of Southern California at Los Angeles, has updated and revised James and Lange's idea with his somatic marker hypothesis—the notion that your feelings strongly contribute to even the most "rational" decision making in everyday life. Scientists used to assume that reason and emotion were qualitatively different psychic spheres. Clearly these spheres could influence each other, but most believed that the thinking, knowing, reasoning part of the mind was in some fundamental way distinct from the mind's feeling, sensing, emotional, and more primitive aspects. But James and Lange, and now Damasio, Craig, and others who follow the neuroscience, argue that it's just not possible to separate them at a deep level.

Emotion is never truly divorced from decision making, even when it is channeled aside by an effort of will. Even a mathematician pursuing the trail of a new proof is driven by a blend of personal ambition, curiosity, and the sometimes spine-tingling Platonic beauty of the math itself. Even a judge who renders a verdict that the law supports but he finds personally distasteful is being driven by a moral emotion about the principle of the rule of law. Even a terrorist coolly gearing up for a suicide attack on innocents is spurred by an intensely felt motivation inspired by his love of God and God's favored people, who also happen to be his own.

Interoception, then, is the font of your complex emotionality. It breathes life into your cortex, which is otherwise rather machinelike in character. Interoception is the fire under the kettle of consciousness; remove the heat, and the system settles into tepid equilibrium.

The Problem of Pain

In May 2001, Michael G. DeGroote was sitting in his basement, watching television, when he felt something unusual in his leg. The retired Canadian billionaire and philanthropist, then sixty-five years old, stood up and tried to walk. But after he toppled over, DeGroote dragged himself to a phone, called an ambulance, and was admitted to a hospital, where he was informed he had suffered a stroke. It turned out that the blood clot to blame lodged not in his cortex, where most strokes occur, but in his thalamus.

The thalamus consists of two bulb-shaped masses of brain matter, each about the length of your thumb, tucked under your two brain hemispheres. Long considered a mere "relay station" between the primitive brain and the more recently evolved cortex, the thalamus turns out to be more like a movie director deciding who gets to say what, when. By setting up recursive loops between itself and nearly all parts of the higher brain, your thalamus plays a major role in regulating your arousal, awareness, and mental activity. If your entire thalamus is knocked out, as can happen after a drowning accident, you will never regain consciousness. But if one small part of your thalamus is injured, as in DeGroote's case, your symptoms will vary greatly depending on the site.

For a couple of days after his stroke, DeGroote's left arm was paralyzed and he had trouble walking, but those problems quickly resolved. DeGroote felt that he had dodged a bullet—until the pain crashed in on him four or five months later.

"My whole left side is affected," DeGroote says. "It's worst in my foot, then hand, knee, torso, and shoulder. It's a burning, icy pain. A stabbing pain. It gets worse every month. I can barely walk anymore."

Other people describe such pain as "like being wrapped in aluminum foil, broiled for a bit, then the foil is attached to electrodes where low voltage is constantly being fed to create a feeling of being wrapped up in electricity, buzzing like a computer that never gets turned off." Another victim writes, "Visualize a sadist with an electric carver, connected to the mains, slashing away, twisting and turning the infernal thing, grinning with delight as I squirm away."

DeGroote, who made his fortune in the solid waste and school bus industries, has what is called post-stroke thalamic pain or central pain.

Central pain is a nightmarish condition. It can afflict large swaths of the body or isolated body parts. There is no external cause, no wound to salve, no tissue damage to heal, no injury to the skin or body. Central pain stems from direct damage to the central nervous system. Stroke is one way, but multiple sclerosis, tumors, brain disorders, spinal cord injury, and head trauma can also bring it on. The pain can be moderate to excruciating, and its severity can wax and wane, but the most constant factor is an icy burning sensation like frostbite.

Half of those who suffer central pain after a stroke have damage to their thalamus, like DeGroote. If they have damage to the right thalamus, they experience a loss of temperature sensation on the left side of their body along with intense burning pain, and vice versa. The cold sensory pathway is wiped out, and the right frontal insula is on fire. Central pain responds only weakly to opiates, antidepressants, and other drugs. Stimulators implanted into the motor cortex can help, but as DeGroote, who has had two such operations, can attest, the pain is never completely gone.

Pain is one of life's greatest mysteries and is among the most powerful motivators of human behavior. Avoiding it, treating it, explaining it, and inflicting it have been central concerns of just about every system of folk medicine, magic, justice, religion, and theology that people have practiced. A few centuries ago, science joined the inquiry, with mixed success. Chemists, and later pharmacologists, gave us an array of pain treatment drugs that revolutionized medicine and surgery. Geneticists have found genes that confer susceptibility to pain. And neurosurgeons in turn have come up with some ingenious ways of alleviating pain under certain conditions. Yet the core explanation for pain has remained elusive. The good news is that this may not stay true much longer.

In the past, neurologists expected the explanation for pain to fall along much the same lines as those for touch and proprioception. Just as your brain contains complete maps of your body's touch receptors and proprioceptors, so too, they reasoned, there should be at least one map of your body's pain receptors. They knew it must be mapped somewhere. (The insula is so deeply tucked away and difficult to study that researchers did not bother to look at it until very recently. The few times Penfield probed it, people said they felt nauseated or sick.) If pain weren't mapped, you wouldn't be able to tell sharp, stabbing pain in your left elbow from hot, shooting pain in your right Achilles tendon. So when you cut your finger, burn your hand, smash your toe, or sprain an ankle, the appropriate subpopulation of pain receptors in the afflicted area must send signals up to the primary map somewhere in the vicinity of the other primary body maps. Pain, in this view, is a variety of touch, of exteroception. It can be localized, scaled, and timed. Yet by focusing on conventional aspects of touch, neuroscientists who went looking for a pain homunculus (and for a temperature homunculus too) always came up empty-handed. Your somatosensory regions do not contain a distinct topographical map of your body's pain receptors. If large portions of your touch maps are wiped out by, say, a massive stroke, you will still be able to feel pain and temperature.

This isn't to say that researchers couldn't see pain having certain effects on the activity of various body maps. Chronic pain can even alter their structure. For example, the common repetitive stress injury called carpal tunnel syndrome leaves a mark on your cortical hand maps. Carpal tunnel syndrome is often caused when repetitive hand motions such as typing lead to a shearing injury in the tissue that lines the tendons in the wrist or forearm. Different people experience it differently. Some feel agonizing pain, some feel pins and needles, others feel a disturbing numbness. For some these sensations are vividly localized in particular joints, while others describe them as just generally afflicting the fingers or hands as a whole. It turns out that each of these symptomologies corresponds to a different kind of change in the hand maps, which can be either expanded, shrunken, or blurred.

Craig, a meticulous anatomist and mapper of all the body's sensory fibers, has shed new light on the enduring mysteries about pain. Conceptually, he says, pain, temperature, sensual touch, and the rest of the ancient somatic senses belong not with exteroceptive touch but with the emotions. Thus pain is a homeostatic emotion like hunger and thirst and the other biological urges that the primate insula represents in vivid high resolution. Pain is primarily processed by the same circuitry that balances your visceral sensations and gives rise to the emotions on which they are based. From there the pain signals percolate through the rest of the body mandala and make their unpleasant effects known far and wide throughout the mind.

The Mind-Body Connection

Have you ever been out in the cold so long that your feet or hands turn numb? If you then plunge them into cold water, they will feel as if they're on fire. The water seems boiling hot. But what if it is 120 degrees in the Arizona sun? Water at the same temperature now feels extremely cool and soothing on your skin. Thus how you evaluate a signal from your body depends on your homeostatic state.

This suggests a new way to look at pain—as an opinion on the state of your body. Of all the somatic senses, pain is the most subjective, the most constructed, the most variable. This is not to minimize its importance, or to say that people in chronic pain just aren't thinking about their pain in the right way. But pain is interpreted with the help of memories, emotions, and beliefs. To some degree, your response to the homeostatic imbalance called pain depends on your attitudes. The anterior cingulate cortex seems to be especially important in interpreting the intensity of pain downward or upward based on context, belief, and expectation.

This is why hypnosis, placebos, and distraction work to deflect or reduce pain. It is also why people's pain thresholds are so context-dependent. When a person wants a tattoo, for example, she can endure intense and prolonged pain that would send her through the roof if inflicted unwillingly. Pain can even become something desired—can even become an addiction, as the practice of "cutting" illustrates. (One hypothesis to explain the surprisingly widespread appeal of ritual self-injury with knives or razors is that the physical pain feels like relief relative to the unbearable weight of psychic, social pain—which is also experienced through the pain maps of the insula and anterior cingulate. This would be analogous to the way a cold bath that would ordinarily make your teeth chatter feels refreshingly warm after a swim in an icy lake.)

Pain, says Craig, is an emotion plus a motivation. It's a homeostatic experience from your body like thirst, itch, or nausea, not an exteroceptive experience like raking your hands through sand or feeling the heft and balance of a hammer. Pain is inherently unpleasant, warning you that your body is threatened. Your normal internal homeostatic mechanisms cannot by themselves bring you back into balance. The rest of your body mandala is mobilized. Your attention is focused on attaining relief or getting help.

Viewing pain as a loss of homeostasis may solve one of the great medical mysteries of our age. Thanks to the seventeenth-century French philosopher René Descartes, Western medicine has viewed your body—the red meat of you—as entirely separate from your mind—the ethereal soul of you. He concluded, somewhat arbitrarily, that the point of brain-soul interface was the pineal gland, a small bulb of neural tissue that dangles from the brain's center. But the mind is not a metaphysical dangler on the brain; it is embodied.

There are many ways your body can lose homeostatic balance. The normal way, the way "nature intended," is through deprivation or physical insult. Not enough water? Not enough salt? Running low on nutrients? Ate something rotten? Too hot? Stepped on a thorn? Your body will let you know, and strong emotions coupled to motivations will mobilize you to take corrective action and restore balance. In most circumstances there are fairly simple corrective actions you can take. Take a drink of water. Eat some of the required nutrient. Sit down and take a breather. Keep off the injured foot for a while.

But other losses of homeostasis can be much harder or nearly impossible to remedy. Anxiety, depression, and other mood disorders have a definite visceral component and may relate to loss of homeostatic control. For example, anxious people are especially sensitive to their visceral

THE POWER OF BELIEF

Your mind and your body are in a constant two-way conversation. Your body talks directly to your brain, and your brain maps those signals, interprets them, and in turn controls and modulates the body. Exteroception is the half of this conversation that dominates our awareness, but the interoceptive half is every bit as vital to our being. Interoception, and the brain maps it feeds into, keep mind and body in tune. When you are healthy, your mind and body are in equilibrium. You feel good. When your mind and body are thrown out of balance by injury or disease, you feel bad.

Sometimes you feel sick because you caught a virus or bacterial infection. Maybe you broke a limb or sprained your ankle. Perhaps you developed a chronic disease with clear causes. This is where modern medicine can help, with its focus on understanding and treating the biology of disease and injury.

But other times you may feel sick and there is no explanation as to why. You visit doctor after doctor but no one can find anything wrong with you. Eventually you seek alternative or complementary treatments—healing touch, yoga, acupuncture, hypnosis, reflexology, or dozens of other practices—and mercifully, gratefully, it makes you feel better.

The reason these diverse techniques so often work has much to do with the power of belief. A belief is a state or habit of mind in which you place trust or confidence in some person or thing. A belief is also the human drive to look for causal explanations in everything you do.

Alternative and complementary medical treatments work extremely well in many cases because they relax you and because you believe in them. Remember, pain is an opinion on the state of the body, not an objective perception. Your beliefs, held in your mind, exert powerful effects on your body. Your beliefs can make you well. And they can make you sick. Beliefs can even kill. In the Caribbean, many people believe in voodoo. When a witch doctor puts them under a curse, in extreme cases they sicken and die.

A lesser degree of this same basic process shows up in hypochondria and somatoform disorders—cases in which people have inexplicable symptoms of ill health such as muscle aches, back pain, nausea, bloating, dizziness, fatigue, or pain in the abdomen, stomach, chest, joints, and so on. People show great variability in how they interpret signals from the body. A small discomfort can be ignored by one person but gets magnified in the mind of another. It drives physicians crazy. A quarter to a half of their patients cannot be helped by conventional medicine. Their suffering is real but much of it is psychically self-inflicted, and the medical profession has no answer to it.

All your body parts send sensory signals to the brain. Most of these signals contribute to unconscious processes like proprioception or routine homeostasis and do not rise to the level of consciousness. But sometimes, in some people, the nervous system's filters for these sensations don't work as well as they're supposed to. When this happens you can interpret these sensations as meaningless or as having pathological significance. You can ignore them, or amplify them into chronic pain.

In some people, researchers have found that immune cells called cytokines—the kind that make you feel sick—can be activated without a pathogen present. Recent research is starting to show that the central nervous system has a lot more active interaction with the immune system than previously thought. Emotions and beliefs, not just bona fide disease, can trigger the sickness response.

Brain imaging studies reveal that these misinterpreted sensations are not imaginary. Parts of the brain that map the state of the body show real changes in activation to unfiltered information. Pain can alter the body schema. A hypochondriac's body maps can be abnormal.

So-called hysterical conversion disorder is even more dramatic. This is where an emotional conflict or stress mimics neurological disease. People become paralyzed, blind, deaf, mute, or have seizures, with no typical injury to the brain. Their nerves and muscles are healthy, yet they show convincing symptoms of a stroke. When researchers imaged the brain of such a woman who was paralyzed on her left side, and asked her to move her left leg, they saw that her motor cortex did not activate. Instead, her right orbitofrontal cortex and right anterior cingulate cortex lit up. Her emotions had paralyzed her body. One to three percent of hospital patients have some sort of conversion disorder.

The ancient Greeks wrote that such patients (all female, of course) had a displaced uterus (*hystera*, the same word root as in "hysterectomy"); hence the term "hysterical conversion." Sigmund Freud pinned conversion to sexual abuse and childhood trauma. But scientists today trace it to genuine changes in how the brain maps the body. For example, the brains of people with hysterical paralysis show underactivity in two brain regions involved in movement. When their symptoms improved naturally over time, the affected regions returned to normal.

Beliefs can also make you well. When a person in a white coat with a stethoscope hanging on his chest hands you a blue pill and tells you that it will calm you down, chances are it will, even though the pill is made of an inert substance. Placebos, as such sham medications are known, are potent medicine. When people suffering from painful knee arthritis underwent sham surgery—meaning the surgeon only pretended to scrape the inside of the knee—a surprising number of them felt better anyway. When Parkinson's patients thought they had received brain implants designed to alleviate their symptoms, but instead got a surgical incision but no treatment, they improved nonetheless. Placebo painkillers, especially sham acupuncture, are notoriously effective in treating disorders of mind and body. (The reason "fake" acupuncture works so well, researchers say, may be that patients have to see a practitioner at least twice a week for their treatments. This raises the question of whether attention from a practitioner is itself a placebo.)

When you expect a medical treatment to work, your body releases painkilling substances and your mind starts to interpret your symptoms differently. The specific contents of your beliefs don't seem to matter much. Whether you believe your witch doctor can drive evil spirits out of you with sorcerous powers, or that your faith healer can open you up to miraculous curative energy sent by God, or that your doctor is offering you the benefits of a new and amazingly effective cutting-edge medical breakthrough, the belief dividend for you is the same. It really doesn't matter what these beliefs purport to be true. Energy fields, astral planar travel, prayer, guided imagery, relaxation techniques—they can all work, if you put your faith in them.

sensations. Amplified awareness of autonomic to ordinary people, places, and things may be what leads them to misinterpret life as being dangerous. When anxious people anticipate something bad about to happen—such as being confronted with creepy pictures of snakes or spiders—their right frontal insulas go into overdrive.

Likewise, in depression, flattened and negative emotions are often associated with bodily depression. People who are extremely depressed also report a blunting of the will to act. They may know what they want or need to do, but they feel "paralyzed" or as if they are sleepwalking through their days.

Chronic stress is a major villain in this play, Craig says. By producing an overabundance of sympathetic activation, stress throws homeostasis out of whack. The result: chronic fatigue, fibromyalgia, back pain, exhaustion, burnout, a foggy brain, insomnia, and the like. Again, in imaging studies of all these conditions, the right frontal insula lights up. People with a painful disorder, irritable bowel syndrome, show underactivation of the right frontal insula in tests of rectal distention.

Could an effort to restore homeostasis treat these symptoms and relieve pain? What if chronic fatigue were caused by something as simple as a salt imbalance? Or a mineral deficiency? Or chronic stress? The goal of any treatment should be to calm down the right frontal insula, Craig says. It is overactive, buzzing, out of control. So the question is, How can it be quieted? How can you turn down the fire inside your brain?

One idea, which has had some success in treating epilepsy, is the controversial vagal nerve stimulator. The vagus is a huge nerve that modulates the brain, heart, stomach, and other organs. The stimulator is essentially a pacemaker for the vagus nerve. The device is implanted under the left collarbone and delivers electrical pulses at a steady thirty cycles per second. It calms the right frontal insula.

Craig notes that many patients and doctors have been disappointed with vagal nerve stimulator therapy for other conditions, such as depression. He suspects a big problem is the stimulator's constant pulse rate; it's a bit like fixing a car's transmission but only restoring second gear. He says vagal stimulators should modulate their pulse rates in harmony with physiological cues from the body. They would deliver fewer, smaller pulses that are timed to activity from the heart and lungs. Until manufacturers improve the devices, he says, their ability to calm the highly sensitive insula cannot be fully realized.

Just about the worst loss of homeostasis is DeGroote's condition, central pain. Normally the insula detects innocuous temperature changes on and within the body. But if you have a lesion in your thalamus and it blocks activity to and from your insula, your ability to sense temperature goes haywire. Your anterior cingulate cortex releases a motivational distress signal of acute pain. This is when you meet the sadist with the electric carving knife. This is why your body burns and freezes in excruciating pain. This is why ice packs, which normally work for most kinds of pain, have no effect.

Since central pain originates in the brain, treatments must aim to correct the loss of homeostasis. One still-untested approach is the body-harmonized vagal nerve stimulator. Another is "gamma knife" surgery, in which twin lesions are made in the thalamus with a focused beam of radiation. This treatment, which is experimental, has been tried on only a few people so far, but with good success.

However, opening up the brain or even implanting small battery-powered devices inside the body are never desirable options. Less invasive means of calming the right frontal insula are neurofeedback and meditation. They have grown extremely popular because, unlike a lot of

THE THERMAL GRILL ILLUSION

Have you ever wondered why an ice pack relieves pain? Why should cold make the hurt go away? It works because a cold object activates fast fibers in your spinal cord while pain travels up to your brain on slow fibers. So when you press a cold pack against a sore muscle, your fast fibers beat out the slow ones. You feel cold, not pain.

But you can upset this system with the thermal grill illusion. All you need are three or more all-metal butter knives, two drinking glasses, and a friend to help. Fill one glass with ice water and the other with hot water (Not boiling! Just hot enough for a nice bath, say). Put half the knives in the cold water and the other half in the hot water, handles submerged. Wait a few minutes. Then have your friend pull the knives out by their blades and alternate them—warm handle, cold handle, warm handle, etc. If you use just three knives, which makes the illusion a little harder to achieve, make sure it's one cold handle between two warm ones. Close your eyes while your friend brings the lined-up knife handles to the inside of your wrist.

Yow! You will feel an intense icy burning sensation far beyond what the knives should be able to produce. For some people it can be quite painful, though rest assured it is harmless.

Here's how it works. Your skin has two types of temperature receptor: one for non-painful heat, one for non-painful cold. Your skin also has a kind of pain receptor that responds equally to extreme heat, intense cold, and hard pinching. These pain receptors are always "on"—always trying to send painful signals brainward. The reason you aren't in searing agony all the time is the receptors that register non-painful cold are also ever active. And again, because the cold signal travels faster than the pain signal and inhibits the pain signal when it arrives in the brain, the pain doesn't filter through to your awareness. When you touch the thermal grill, however, the alternating warm-cold-warm pattern throws the system out of balance: The warm receptors interfere with the nearby cool receptors, slowing their rate of firing. The cool signals don't arrive in time to block the pain, so icy burning pain is what you feel.

Central pain is related to the thermal grill illusion. Your insula contains temperature maps and pain maps of your body. But when the insula or the part of the thalamus that projects to it is damaged, the non-painful cold information can no longer enter your brain. You feel constant burning pain instead, and in this case you can't just take your wrist away from some butter knives to make it stop.

self-help advice, which leaves no trace in the brain aside from verbal memories, they have been proven to dramatically reshape brain activity and structure.

For example, Dr. Sean Mackey, an assistant professor of anesthesia and pain at Stanford University, puts chronic pain patients into a brain scanner and shows them a computer-animated flickering flame, which he tells them represents the level of their pain. And indeed it does: The flame's size and intensity directly reflect the level of activity in their anterior cingular cortex. While watching the flame, patients are instructed to lower it as far as possible. It is up to each person to find a way to do this. Many find that mental imagery helps. For example, one woman thought of snowflakes and little men marching on her back, scooping the pain away. Whenever activity in the anterior cingulate cortex diminishes, the flame dims. This new and potent form of neurofeedback allows most people to significantly quench their pain levels.

Brain-derived biofeedback also shows promise for boosting the emotional and empathic function of the right insula. In a pilot study at the University of Tübingen in Germany, Niels Birbaumer and Ranganatha Sitaram showed volunteers a biofeedback display linked to the activity in their right insulas. After some practice, they were able to dull their gut reactions to negative and disgusting imagery.

This result by itself could lead to treatments for post-traumatic stress disorder, chronic anxiety, depression, phobias, and many other conditions. But then Birbaumer and Sitaram took it further and brought in three convicted psychopaths, whose abnormally low levels of right insula activity is part and parcel of their cold-bloodedness. One of these psychopaths, though not the other two, was able to use the neurofeedback loop to nudge his insula activity upward. The result is entirely preliminary, but potentially far-reaching.

Meditation also exerts control over both pain and emotion. In one study, people who had practiced meditation for thirty years showed a 40 to 50 percent lower brain response to pain compared with healthy controls. Meditation is also a great antidote to heart disease for some people.

When you take six breaths a minute, rather than the usual ten to twelve, you can steer your autonomic nervous system back toward balance. The effects filter up from your body into your right frontal insula.

Active, cultivated awareness of your internal sensations can lead to amazing results. Experienced meditators like yogis and lamas actually gain conscious control over their heart rates, oxygen consumption, and other basic autonomic functions. They also say they feel extremely happy and emotionally stable. And just as a bodybuilder can point to his bulging muscles as proof that he hits the gym regularly, an experienced meditator shows structural brain changes reflecting his long hours of breathing and mindfulness. A recent study by Sara Lazar at Massachusetts General Hospital found that the right frontal insula and left prefrontal cortex (which is associated with feelings of joy and happiness) are larger and thicker in people who meditate regularly. Striving to tune up the body maps of your right insula may turn out to be one of the best investments in yourself you can make.

THE YOU-NESS OF YOU

I f your body sense is so morphable, how do you keep track of where your "true" self begins and ends? How do you recognize yourself as being separate from others? How do you arrive at the feeling of being sentient and psychically self-contained?

Think about it. Your mirror neurons provide a meta-mapping between your own actions and those of your fellow human beings, but in doing so, they seem to make you surrender some of your own identity. For a fleeting moment you are that guy in the movie getting kicked in the groin, which is why you are tempted to gasp and double over. And you are that starving African orphan on TV—but you can't bear it, so you flip the channel to mingle identities instead with the beautiful charismatic people in a sitcom. And in a not-too-remote corner of your body schema you are that rampaging first-person shooter in "Grand Theft Auto," enjoying the sweetness of forbidden transgressions.

And how easy it is for you to attribute sensations to the tip of a rake. Your mind doesn't have any trouble allowing sensations to emanate from rubber hands and umbilical tentacles. Your brain is perfectly willing to let your body maps be co-opted, stretched, erased, or dramatically repurposed in response to quite simple tricks involving buzzers, mirrors, and virtual reality displays.

But if your body sense is so labile, so willing to imitate and share in the identity of others, so easily seduced by tools and cyberspatial illusions, why doesn't the "you-ness" part of you ever simply get lost? What accounts for that kernel of selfhood that you feel at the center of your being, to which you always have reference and always return? Is there a locus of your core consciousness, a foundation for experiencing yourself as an independent being? What keeps your mind embodied in your particular body?

A new discipline that's been dubbed "the neuroscience of the self" is beginning to find answers to questions like these. In laboratories around the world, researchers are gaining glimpses of how each of us builds up the sense—or perhaps it's an illusion—that we are separate individuals with self-agency, self-awareness, and free will.

Start with a mirror. When you were about fifteen months old, you began to recognize your reflection as being your own. You'd stand on your plump, wobbly legs, gaze at your chubby cheeks, and know that it was you looking back, making those funny faces. Mirror self-recognition is a hallmark of socially advanced creatures. Only humans, the great apes, elephants, and possibly dolphins and whales have the ability to recognize themselves in mirrors. As you grow up, your face and body change drastically, but you still know it is you. When you get those first strands of gray hair and crow's-feet, it is still you looking back. So a first and obvious answer to how you know yourself is that you have been tracking your face and body in mirrors for as long as you can remember. While your features change over time, you are the same person inside. Your memory tells you so.

Another answer has to do with the barrage of sensory feedback that your brain receives from your body each day. Every time you see or move your hands, forearms, trunk, legs and feet, and other body parts, your brain maps know what is happening, thanks to your somatic senses—especially touch, balance, proprioception, and interoception.

Two areas in the back of your brain, in your parietal and temporal regions, specialize in multisensory body-related information. One is called the EBA, or extrastriate body area. It responds to images of human bodies and body parts. If you look at another person's foot, arm, hand, buttock, or any other body part (except the face, which has its own special area), your EBA lights up. It also lights up when you move your body and when you imagine moving your body. So here is one important clue to the nature of self-recognition: Your EBA tracks other people's bodies in addition to your own, but because your EBA is directly integrated into your own body mandala, it also has access to the sensory and motor activity of your body. By matching this data with its own body part perceptions, the EBA is an important element in your ability to keep track of which hands and arms are your own.

A second area, the TPJ, or temporal parietal junction, works closely with your EBA to maintain your sense of corporeal ownership. Remember Heidi? She is the Swiss woman who had an out-of-body experience when her doctors zapped her right angular gyrus with an electrode. It turns out that the right angular gyrus, which is a part of your TPJ, is an area that gives you the sense of being localized in your own body. Zap it and you may leave your body. So the TPJ and EBA, in ways that are just beginning to be explored, play a critical role in self-recognition, self-awareness, and knowing where your body is located in space.

At UCLA, Dr. Marco Iacoboni recently carried out an experiment to see what would happen to personal identity when he temporarily disabled the right angular gyrus of eight volunteers with a transcranial magnet. The magnet produces a "virtual lesion," which means it temporarily stuns and fatigues the targeted population of neurons.

Six women and two men came to Iacoboni's laboratory, where they were shown six morphed images of themselves and a close personal friend or colleague. A morphed image is a composite of two people blended to various degrees. If you were in the experiment, the six images would be 100 percent you; 80 percent you and 20 percent your friend; 60 percent you and 40 percent your friend; 40 percent you and 60 percent your friend; 20 percent you and 80 percent your friend; and 100 percent your friend. Each face was presented ten times in random order for one second. Subjects pressed one button if they thought the image looked more like them and a second button if the image looked more like the other person.

The task was easy, Iacoboni says. Most people have no trouble perceiving their own face when the composite is under 50 percent. When the composite is more than 50 percent, they know instantly it is their friend or colleague.

Then Iacoboni ran the magnet over the right hemisphere for twenty minutes. When the right angular gyrus was disturbed, he says, the people could no longer distinguish self from other. In a separate part of the study he found that knocking out the left angular gyrus produced no effects on self-recognition.

Your right hemisphere is the big kahuna when it comes to providing circuitry for telling yourself apart from others. But why this might be so, and precisely how it is carried out, is still high on the research agenda.

As for your mirror neurons and why you don't confuse yourself with others, scientists do have an answer. The rubber hand illusion explains how. Recall that in the illusion, your hand is hidden from view and stroked while you look at a rubber hand being stroked with the same rhythm. The rubber hand feels as if it belongs to your body. But if the rhythm is out of sync, or if the rubber hand is pointing in a different direction than your real one, you do not have that sensation. It's just a Halloween prop. Your sense of owning the rubber hand requires congruence of vision, touch, and proprioceptive stimulation.

In new work carried out in Britain, Germany, and Italy, researchers replaced the rubber hand with the real hand of an experimenter. Your hand is hidden and stroked while another person's nearby hand is stroked with the exact same rhythm. In this condition, you get the weird feeling that the other person's hand belongs to your body. But if the other person moves his fingers unpredictably, the illusion is broken. Or if your motor cortex is zapped by a magnet while you watch the other hand, the illusion is also broken. Brain imaging shows the difference between the two conditions: When you watch the hand and think it belongs to another person, your motor system is activated. But when you think the other person's hand belongs to you, your motor system is suppressed.

Other brain systems play a part in your self-awareness. One of these crucial circuits is centered on the right frontal insula, anterior cingulate cortex, and a few associated structures. As Dr. Bud Craig puts it, this is the circuit where "the emotional me" and "the material me" get united. Your degree of conscious awareness throughout each day is based on changes in your body awareness across time. A refined and integrated image of the state of your body provides the basis for your awareness of your physical self. Input from your body is the basis for your sentient self.

While all the brain regions just mentioned play an important role in producing your sense of self, the search for a nexus of you has a broader answer.

Yes, you are morphable. But you are also stable. And in the larger picture of your brain-body system, the flexibility is minor in comparison to the stability. Many of the circuits within your body mandala can be reorganized by neuroplasticity. Your body schema is willing to make some really permissive interpretations of novel patterns of sensory input in order to maintain a sense of coherent embodiment. Remember the lobster legs? The shrinking waist? Nevertheless, the core infrastructure of your brain and its body-mapping system is more or less fixed. Your brain was created by your genes starting when you were a fetus and it congealed into the macro-configuration it has today and will always have. You can grow new connections between brain maps, but you can't grow a whole new lobe. Learning and plasticity can make crucial and useful adjustments to the way information flows around the myriad circuits of your brain, often in useful and delightful ways, but at the end of the day, the flexibility is fairly minor compared with the stable long-term configuration bequeathed by your human and primate ancestors.

Illusion Redux

So, is the self ultimately "just" an illusion? Are we, in the words of the late Nobel laureate Francis Crick, "just a pack of neurons," or, to rephrase him, "just a pack of illusions"? According to the neuroscience of body maps—and, incidentally, the majority of Eastern religions—in many respects, yes.

But how to square that notion with common sense? Can the self really be an illusion? After all, you can pinch yourself, you can reach out and move objects, you can change people's minds, you can choose among entrées on the menu. You are a flesh-and-blood person with all your faculties. You are demonstrably an independent being unto yourself. And crucially, you clearly have the precious faculty of free will. The you-ness of you really, really doesn't feel like an illusion. But of course, that is how illusions are: They appear convincingly to be a certain way, but the underlying reality may be very different.

A key point is that your mind feels like a seamless whole when "all your faculties" are working. But if your body mandala were to go on the fritz in one of a hundred ways, whether through damage to one map or several, or through a severing of between-map connections, you might suddenly experience extra arms, a phantom leg, autotopagnosia (where you can point to your watch but can't find your wrist), hemineglect (where half the universe winks out of your awareness), alien hand syndrome, and all manner of delusions and misperceptions. Case studies of brain damage like these are one of the biggest philosophical, not to mention logical, arguments against the idea of a unitary psychic core. When certain parts of the brain break, certain parts of the mind break; the illusion is spoiled, and the underlying multifariousness of the psyche is exposed.

The illusion of the self isn't that there is no such thing as you. Nor does the illusion of free will mean that you cannot make choices. Instead, the illusion is that the self and free will are not really what they seem to be from your, the "end user's," perspective. The illusion of free will is that free will has infinite scope, rather than being a flexible set of feedback loops between higher-order body maps and emotional and memory-storage systems in the brain. The illusion of the self is that self is a kernel, rather than a distributed, emergent system.

Remember from chapter 2 how the philosopher's "homunculus fallacy" is to ask where your sense of self "resides" in your brain? This is the wrong way to ask the question. There is no central address in the brain, no point where all the information "comes together" to produce the feeling of undivided sentience you enjoy and take for granted. It's all distributed, among lots of sensory maps and motor maps and other brain areas. Localizations of psychic functions are better said to exist in loops of information processing, or circuits, rather than specific points. Some of these maps and circuits are just more important to you than others.

In much the way people used to wonder where the sun went while it was underground at night, many people continue to wonder where the core psychic self really is. But it apparently arises "merely" from the sum of brain activity distributed across dozens of maps and other brain regions. It is an orchestra without a conductor or a fixed score, but whose players are so good at collaborative improv that wonderful music keeps flowing out of it. Just as the orchestra has no score and no conductor, the mind has no kernel, no "little man" sitting at the center of the fray directing the action. But it is teeming with noncentral "little men," the brain's motley team of homunculi, who form the backbone of the whole production. And you, thankfully, have the irreducible illusion of being the conductor of your life's music in all its complexity, emotional nuance, crescendo and diminuendo—the ballad that is the you-ness of you.

ACKNOWLEDGMENTS

—but first, a note to our readers who are scientists or philosophers

To convey the excitement of your work to a general audience within the sweeping synthesis of this book, we have vastly oversimplified the science. Lost in translation is any mention of the basal ganglia, precuneus, superior colliculus, and a host of other brain regions that help us make sense of our world. Missing are references to Husserl, Merleau-Ponty, subjectivism, and qualia. Certain details and caveats that a specialist would consider vital have been condensed, glossed over, or shoehorned into metaphors. And finally, many researchers whose work contributed to this book have not been credited in the style becoming academic papers. We hope you understand that we hold the rigors of science and philosophy in the highest regard. Any misrepresentations or perceived slights are unintended.

And now we extend our heartfelt thanks to many of the people who made this book possible. First and foremost, we are grateful to our literary agent, Jim Levine, who worked with us every step of the way. We want to especially thank Caroline Sutton, our editor at Random House, her assistant, Christina Duffy, and production editor Beth Pearson for all their support and hard work. Many others assisted along the way, including: Charles Adler, John Allman, Jeremy Bailenson, Janet Bailey, Anna Berti, Megan Biesele, Edoardo Bisiach, Dennis Blakeslee, Olaf Blanke, Peter Brugger, Victor Candia, James Collins, Arthur "Bud" Craig, Hugo Critchley, Barbara Davis, Cornelia Dean, Michael DeGroote, Jeff Della Penna, Lindsay Edgecombe, John Flanagan, Ken Ford, Scott Frey, Martin Grunwald, Edward T. Hall, Peter Halligan, Riitta Hari, Joe Havlick, Nicholas

Holmes, David Howes, Marco Iacoboni, Atsushi Iriki, Margie Jacobson, Christian Keysers, Herbert Killackey, Günther Knoblich, Karen Kovach, Leah Krubitzer, James Lackner, Jaron Lanier, Peter Levine, Sara Lippincott, Mike Merzenich, John Milton, Edvard Moser, Aimee Mullins, Paolo Nichelli, Miguel Nicolelis, Richard Nisbett, Paula Palmer, Alvaro Pascual-Leone, Jessica Phillips-Silver, Seth Pollak, V. S. Ramachandran, Richard H. Ray, Giacomo Rizzolatti, Jeffrey Ross, Toni Sciarra, Lydia Segal, Stephanie Sogg, Jennifer Stevens, William Straub, Jamie Ward, Margaret Wertheim, Alison Winter, Allan Wu.

AFFORDANCES: properties of objects and features of the environment that a creature perceives directly in terms of its own ability to interact with them.

ALICE IN WONDERLAND SYNDROME: a disorder in which people experience a distorted sense of their hands or faces.

ALIEN HAND SYNDROME: a disorder in which a person's hand seems to have a mind of its own.

AMYGDALA: an ancient brain structure important for linking strong emotions to experiences and memories.

ANOREXIA NERVOSA: an eating disorder of self-starvation and distorted body image.

ANTERIOR CINGULATE CORTEX: a high-level body map involved in several crucial mental functions, including the ability to recognize, correct, and learn from mistakes; to plan and execute actions with respect to emotions and goals; and to modulate pain sensations based on context and expectation.

APRAXIA: a disorder characterized by the loss of the ability to carry out learned purposeful movements, despite having the desire and ability to perform the movements.

AUTISM: a developmental disability that affects social interaction, communication, and imaginative play.

AUTONOMIC NERVOUS SYSTEM: the part of the peripheral nervous system (qv) that regulates organ function, metabolism, and homeostasis.

AUTOSCOPY: an experience of disembodiment in which people see themselves as doubles.

AVATAR: the computer-animated representation of one's body in virtual reality.

BIOFEEDBACK: visual or auditory readouts that track a person's heart rate, brain wave activity, or other physiological variables, which the person can use to gain control over the autonomic nervous system (qv).

BODY DYSMORPHIC DISORDER: a belief that certain of one's body parts are grotesque.

BODY IMAGE: one's perception of and beliefs about one's own body's appearance.

BODY INTEGRITY IDENTITY DISORDER: a condition in which people desperately want to amputate perfectly healthy limbs.

BODY SCHEMA: one's perception of one's own body's felt position, movement, and capabilities.

CENTRAL NERVOUS SYSTEM: the brain and spinal cord (cf, *peripheral nervous system*).

CENTRAL PAIN (POST-STROKE THALAMIC PAIN): searing pain in the body that stems from direct damage to the central nervous system rather than to any of the body's tissues.

CEREBELLUM: an older part of the brain involved in motor coordination and cognition.

CEREBRAL CORTEX: the thin sheet of tissue in which most of your body maps are located; it is folded and crumpled around older brain structures.

DEPERSONALIZATION SYNDROME: a disorder involving distorted vestibular signals.

DYSTONIAS: body map disorders involving abnormal muscle movements.

EFFERENCE COPY: a sensorimotor prediction that is automatically created along with any action you take; it helps your body mandala keep track of which sensations and movements are self-generated and which are not.

EXTEROCEPTION: the ability to perceive the world outside the self through vision, hearing, smell, touch, and voluntary movement (cf, *interoception*).

EXTRAPERSONAL SPACE: the volume of space beyond peripersonal space (qv).

EXTRASTRIATE BODY AREA (EBA): a brain region that responds to images of human bodies and body parts.

FAUX PROPRIOCEPTION: a brain circuit that mimics motor actions in the imagination.

FINGER AGNOSIA: the inability to distinguish the fingers on your hand.

GRID CELLS: neurons related to place cells (qv) that map space in terms of an imaginary triangular lattice, without regard to landmarks or other features of the environment.

HEMISPATIAL NEGLECT: a disorder caused by damage to the parietal lobe in which one loses the ability to perceive the left half of space, the left half of his or her body, or both.

HIPPOCAMPUS: an ancient brain structure involved in many crucial functions, including memory storage and spatial navigation (cf, *grid cells* and *place cells*).

HOMEOSTASIS: internal balance of key life functions such as temperature stability, energy usage, and nutrient intake.

HOMEOSTATIC SELF-REGULATION: the body's ability to achieve and maintain homeostasis (qv).

INSULA: a map-rich brain area in which visceral and homeostatic (qv) information is processed; it plays key roles in emotional awareness, empathy, and physiological self-regulation.

INTEROCEPTION: the ability to read and interpret sensations arising from the viscera and internal tissues of the body (cf, *exteroception*).

MANDALA: a geometric pattern of images that maps out the universe from a human perspective; used in this book as a metaphor for one's integrated network of body maps.

MIRROR NEURONS: a special set of cells within certain high-level body maps that represent actions performed both by oneself and by others; hence, they are key to many higher mental functions, including imitation, empathy, and the ability to read one another's intentions.

NOCICEPTORS: nerve cells in your skin that carry information about different kinds of pain, tickle, and itch.

ORBITOFRONTAL CORTEX: a brain region critical for self-discipline and for setting plans and priorities in relation to rewards and punishments.

PARASYMPATHETIC NERVOUS SYSTEM: the "rest and digest" part of the autonomic nervous system (qv), which calms the body and the emotions and controls functions relating to energy conservation, eating, elimination, social activity, and sex.

PERIPERSONAL SPACE: the bubble of space around a person's body that his brain includes as part of him in its map of his body.

PERIPHERAL NERVOUS SYSTEM: the part of the nervous system that suffuses the body's organs, tissues, and skin.

PLACE CELLS: neurons related to grid cells (qv) that map space with reference to landmarks and other features of the environment.

PLASTICITY: the process by which brain structures change in response to learning and experience.

PREMOTOR CORTEX: a body map that helps plan one's actions.

PRIMARY MOTOR MAP: a brain map that sends signals out to one's muscles and creates one's ability to move and assume complex positions in space.

PRIMARY VISCERAL MAP: a patchwork of small maps in the insulas (qv) that represents one's heart, lungs, liver, colon, rectum, stomach, and other internal organs.

PROPRIOCEPTION: one's internal sense of where his body parts are located in space and how they are moving.

PROPRIOCEPTORS: nerve cells in the muscles, tendons, cartilage, and joints that measure stretch and body position as one moves.

RECEPTIVE FIELD: the region of sensory space and/or the portions of other brain maps from which a sensory neuron gets its information.

SECONDARY SOMATOSENSORY CORTEX: a touch map that discriminates higher levels of shape, texture, and motion analysis than the primary touch map.

SENSORY ANTHROPOLOGY: the study of how cultures stress different ways of knowing through the senses.

SOMATIC MARKER HYPOTHESIS: the theory that emotion (a) derives in large part from body states and (b) plays an important, largely underappreciated role in rational thought and decision making.

SOMATIC PSYCHOLOGY: a branch of psychology that tracks the body's felt sensations as a way of addressing trauma.

SOMATIC SENSES: senses brought to a person by receptors that suffuse the body's skin and inner tissues, including touch, temperature, pain, position and motion in space, and balance (cf, *special senses*).

SOMATOTOPY: the orderly mapping of one's body on the surface of one's brain.

SPECIAL SENSES: vision, hearing, taste, and smell (cf, *somatic senses*).

SUPERIOR TEMPORAL SULCUS (STS): a brain region that specializes in detecting biological motion, such as walking or reaching, as opposed to natural, inanimate motion, such as passively swaying or rolling.

SYMPATHETIC NERVOUS SYSTEM: the "fight or flight" part of the autonomic nervous system (qv), which gets the body revved up and ready for violence or intense physical (or emotional) activity.

SYNESTHESIA: a congenital cross-wiring of the senses that may, for example, unite perceptions of colors with tones, or images with words, or textures with tastes.

TEMPORAL PARIETAL JUNCTION (TPJ): a brain region that processes information about faces, bodies, and one's own body and its position in space.

THERMORECEPTORS: nerve cells in the skin that carry information about heat and cold.

TOUCH MAP: a map of one's body surface in a brain region that receives touch sensations, such as pressure and vibration, from the skin.

TOUCH RECEPTORS: nerve cells in the skin that send information about pressure to one's touch maps.

TRANSCRANIAL MAGNETIC STIMULATION: a technique for probing brain function using powerful electromagnets held directly over the head.

VAGAL NERVE STIMULATOR: a small battery-powered device that can be implanted in the body to serve as a pacemaker for the giant nerve that carries visceral sensations to the brain.

VESTIBULAR SENSE/SYSTEM: one's sense of balance.

VON ECONOMO CELLS (INTUITION CELLS): a special class of cells found in the cortexes of only the most mentally and emotionally advanced mammals, which play a key role in the ability to achieve fast, intuitive judgments and insights.

INDEX

page 13 Mandala: Reprinted with permission from www.thangka-center.de.

page 21 Homunculus sculptures: Reprinted with permission from the Natural History Museum, London.

page 25 Raccoon photograph: Courtesy of the United States Fish and Wildlife Service.

page 25 Raccoon body map: Reprinted from *Neuroscience* 7:915–36 (1982), J. I. Johnson, E. M. Ostapoff, and S. Warach, "The anterior border zones of primary somatic sensory (SI) neocortex and their relation to cerebral convolutions, shown by micromapping of peripheral projections to the region of the fourth forepaw digit representation in raccoons," with permission of Wiley-Liss, Inc., a subsidiary of John Wiley & Sons, Inc.

page 25 Rat body map: Reprinted from *Journal of Comparative Neurology* 229:199–213 (1984), J. K. Chapin and C. S. Lin, "Mapping the body representation in the SI cortex of anesthetized and awake rats," with permission of Wiley-Liss, Inc., a subsidiary of John Wiley & Sons, Inc. (Note that while the text in this section refers to mice, the body map presented was derived from lab rats. Given how closely related mice and rats are, the body map differences between them are negligible for the purposes of this book.)

page 26 Star-nosed moles (photograph and body map): Reprinted from *Current Biology*, vol. 15, no. 21 (2005), pp. R863–64, Kenneth C. Catania, "Star-nosed moles," with permission from Elsevier and the author.

page 95 Aimee Mullins: Photograph by Howard Schatz from Howard Schatz and Beverly Ornstein, *Athlete* (HarperCollins) © 2002 Schatz Ornstein.

page 101 Eeva's self-portrait: Reprinted from *Neuroscience Letters*, vol. 240, pp. 131–34 (1998), Riitta Hari et. al., "Three hands: fragmentation of human bodily awareness," with permission from Elsevier.

page 104 Carol's self-portrait: Reprinted from *Neurocase*, vol. 11, no. 3, pp. 212–15 (2005), Giovanna Zamboni, Carla Budriesi, and Paolo Nichelli, "See-

PHOTO: © URSULA COYOTE

PHOTO: © INNA ZAVADSKY

Sandra Blakeslee is a science writer and longtime contributor to *The New York Times*. While she specializes in the brain sciences, her articles cover a wide range of topics, from Antarctic ice fields to Tasmanian devils. She is the co-author of numerous books, including *Second Chances* and *The Unexpected Legacy of Divorce* with Judith Wallerstein, *Phantoms in the Brain* with V. S. Ramachandran, and *On Intelligence* with Jeff Hawkins. She lives in Santa Fe, New Mexico.

Matthew Blakeslee is a freelance science writer based in Los Angeles. This is his first credited book. He is the fourth generation of Blakeslee science writers. His great-grandfather, Howard Blakeslee of the Associated Press, was a founder of American science writing. Howard's son Alton (Sandra's father), was science editor of the Associated Press. Born and raised within a science writing tradition, Sandra and Matthew have formed what may be the world's first mother-son neuroscience writing team.

Printed in the United States
by Baker & Taylor Publisher Services